T0339442

URBAN GOODS MOVEMENT: A GUIDE TO POLICY AND PLANNING

This book is dedicated
to the memory of my father,
Ernest Ogden
1912-1988

Urban Goods Movement: A Guide to Policy and Planning

K.W. OGDEN

Professorial Fellow
Transport Group
Department of Civil Engineering
Monash University
Melbourne, Australia

Routledge
Taylor & Francis Group

LONDON AND NEW YORK

First published 1992 by Ashgate Publishing

Published 2017 by Routledge
2 Park Square, Milton Park, Abingdon, Oxon OX14 4RN
711 Third Avenue, New York, NY 10017, USA

First issued in paperback 2017

Routledge is an imprint of the Taylor & Francis Group, an informa business

A CIP catalogue record for this book is available from the British Library and the US Library of Congress.

ISBN 13: 978-1-138-26898-2 (pbk)
ISBN 13: 978-1-85742-029-6 (hbk)

Contents

List of tables

List of figures

Foreword

Professor Ken Ogden has made many contributions to the field of freight transportation in urban areas through research, teaching, publications, and presentations during the last two decades. This book, which is titled *Urban Goods Movement: A Guide to Policy and Planning*, is perhaps his greatest contribution. It is a pioneering work.

It may be surprising to many that a comprehensive book on urban freight transportation is hard, if not impossible, to find. Ken Ogden's work is courageous because the subject is not a popular or 'hot' topic. As he points out in the very beginning, 'freight transport is absolutely essential to modern urban civilization', and yet it is a neglected subject. Planners and engineers of public agencies in most cases are busy taking care of the needs and complaints of automobile users and transit riders. Private freight companies do not complain loudly, and so the needs of urban freight are rarely examined in the urban transportation planning process. In some cases planners and engineers adopt a negative approach towards truck related activities. Instead of trying to accommodate trucks to reduce costs, public officials in some communities have attempted to ban trucks on freeways and/or the central business districts with the notion that such policies would be beneficial to the public. Academicians also seem to be obsessed with passenger transportation, and have practically ignored the significance of urban freight transportation. Most of the text books on urban transportation planning have little information on urban goods movement, and the time allocated on this topic in classrooms is usually minimal, if any at all. Of course there are exceptions, and Ken Ogden's book is such an exception.

The book begins with background information on urban freight. It describes the characteristics and role of urban freight. It then explains the urban freight system including the physical distribution process and the role of various participating groups or 'actors'. The first five chapters would help a student of urban freight and a neophyte freight transportation planner develop a sound understanding of the urban freight transportation system. In the subsequent chapters, Professor Ogden provides exhaustive information on urban freight related issues, planning techniques and strategies. The latter chapters will be invaluable for practicing planners and engineers. In the discussion of strategies there are numerous examples of actual practice in different urban areas. There is also a separate chapter on selected case studies involving policies towards urban freight transportation. The planning techniques that are discussed include mathematical modelling for demand estimation. The chapter on the implementation of freight planning and policy deserves a careful study by practitioners because it is full of practical suggestions, and it would help them adopt a realistic approach and avoid many pitfalls.

One of the assets of the book is the quantitative information it provides on various items of interest. Wherever possible, be it the size of trucks or the number of truck loading bays/spaces for different land uses, the book quotes typical values. Another asset of the book is the references it provides on almost every topic discussed. Each chapter is comprehesively referenced. I am amazed by the thoroughness of the referencing work which reflects the scholarship and care devoted to this work. Professor Ogden evidently has been accumulating reference materials over a long period of time from a variety of sources in different countries. I have met him many times in conferences in the United States of America on the subject of urban goods movement. It appears that he utilized these visits and periods of work in the USA to build up his library of reference materials.

The title of the book suggests that its emphasis is on policy and planning. The title is faithful to its content. The book is not meant to be a design manual for freight related physical facilities such as truck and intermodal terminals. However, it does not ignore the design aspects entirely, and it contains sufficient information on the functional aspects of terminals and guideways for a planner to develop a better understanding of the physical components of an urban freight transportation system.

The book is published in Australia, Great Britain, Singapore and USA, but its relevance and application are not limited to any particular country. There are probably as many examples and references drawn from cases in the United States as elsewhere. There are also references to cases and research in Europe. It is an international book, and it should be available in every library in the world.

I sincerely hope that transportation planners and engineers of all countries will read this book, and that urban freight transportation will be given the recognition it deserves.

Arun Chatterjee
Professor of Civil Engineering
The University of Tennessee
Knoxville

Professor Chatterjee is Chair of the Urban Goods Movement Committee of the Transportation Research Board, National Research Council, USA, and a former Chair of the Urban Goods Movement Committee of the American Society of Civil Engineers.

Preface

Transport involves the movement of both people and goods. Those responsible for urban transport policy and planning have long acknowledged the former and developed explicit ways of treating it. They are less sure about the latter. In part at least this stems from a lack of day to day experience with urban goods movement problems, the lesser political sensitivity of freight transport, and a reluctance to intervene (for good or ill) in the activities of what is essentially a private sector concern. However, in part it probably stems also from an ignorance of the subject and its importance in economic, social and environmental terms, and an uncertainty about what could be done in policy or planning terms.

Many cities around the world have tackled aspects of urban freight, in an attempt to resolve some particular local issue or to use freight policy to contribute to a broader transport or urban objective. Many disparate research and planning studies have been undertaken, and a number of significant conferences have been held. With over twenty years of experience in this field, I knew of many of these studies and activities, and it seemed to me that what was needed was a book which brought together much of this knowledge and experience, so that those responsible for urban transport planning and policy could have a comprehensive, detailed and practical source of information on urban freight. This book, therefore, attempts to satisfy this aim.

I have written the book with the practicing professional in mind. It is directed towards a specialist audience, such as might be found in an urban transport planning agency, a local government traffic engineers office, a road authority, or a planning or engineering consultancy. It would also be relevant to a graduate course in transport planning or policy. However, I hope that it is intelligible to the interested layperson, and of interest to all who have a concern for contemporary issues in urban development.

As mentioned, the book has arisen from my own research interest in this field. However, the subject matter does not constitute the output of a specific research project, but rather aims to reflect the current state of knowledge and understanding about urban freight, its importance, and ways of accommodating it within urban policies. While inevitably much of my own work is reflected where appropriate in the text, the book aims to bring together the contribution of many of those who have studied and written about the subject. In keeping with this aim therefore, I have extensively referenced all sources, so that those who may wish to learn more about any one specific part of what is, after all, a vast topic, may have some point of entry into the literature.

The book aims to be international in scope and perspective. Although the actual freight movement patterns and specific freight issues in any urban area reflect the needs and concerns of that area at that time, there is nevertheless a degree of commonality about many of the problems, issues, and solution strategies which makes an overview relevant and useful. Thus, I have aimed to bring to bear some of my own experience based upon personal research in Australia, the United States, Britain, Canada and The Philippines, coupled with personal contact with other researchers and government officials made in the course of my professional career.

A substantive draft of the book was written in 1990-91 during a period of sabbatical leave from Monash University, spent at the University of California, Irvine on a Fulbright Fellowship. I therefore wish to acknowledge with gratitude all of those who made this leave possible: The Australian-American Education Foundation in Canberra and the Council for International Exchange of Scholars in Washington; Medhat Haroun and Stephen Ritchie in the Department of Civil Engineering at UC Irvine; and Eric Laurenson at Monash University. Thanks are due also to Bill Young and Michael Taylor for carrying my teaching and other workloads at Monash University during my absence. The book itself could not have been written without the invaluable contribution of the library staff of the UC Institute of Transportation Studies, especially Evelyn Wilkinson at Irvine and Michael Kleiber and his staff at Berkeley, and Will Recker, ITS Director at Irvine.

I am indebted to a number of people who have made comments or provided advice on specific parts of the draft manuscript, in particular Darrell Bowyer, Jim Cooper, John Exnicios, Rey Huck, Ed Morlok and Carol Walters. There are countless people who have contributed to my understanding and knowledge of this subject over many years. I could not possibly list them, as I would do too many people an injustice by omitting their names, so a collective "thank you" must suffice. I would be remiss however if I did not mention Arun Chatterjee, who kindly agreed to write the foreword to this book.

A special appreciation is due to Irene Sgouras, who prepared the camera-ready pages, based upon my oft-scruffy WordPerfect files. I thank Robert Alexander for preparing the line drawings, Don McCarthy for preparing the photographic prints, and Robert Morgan for taking a couple of photographs for me on one of his trips to Britain. I also thank John Hindley from Gower Publishing Group for his advice and encouragement.

Finally, to my wife Elaine, and sons Marcus, Matthew and Nicholas, I say thank you for bearing with me during the time I spent writing and editing the manuscript.

Ken Ogden
Melbourne
August, 1991

PART A

POLICY: ISSUES AND OBJECTIVES

1 Freight in urban areas

Introduction

Freight transport is absolutely essential to modern urban civilisation. The very concept of urbanisation requires a freight system to sustain it, since urbanisation means that large numbers of people are accumulated in areas remote from their sources of food, sources of raw materials for industry, markets for industrial products, and places to dispose of their waste. No urban area could exist without a massive, sustained, and reliable flow of goods to, from, and within it.

Facilities for the movement of goods must therefore be provided in any urban area. In western industrialized countries, both the public sector and the private sector have important roles to play, the former in the provision of infrastructure and the establishment of a social and legal framework within which transport can occur, and the latter in the provision of most of the industrial resources (vehicles, terminals, etc) necessary to supply the service.

For these reasons alone, goods movement deserves explicit consideration in urban transport policy, planning and facility design. However, in addition, the explicit consideration of urban goods movement has the potential to contribute in a useful and positive way to achieving both the goals of urban transport and some of the broader goals of urban policy and planning.

This book aims to contribute to this objective. It is based upon the proposition that there are likely to be benefits to the community at large if explicit consideration of freight is included within urban policy, planning and design processes, and it attempts to show some of the key ways in which this may be done.

It is directed primarily at professionals with responsibility for urban policy, transport planning, and transport or traffic engineering. This is not to deny that other perspectives are equally valid or important; indeed, as we will see shortly there are very many valid perceptions of urban freight and the issues related to it. However, the contribution of the aforementioned professionals is important, and there are few comprehensive, recent guidelines to assist in urban freight policy and planning.

The balance of this opening chapter introduces some of the issues and problems in urban goods movement; many of these will be discussed in more detail in later chapters. It also presents a brief historical perspective of the field of study of urban goods movement, and concludes with an overview of the structure of the book.

Problems and issues

To a greater degree than in urban passenger transport, the urban freight task is enormously complex and heterogenous.

It is difficult to identify common features between the requirements of different users and different vehicle operators. What is common between, for example, the nature of trips undertaken by tipper trucks, courier vans, fire trucks, tractor semi-trailers, plumbers trucks, post office vehicles and twin or triple trailered trucks? Or what is common between the requirements of those transporting pre-mixed concrete, parcels, oil drilling pipes, milk and garbage? Again, where is the commonality between the process of delivering goods to warehouses, factories, shops, offices, transport terminals, construction sites, homes, at the roadside, or the waterfront?

This complexity and heterogeneity means that there are a multitude of 'actors' in the urban freight scene, and therefore a multitude of perceptions of 'the problem'. The motor car driver sees trucks as a nuisance on the roadway; the driver looking for a downtown parking spot resents all the space devoted to loading zones; the retailer values the goods the truck brings, but regrets the fact that the loading zone takes away car parking space for potential customers; the office building owner or developer sees the provision of loading docks as dead space, and would rather have the deliveries made from the curb; the road user is frustrated at having to wait at railroad level crossings while freight trains pass through.

On the other hand, the truck driver views private motorists as menaces as they travel too slowly, force an awkward lane change on the freeway, or as they change lanes into the truck's braking space ahead of a red traffic light. The trucking company sees private cars as a problem, creating too much congestion and pushing up operating costs. Industry seeks to have a regular supply of components, and sees urban freight problems in terms of lost production if 'just in time' deliveries are delayed by traffic congestion, vehicle breakdowns, strikes, etc. Pedestrians see large trucks as a threat, and a producer of foul emissions and noise. Urban residents want to keep trucks out of their streets, to minimize noise, air pollution and help preserve the ambience of their locality. Pavement engineers see trucks breaking up their roads and streets, while traffic engineers are concerned about catering for trucks at traffic signals, intersections, and at loading and parking areas. To the urban planner, the problems of providing adequate road space or sufficient loading docks are day to day problems, while in the longer term they worry about the effect of freight on urban form and structure, and the consequences of freight transport costs on the economic viability of industries in their region.

These are cameos of course, but they serve to underscore the vast range of activities encompassed within urban freight, and the considerable variety of problems and issues associated with it. It is hardly surprising that just as there is no one 'problem', there is no single panacea for dealing with those problems, but rather a range of strategies, each applicable to particular cities for particular issues at a given time.

At the risk of over-simplifying matters, it is however suggested that urban freight issues can be categorized into three main areas, namely those related to economic development, transport efficiency, and the minimization of adverse impacts.

Economic development

The first set of issues are those related to the contribution which the goods transport sector can make to the economic development of an urban area. Various studies have shown that urban goods movement is a very significant component of a nation's economy. For example,

-   A US study using 1972 data (Kearney, 1976, p 4) estimated that the cost of moving goods within urban areas was equal to nearly 5 per cent of gross domestic product (GDP), and further that the four

5

domestic transport components (passenger and freight, intra-city and inter-regional) were approximately of equal magnitude.

- A Canadian study (Lea, 1971) estimated the costs of person and freight transport for three representative cities. Their results indicated that:

  • the costs of freight transport were significant (6 per cent of income in the smallest city, and 18 per cent of income in the largest (population 2 million));

  • the total national cost of goods transport was nearly as great as the cost of person movement;

  • the cost of goods transport increased faster with city size than did the cost of person movement, with the result that in the largest urban areas, the cost per head of freight transport was 55 per cent greater than the cost of person transport.

- An Australian study (Bureau of Transport Economics, 1978) also found that the total national costs of urban passenger and urban freight transport were similar.

- In Britain, Hall (1982) has estimated that about 10 per cent of GDP is spent on freight transport (and, again, about 10 per cent on passenger transport), but this estimate increases to 17 per cent if inventory and warehousing costs are considered.

The consistency of the conclusion that the costs of urban freight and urban passenger transport are comparable is striking. In view of this, it is hardly surprising that, as the Kearney report noted (op cit, p 6) 'local officials are concerned about the economic competitiveness of their cities vis-a-vis other cities'.

Freight efficiency

There are a range of concerns related to effective and efficient delivery of goods within an urban area. These include both public and private sector responsibilities. Those in the public sector include:

- the provision for trucks in infrastructure design (e.g. roads, bridges);

- the provision of adequate off-street loading docks in new developments, or the allowance for on-street loading and unloading in older areas;

- the provision of intermodal container transfer facilities at or near major ports;

- allocation of land for freight terminals, in appropriate places and with adequate controls on abutting development to allow 24 hour operation;

- the introduction of measures aimed, directly or indirectly, at improving the fuel efficiency of trucks, including linked traffic signals, fuel efficiency targets, urban freeways linking industrial areas, or relocation of freight terminals;

- the provision within general regulations covering vehicle mass and dimension limits of a facility to allow for the movement of 'oversize' vehicles where the nature of the load dictates the necessity to do so.

These may be considered in some senses to be routine, but the very fact that such provisions exist indicates the necessity to consider goods movement as an integral part of urban area planning and policy, and perhaps to examine existing practices to see if they are still appropriate.

Minimization of adverse impacts

The third general category of issue includes those aimed at minimizing the adverse effects of urban goods delivery. These might include:

- attempting to reduce traffic congestion by introducing controls on truck operating hours;

- reducing vehicle emissions from trucks by introduction of emission control standards, etc;

7

- similarly, the control of truck noise by either vehicle-based methods or operational methods such as restrictions on truck operating hours or access;

- preservation of local amenity by limiting truck access to residential areas;

- various measures aimed at minimizing truck involvement in road crashes.

Once again, these measures are widely practiced. However, in many cases their introduction may not have been associated with a full and complete analysis of the consequences, and in some cases at least it could be argued that the policies have been counterproductive. In few cases where such policies have been introduced has there been a clear assessment of the costs to the industry and (because such costs get passed on to the ultimate consumer) the cost to the community.

Historical perspective

It is often helpful in the introduction to a new subject to understand a little of its historical background. This helps to put current knowledge and understanding in perspective, and may perhaps give a clue to possible future developments.

A useful starting point for urban goods movement is with two seminal conferences convened in 1970. The first was held under the auspices of the Organisation for Economic Cooperation and Development (1970) in Paris, and the second by the US Highway Research Board (1971) at the request of US and Canadian transportation agencies.

These conferences arose essentially from a recognition that the great burst of transport planning studies in urban areas worldwide in the previous 10-15 years had almost completely neglected urban goods movement. Both conferences reviewed what little information there was about urban goods movement, and made recommendations in terms of the need to build a better understanding of it, and to attempt to incorporate freight in the mainstream of urban transport planning.

The US and Canadian federal governments were active in sponsoring urban goods movement research and planning studies during the 1970s. Transport Canada in particular funded a series of studies aimed at improving the level of knowledge about truck and freight flows, or investigating specific proposals for improvement. These studies are reviewed in Wood (1979) and an overview of Canadian freight research in the 1970s is given in Wood, Suen and Ebrahim (1982).

In the US, the Federal Government also funded a number of research and investigation projects, of which probably the two most significant were an overview of urban freight costs, problems and opportunities (Kearney, 1975, 1976), and a reference guide for use by local and state officials in appraising freight problems and devising solutions to them (Christiansen, 1979). Although there was a lot of emphasis on attempting to redress the perceived neglect of goods movement in urban transport planning, probably the most useful material was concerned with the inclusion of trucks in Transportation Systems Management (TSM) guidelines, especially related to traffic engineering measures (Hedges, 1985).

In Britain, the Transport and Road Research Laboratory undertook a number of detailed studies focussed on freight problems and opportunities in specific urban areas during the 1970s (Corcoran and Christie, 1978).

In 1973, the first of what was to be an irregular series of conferences on goods transportation in urban areas was convened. This series, although held in America (under the auspices of the Engineering Foundation), have all been international in scope, and probably provide a good chart to the changing emphases and concerns. The conferences dates and references were as follows:

1973, South Berwick, Maine (Fisher, 1974)
1975, Santa Barbara, California (Fisher, 1976)
1977, Sea Island, Georgia (Fisher 1978)
1981, Easton, Maryland (Fisher and Meyburg, 1982)
1988, Santa Barbara, California (Chatterjee, Fisher and Staley, 1989)

It is interesting to note the changing emphases over time, as reflected in the topics considered by the 'probe groups' which have been a feature of each conference. These are listed in Figure 1.1. Although perhaps not too much should be placed upon this analysis, nevertheless as an indication of what were regarded at least by the conference organisers as current issues, we may discern the following:

9

1973: Urban goods movement considerations in urban transportation planning studies.

The use of regulatory powers in improving urban goods transportation.

The location of freight terminals in urban areas.

Issues in urban rail relocation.

Consolidated terminals for pickup and delivery in urban areas.

1975: Intermodal considerations.

Assessment of planning and modelling methodologies.

Improving urban goods movement systems through operations management.

Economic issues in urban goods movement.

Impact on urban goods movement of reconstructed rail services.

Opportunities for capital and institutional improvements in urban goods movement.

1977: Traffic engineering and design to facilitate urban goods movement.

Impact of local government regulations.

Interface between federal regulations and urban goods movement .

Goods movement considerations in metropolitan planning.

Locating and servicing major freight generators in urban areas.

1981: Integration of urban goods movement into the urban transportation planning process.

Freight movement in relation to land use, planning, terminal facilities and the environment

Fuel conservation and contingency planning.

The role of regulation in urban goods movement.

Research issues.

1988: Truck accommodation in urban areas.

Urban intermodal freight movements.

Data requirements for policy, planning and design.

Figure 1.1 Probe groups, conferences on goods transportation in urban areas

- an on-going concern with terminals and freight facility location;

- a concern during the 1970s with incorporating freight into the urban transport planning process - a concern which gave way in the last conference to one focussing on data and information requirements;

- an emerging concern in later conferences with traffic management;

- an early concern with rail in the context of urban goods movement, which later disappeared or became absorbed within broader terminal issues;

- a concern with regulations and their effects, which was not present in the last conference, and

- perhaps surprisingly, only a fleeting concern with environmental, social and energy impacts.

The inclusion of freight in urban transport planning and modelling never really got off the ground. Some urban areas have explicitly considered freight in their transport planning procedures; Chicago and London would probably be the two foremost cities in this regard. However, even here, the models used for this task are quite primitive, and indeed it would probably be true to say that in those urban areas which have included freight in their transport planning activities, goals other than those related to the urban transport system dominated.

For example, Chicago has been concerned to maintain its role as a transhipment point for the American midwest, and is thus concerned about freight movements between terminals; London has been concerned about managing environmental problems while maintaining its industry and trade base; Melbourne is concerned to maintain its viability as Australia's leading manufacturing centre; Los Angeles is primarily concerned with problems of air pollution and has included urban trucking as one of the targets of a broader air quality program, and so on.

The decade of the 1970s was clearly the time of major activity: many studies, much research, and lots of conferences. The decade of the 1980s may be described as a time of consolidation. While many of the aspirations of the early 1970s did not come to fruition, there has been at least in some quarters a clearer recognition of the role of freight, and ways of accommodating it. This is perhaps most obvious in the area of traffic management.

It is interesting to conclude this historical overview with the output of one of the probe groups at the aforementioned 1988 conference on goods transportation in urban areas. This group identified a number of changes in the context within which urban goods movement must take place in the years ahead. These included the following (Anon, 1989b, p 15):

-   the increasing suburbanisation of urban freight;

-   increasing containerisation of freight moving to, from and within urban areas;

-   freight issues associated with the construction and on-going use of 'megaprojects' in urban areas;

-   the proliferation of service industries, and their effects on vehicles, goods movements, and employment;

-   the evolution of 'just in time' management strategies with their effect on vehicles, shipment sizes, and schedules;

-   deregulation and the effect on entry of new firms to the industry and the departure of existing ones;

- increased awareness of hazardous materials in transport and handling;

- the issue of waste disposal in urban areas;

- the onset of a period of rebuilding of infrastructure, and the problems of operating vehicles and maintaining schedules as facilities (especially highways) are reconstructed under traffic;

- increased pressure for parking in some locations from high density commuting;

- the increasing community awareness of the road freight industry.

Definition and scope of urban goods movement

Definition of urban goods movement

There is a temptation to attempt to form a comprehensive definition of the term urban goods movement.[1] Others (e.g. Watson, 1975, p 4) have agonized over the definition, and played with the meaning of words like 'urban', 'goods', 'movement', etc.

If we were to attempt such a definition, we would probably end up with something quite unwieldy like the description contained in a publication of the US Department of Transportation (1973):

The transportation of, and terminal activities associated with, the movement of things as opposed to people in urban areas. It includes movement of things into and out of the area, through the area, as well as within the area by all modes, including transmission of electricity to the extent that it relates to the transportation of fuels, pipeline movement of petroleum, water and waste, and collection of and movement of trash and mail, service truck movements not identified with person movements, and even some person trips which involve substantial goods movements such as shopping trips. Activities involving urban streets, waterways, railroads, terminals, loading docks, and internal distribution systems including elevators and related facilities must all be considered in fostering greater efficiency in the movement of urban goods.

13

This is clearly an overkill for definitional purposes, although it does serve to highlight that the boundaries of urban freight analysis are not crisply defined. As House (1979, p 4) has correctly asserted, 'the definition of urban goods movement is essentially arbitrary'. Thus for the purposes of this book, we will not attempt to develop too tight a definition, but merely describe our interest as being concerned with:

the movement of things (as distinct from people) to, from, within, and through urban areas.

Whether we are specifically interested in any aspect that might fall at the boundary of that definition then becomes an essentially pragmatic question depending upon whether it is useful to include it or not.

For most practical purposes, our interest is with urban trucks. In most modern western urban areas, urban trucks dominate internal goods movement (i.e. freight movements with both ends in the urban area). Maintaining our attitude of pragmatism, we could then say that we are interested in non-truck modes to the extent that they are helpful to our particular interest. For example, in some urban ares such as New York, movements by barge and other marine modes is significant (see Chapter 2), and clearly therefore that would be pertinent in any analysis of freight in that urban area. In most other urban areas it is simply not an issue.

Similarly, our interest in non-road modes bringing products to and from an urban area translates to an interest in intermodal freight terminals (seaports, rail terminals, airports, trucking terminals). For most purposes, we need not concern ourselves with movement of goods by pipeline. As Button and Pearman (1981, p 2) have remarked, 'these are essentially technical debates ... and the activities of public utilities seldom interact (except during their installation) either with each other or with other forms of transport.' However, once again, this exclusion is for reasons of pragmatism, not concept, and if it was helpful in any specific instance to consider urban pipeline movements, then one should by all means do so. Interestingly, in simple terms of their contribution to the total urban freight task, pipelines absolutely dominate; the Tri-State Transportation Commission (1968) has noted that for the New York area in the 1960s, water pipelines conveyed about 210 tonnes per capita per year, while the next largest commodity (building materials) was only 2–5 tonnes per capita per year.

If our primary interest therefore is with movement of goods by truck within urban areas, our pragmatism would dictate that we are in fact interested in truck movements, whether or not they are associated with freight activities. If we are concerned for example with traffic design or analysis of highway capacity, it is in fact the truck not the freight which is our primary concern. In practice, this means that we are likely to be interested in the trucks engaged on service type functions (e.g. plumbers trucks, utility maintenance trucks), and that we need to be careful about the definition of a truck to be sure that we exclude vehicles which are essentially for the movement of people (e.g. pick-up trucks). This can create a difficulty, since for some purposes we are likely to be quite interested in certain aspects of freight which involve small vehicles, such as courier deliveries. Once again, let pragmatism reign, and include any vehicles or goods which are relevant to the particular purpose at hand, and exclude it otherwise.

In general however, we might say that for practical purposes in most western cities, internal urban goods movement (i.e. that with both origin and destination within the one urban area) is synonymous with urban trucking.

Finally, it is important to note that our emphasis on *urban* goods movement, which implies a distinction between urban and non-urban activities, is really only relevant to geographically large areas, such as the United States, Canada, Australia, or continental Europe. It is not so meaningful in a smaller country, such as Britain. Hall (1982, p 5) has explained the reasons for this quite well:

> The distribution systems operated in Britain do not correspond to those of much of the US or Canada where there is a valid distinction between interstate, intrastate and intra-urban goods transport, largely because of the much greater distance between settlements. In Britain, except at the higher scale of settlement, the pattern is not one of trunk haul to the periphery of the settlement and then separate distribution within it; for most commodities the freight distribution system will include 8 to 16 depots from which onwards delivery is made. Thus any one urban area might be serviced with some goods only by local delivery vehicles, while for others a depot may be sited in an area and both trunk and delivery vehicles will operate within it.

Scope of urban goods movement analysis

As noted above, this book is primarily aimed at professionals having responsibility for aspects of urban policy, transport planning or traffic

15

engineering. While in most western countries, the carriage of goods within urban areas is carried out by the private sector, there is an important public sector role, and this book aims to explore that role and assist in its execution. The public sector plays several roles in urban goods movement.

Given the symbiotic link between urban freight and urban trucking as discussed above, the first and most obvious interest of the public sector is with the provision and maintenance of the urban road network. This extends to such aspects as transport planning, road construction and maintenance, traffic control, and traffic engineering.

Government has an interest in economic development, and as discussed above, an efficient urban goods movement system can contribute to economic growth, while conversely an inefficient system can retard it.

In most countries, the use of land is controlled, to a greater or lesser extent, by government, and thus there is an interest in and responsibility for such freight-related aspects as location of freight-generating activities (including, but not only, freight terminals), site access, provision of adequate freight facilities such as off-street loading docks, etc.

The transport sector in most countries is regulated to some extent, and while the urban component is usually subject to less regulation than longer distance or international movements, there are nevertheless a range of qualitative regulations (e.g. those covering vehicle mass and dimensions, safety, noise, emissions) and sometimes quantitative regulations (e.g. entry to the industry, rates) covering aspects of urban freight.

Finally, it is important to note that freight often has significant externalities – i.e. impacts upon other parties or the public in general - and it is part of the role of the public sector to ameliorate these or deal with the consequences. Examples include noise, emissions, safety, etc.

The focus of the book is therefore upon issues such as these. Aspects which are the concern essentially of the private sector, or more correctly, with the organisation and management of the freight task itself, are beyond the scope of the book.

Format of the book

The book aims to present, in a logical fashion, the conceptual underpinning of freight, the objectives of the freight system from a public sector perspective, and a review of public sector initiatives which may contribute towards those objectives.

The book is arranged in three parts. Part A (Chapters 1–5) is concerned with *policy*, and analyses the issues and objectives of urban goods movement. More specifically, these chapters discuss the subject matter as follows:

In Chapter 2, we briefly review the dimensions of the urban freight task, to assist in giving an understanding of its scope and nature.

Chapter 3 reviews the urban freight system, explaining the role of transport within a broader logistics management context, and discussing the role and perspective of the many 'actors' in the urban freight system. Freight as an economic activity is emphasized, and its supply and demand manifestations are examined.

Chapter 4 proceeds from this broad conceptual framework to consider freight policy and planning, from a public sector perspective. An overall goal of freight policy is postulated, and the role of government in pursuing that goal is discussed.

In Chapter 5, the objectives of urban freight are reviewed. These are considered in six areas: economic objectives, efficiency objectives, road safety objectives, environmental objectives, infrastructure objectives, and urban structure objectives.

Part B of the book is concerned with urban goods movement *planning*, and reviews in detail the various strategies for improvement of the urban goods movement system. Following the general theme of the book, attention is predominantly focussed upon those strategies which are essentially within the public sector, or which public policy or planning can influence. However, for completeness, brief mention is made, especially in Chapter 12, of some strategies which are more the responsibility of the private sector.

Seven types of strategy for pursuing urban goods movement objectives are outlined in chapters 6-12. The discussion reviews in detail the range of possibilities in each, and attempts to summarize previous experience where such experience has been documented. Where relevant and where examples exist, quantitative results are presented. These strategies are:

Chapter 6   traffic management
Chapter 7   location and zoning of land use

Chapter 8   infrastructure
Chapter 9   licensing and regulations
Chapter 10   pricing
Chapter 11   terminals and modal interchange
Chapter 12   operational strategies

Finally in Part B, Chapter 13 discusses the role of models in urban freight planning, and reviews various models which have been developed and used to analyse urban truck trips and commodity movements.

Part C of the book discusses the *implementation* of urban goods movement planning and policy. Two chapters comprise this Part. Chapter 14 discusses implementation in terms of the ways in which the various strategies for assisting goods movement in urban areas may be introduced. Chapter 15 presents some case studies describing how various urban areas around the world have made specific provision for urban goods movement in planning or policy areas; these case studies include:

- New York City (freight activity in the garment centre);
- Dallas, TX (provision of loading spaces);
- Los Angeles, CA (peak hour truck restrictions);
- Los Angeles, CA (transport corridor to the port area);
- Dallas, TX (hazardous materials truck routes);
- Melbourne, Australia (freight needs in road investment);
- Perth, Australia (routes for large combination vehicles);
- London, England (environmental controls on trucks);
- Tokyo, Japan (facilitating urban freight distribution).

Notes

1. The terms 'urban goods movement' and 'urban freight' are essentially synonymous, as used throughout this book. The former is in common usage as a generic term for this field of study, while the latter has the advantage of being shorter, and perhaps more elegant.

2 A profile of urban freight

Introduction

It would be helpful if we could present a comprehensive, up to date profile of freight activities in urban areas. Ideally, we would present summary statistics which would both underscore the importance of the subject, and highlight the significance of freight in the overall urban transport scene. It would be good also to present some recent statistical information that could be used to assist directly in policy and planning activities.

The reality is that our analysis will fall considerably short of that ideal. There is one reason for that – there is a great dearth of useful, up to date information about urban goods movement activities. One urban area only – Chicago, USA – has reasonably comprehensive recent information, based upon a commercial vehicle survey conducted in 1986 (Rawling, 1989). Apart from Chicago, there is only very patchy and incomplete information for other urban areas based upon fairly recent data.

Of less recent vintage, and therefore of less current value, there is a quite considerable body of information dating from the 1970s. A number of urban areas around the world collected data on aspects of urban goods movement; those with fairly comprehensive information bases included:

- Chicago, USA (Blaze, Halagera and Miller, 1973, based on 1970 data);
- Calgary, Canada (Transportation Development Agency, 1974, based upon 1971 data);
- Vancouver, Canada (Swan Wooster, 1979, based upon 1975 data);
- Melbourne, Australia (Ogden, 1977b, based upon 1964 data);
- New York metropolitan area (Tri-State Transportation Commission, 1968, based upon 1965 data);

- Auckland, New Zealand (Smith and Douglass, 1982, based on 1973 data);
- London, England (Hasell, Foulkes and Robertson, 1978a, based on 1975 data).

During the 1960s and 1970s, many other urban areas assembled partial data on truck and commodity flows, collected in the course of major metropolitan transport studies which were in vogue at the time. Moreover, there had been a number of attempts to collate and interpret much of this urban freight information in a way that enabled good insight to be gained into the nature of the activity (e.g. Smith, 1969; Chappell and Smith, 1971; Bolger and Bruck, 1973; Kearney, 1975, 1976; Christiansen, 1979; Hasell, Foulkes and Robertson, 1978a; Levinson, 1982).

Unfortunately, such information has a fairly short 'shelf life'; it becomes stale and possibly even dangerous after a few years. Changes in the freight system and the tasks which it undertakes mean that data more than a few years old should not be expected to be reliable or informative, at least in fine detail; broad indicative information is possibly more robust, but even this should be used with caution, as we will see in the following analysis.

In this chapter then, we are unable to present a profile of urban goods movement in too much detail. Comments based upon data which pre-dates about 1980 are presented only for indicative purposes, and, as mentioned, there is not much post-1980 data. Rather than present an extensive discourse based upon old and therefore not very useful data, the discussion is kept short where there is little or nothing recent, and the reader who wishes to learn what we knew about urban freight in the 1970s is referred to the references cited in the text.

It should be emphasized that the problem is with data on *urban* freight. Many countries or states have quite comprehensive data on overall freight activities, but most do not isolate the movements to, from, or within urban areas. Similarly, data related to truck fleets and their use are published at aggregate levels, but only rarely do they identify urban uses within this.[1]

One thing which these aggregate data do however is to enable us to estimate the relative significance of urban freight in relation to the overall national freight task. Some indicators here are:

- In the USA in 1988, travel by all trucks nationwide totalled 934 billion[2] vehicle km (580 billion vehicle miles). Of this, 471 billion vehicle km (293 billion vehicle miles), or 50.5 percent, was in urban areas greater than 5,000 population, (Department of Transportation, US, 1989, p 172).

- In Australia in 1988, travel by all trucks totalled 11.9 billion vehicle km (7.4 billion vehicle miles), with 42 percent of this in so-called 'capital cities', i.e. the major metropolitan areas of each state. Further, of the total road freight task measured in tonne kilometres, 26.4 percent was within these urban areas, and in terms of tonnes, the capital cities accounted for 34.6 percent (1985 data) (from microfiche tabulations of Surveys of Motor Vehicle Usage conducted by the Australian Bureau of Statistics)

- In Britain in 1989, of a total of 132.1 billion tonne km of road freight transport, 30.0 percent was carried less than 100 km. While this would not all be intra-urban activity, much of it would be. In terms of tonnes lifted, 76 percent of 1704 billion tonnes was attributable to goods moved less than 100 km (Department of Transport, 1990, pp 89–90).

There are several measures of the urban freight task, and a number of parameters of interest. The measures include:

- tonnes lifted, which is a measure of freight demand, and relates particularly to terminal activities and industrial output; since it does not include any reference to distance travelled, it does not relate strongly to the transport system;

- tonne kilometres (or ton miles), which is a more relevant measure of the demand for goods movement so far as transport system needs are concerned; it affects both the freight industry and the road system, since tonne kilometres bears some relationship to the axle loads placed on the road pavement;

- value of goods moved, which is a measure of industrial output, and thus of the importance of such things as congestion costs; this value is not usually measured for domestic or urban goods movement, but is available for international freight;

- volume of goods moved, which would be another potential measure of freight demand if it was available; however, no information is available on this factor for urban freight activities;

- various measures of truck activity, which are supply-side variables indicating how the road freight system copes with the demand variables as outlined above; data on these aspects are more readily available, and several of them are reviewed in this chapter.

There are four freight system parameters of interest; these are reviewed below. They are:

- the economic significance of urban freight;

- characteristics of the urban truck fleet;

- characteristics of trips made by that fleet, and

- characteristics of the demand for goods movement (as distinct from the characteristics of the truck fleet and its activities, which are supply-side variables: see Chapter 3).

Economic significance of urban freight

In Chapter 1, we discussed the economic significance of urban freight in terms of shares of gross domestic product (GDP). To briefly recapitulate, urban freight costs have been estimated at around 5 percent of GDP; urban freight costs are of comparable magnitude to urban person transport costs, and urban freight costs increase with the size of the urban area at a greater rate than do the costs of urban person movement. Each of these conclusions serves to underscore the importance of urban freight, and the potential value of targeting it for specific treatment in a policy or planning context.

It is also of interest to consider urban freight costs as a component of the value of particular products. Various studies have attempted to do this, but a word of warning needs to be sounded in interpreting these studies, in that there are variations in what has been measured. On the cost side, some have considered transport costs, while others have considered all logistics costs. As an index, various measures have been used, such as value of product, cost of production, selling price, etc. These differences make comparisons difficult, but the results are of interest. Two fairly recent examples will be given here.

Table 2.1 shows the results of an American study which examined transport costs (inbound and outbound) as a proportion of product prices. This shows that transport costs vary significantly between industries, with the importance of transport declining as the product value increases.

Table 2.1
Transport costs for a selection of US industries in 1982
as a percentage of product prices

Industry	Inbound and outbound transport costs (percent of product costs)
stone, clay and glass	27
petroleum products	24
lumber and wood products	18
chemicals	14
food and kindred products	13
furniture and fixtures	12
paper and allied products	11
primary metals industries	9
textile mill products	8
fabricated metal products	8
miscellaneous manufacturing	8
transport equipment	8
rubber and plastics products	7
tobacco manufacturing	5
machinery (excl electrical instruments)	5
instruments	4
apparel and other textiles	4
printing and publishing	4
electrical and electronic machinery	4
leather and leather products	3

Source: Anderson (1983).

An Australian study (Gilmour, 1987) considered the total logistics costs, and expressed them as a proportion of sales value (Table 2.2). This shows that transport, on average, accounted for 2.7 percent of sales, while other logistics costs accounted for a further 18.4 percent of sales.

In summary, transport costs for manufactured goods are typically of the order of 2–8 percent of the cost of production, with transport's contribution declining as the product value increases. Unprocessed goods, or goods with a low ratio of value to bulk such as quarried products, have a much higher transport cost component; indeed, one study (Department of Transportation, US, 1972) found that transport costs represented over three-quarters of the final demand price for gravel, sand and stone.

Table 2.2
Logistics costs for Australian companies in 1985
as a percentage of sales

Activity	Costs (percent of sales)
transport	2.7
receiving and despatch	1.0
warehousing	2.2
packaging	3.2
inventory	7.2
order processing	2.0
administration	2.8
total logistics	21.1

Source: Gilmour (1987), p 7.

The truck fleet

As noted in Chapter 1, the truck dominates internal urban freight movements in modern industrial countries. In this section, we present a profile of the urban truck fleet, while in the next section the trips made by that fleet are reviewed.

Types of truck

Early US data suggested that for large urban areas, with populations in excess of 1 million, the truck ownership rate was fairly constant at about 25–30 trucks per thousand population (Smith, 1969). However, typically more than half of these were small trucks, which were used either for person transport, or for service and utility functions, and make only a small contribution to the urban freight task (Staley, 1982).

In Chicago in 1986, the total truck population was about 360,000 (Rawling and Reilly, 1987). However, 67 percent of these were small trucks and vans, with gross vehicle mass less than 8,000 lb (3.6 t). Light trucks (8,000 – 28,000 lb (12.7 t)) comprised 13 percent of the fleet, medium trucks (28,000 – 64,000 lb (29 t)) comprised 6 percent, and heavy trucks comprised nearly 14 percent. This last category consisted almost entirely of articulated trucks.

Truck ownership

Truck ownership may be broadly divided into four classes, as follows[3]:

- trucks owned by commercial carriers (referred to in some parts of the world as for-hire carriers or hire and reward carriers) who carry freight for others;

- private carriers (referred to also as ancillary carriers, or own-account carriers), who carry their own goods as an adjunct to the main business of the firm (e.g. a retail store or a farm);

- personal use, which are trucks owned and operated in a similar manner to an automobile; as noted above, they may or may not carry freight and if they do it tends to be items such as tools of trade or building materials;

- government, which includes trucks used by government at all levels in carrying out its various functions.

Recent data are not available showing the distribution of the ownership of the urban truck fleet amongst these four groups, but early data (e.g. Smith, 1969) indicated that about one-half of the urban truck was private, one-third personal, and commercial and government were each less than ten

25

percent. In Los Angeles in 1987, 25.6 percent of non-government heavy trucks (>11.8 t (26,000 lb)) were operated by commercial carriers, 17.6 percent by the construction industry, 16.5 percent by manufacturers, 15 percent by the wholesale trade, 11.3 percent by the agriculture sector and 9.5 percent by retailers (Cambridge Systematics, 1988a, Technical Memorandum 3–2).

These data are important, because they reveal that, contrary perhaps to expectations, only a small proportion of the urban truck fleet is owned by commercial for-hire carriers; the great majority of urban trucks are operated by firms whose main activity is not transport, but which operate trucks in order to carry their own goods. This is true of both large and small trucks.

Truck usage

The average daily distance travelled in Chicago in 1986 by the four truck size categories described above is shown in Table 2.3.

Table 2.3
Truck usage patterns by truck type, Chicago, 1986

Truck type	Average daily distance distance km (miles)	Average daily trips (number)
small trucks and vans	90 (56)	6.9
light trucks	91 (57)	7.9
medium trucks	116 (72)	9.3
heavy trucks	173 (108)	5.9

Source: Reilly, Rosenbluh and Rawling (1987), p 36, 41.

It is interesting to note that these figures are considerably higher than those observed in the US in the 1960s, by a factor of about 2 (Smith, 1969). However, as will be seen later, the number of trips made in a day has changed little, so what is probably being indicated here is more a·change in urban structure and a change in the location of freight generators, with longer hauls between shippers and receivers. Also, the Chicago data may have included some trips by trucks which passed through the area, and since it is reasonable to suppose that these would be longer than internal trips, they may have inflated the overall average (op cit, p 41).

The above data suggest that larger trucks are more heavily utilized, as might be expected given the greater capital investment implied by the truck size. This is also revealed in Australian data for 1987–88, which shows that the average distance travelled per year by articulated trucks in capital cities was 27,500 km (17,100 miles), and for rigid trucks 20,200 km (12,500 miles) (Australian Bureau of Statistics, 1990, Table 12).

Another measure of truck usage is the time spent travelling. There is no recent data on this, but early US data reported by Smith (1969) indicated that the average utilisation was 175 minutes per day, with light trucks spending more of the day at rest than heavy trucks. Ogden (1977b) showed that for Melbourne, Australia in the 1960s, commercial (hire and reward) trucks were more heavily utilized than other trucks, but still managed only 3.6 hours per day. Christiansen (1979, p II–28) has reviewed data from various US cities, and has shown that dwell time (i.e. time spent picking up or delivering goods) is typically in the range 15–25 minutes.

Trips made by trucks

The preceding section has reviewed the characteristics of the urban truck fleet. In this section, the characteristics of trips made by that fleet are reviewed.

Trip generation

In Chicago in 1986, the average number of trips made per day by the various categories of truck was as shown in Table 2.3. These results are comparable with earlier US studies, which indicated an average trip generation rate of around 6 trips per day (Smith, 1969). The Chicago results also showed a very wide dispersion in the distribution of the number of trips per day, no doubt reflecting different usage patterns. Overall, truck trip generation in Chicago was about 300 trips per day per thousand population.

27

Trip purpose

No recent data are available on truck trip purpose. Early US studies (e.g. Smith, 1969) indicated that about half of all urban truck trips were pick up or delivery, about 10 percent were service trips, and the rest included a range of business, construction and private uses. Table 2.4 shows data for Dallas, Texas (central business district only) and the Chicago study area, as reported by Christiansen (1979).

Table 2.4
Distribution of truck stops by purpose,
Dallas and Chicago

Purpose	Dallas CBD, 1972 (percent of stops)	Chicago, 1970 (percent of stops)
pickup	16	20
delivery	59	55
pickup and delivery	10	8
service	5	17
other	10	–
total	100	100

Source: Christiansen (1979), p II–26.

Commodities carried

The relationship between truck trips and the commodities carried on those trips is not very meaningful. A given commodity consignment may be associated with several trips, and conversely a trip may not involve any commodity at all. However, it is of interest to note the distribution of commodities carried on truck trips. Table 2.5 lists the distribution of commodities carried as a percentage of internal truck trips in Chicago in 1986.

Table 2.5
Distribution of commodities carried on trips, Chicago, 1986

Commodity	Trips (percent)
parcel post and express	19.4
printed matter	12.1
electrical machinery	19.3
mail	9.5
food and kindred products	9.0
empty trucks	7.8
service equipment	3.7
waste and scrap	3.0
loaded tankers, tailers	2.7
fabricated metal products	2.4
machinery, except electrical	2.0
household goods	1.9
miscellaneous manufactures	1.5
chemical and allied products	1.6
furniture and fixtures	1.4
stone, clay, glass and concrete products	1.4

Source: Rawling (1989), p 115.

The very low proportion of empty trips seems surprising in this data; work elsewhere in earlier years showed more like one-quarter of truck trips to be empty (e.g. Smith, 1969, Transportation Development Agency, 1974). Also, the high proportion of mail did not show up in earlier work. Perhaps the definition of 'trip' is different. In any case the definition of 'commodity' certainly matters; since the Chicago differentiates machinery into a wide range of categories, only one type (electrical) shows up as important.

This is apparent if the Chicago results are compared with another comparatively recent study, that of commodities carried on trips using selected bridges and tunnels in New York (Strauss-Wieder, Kang and Yokel, 1989). Although this was not a metropolitan area-wide study as in

Chicago, the distribution of commodities carried on truck trips is still of interest (Table 2.6). (Note that in this study, there were no empty trucks recorded; presumably the results reported were for loaded trucks only.)

Table 2.6
Distribution of commodities carried on selected tunnels
and bridges, New York, 1985

Commodity	Trips (percent)
food	22.3
miscellaneous freight	9.2
paper	8.5
furniture	5.7
apparel	5.3
chemicals	4.9
metal products	5.6
concrete and clay products	3.6
transport equipment	3.5
electrical machinery	3.5
all other	28.1

Source: Strauss-Wieder, Kang and Yokel (1989), p 88.

Trip length

Reilly, Rosenbluh and Rawling (1987, p 36) have presented results showing the average trip lengths for trucks in Chicago in 1986. These were as follows:

small trucks and vans	17.7 km (11.1 miles)
light trucks	15.5 km (9.6 miles)
medium trucks	16.9 km (10.5 miles)
heavy trucks	40.0 km (24.9 miles)

These trip lengths are very much longer than those reported in other cities or even in Chicago in 1970. Rawling (1989, p 101) attempted to explain this in terms of different data bases, different trip definitions, and changes in urban structure. Also, as noted above, they may have included some 'through' trips (i.e. trips with neither origin nor destination in Chicago). Whatever the reason, the difference is so great that these results should not be considered applicable to other urban areas. For example:

-   Smith (1969) found an average truck trip length across 11 US cities in the 1960s to be 5.6 km (3.5 miles);

-   Ogden (1977b) found an average of 5.1 km (3.2 miles) for Melbourne, Australia in 1963;

-   Christiansen (1979, p II–31) reported an average across several US cities in the 1970s of 4.9 km (3.0 miles) for light trucks, 5.7 km (3.5 miles) for medium trucks, and 11.3 km (7.0 miles) for heavy trucks; the overall average truck trip length for these cities was 5.2 km (3.2 miles).

Average trip lengths for heavier vehicles tend to be longer, probably because the smaller vehicles are more likely to be engaged upon pick up and delivery operations. The Chicago data show a very wide dispersion of trip lengths, with heavy trucks in particular showing little tendency to peak. As a result, mean values are not very meaningful.

Hourly variations

Truck traffic is not peaked, at least not to the same extent as car travel. Figure 2.1 shows the distribution of truck trips by time of day in the Chicago study (Rawling, 1989). The distributions for light and medium trucks are quite similar, showing a fairly uniform rate of trip generation between about 9 am and 2 pm, with about 9–10 percent of total daily traffic in each hour at that period. Heavy truck traffic is not peaked either, but shows a fairly uniform rate of activity between 8 am and noon, with about 7 percent of total daily generation in each hour; as a corollary, heavy truck traffic is greater at night with between 1 and 3 percent of daily traffic generated in each hour between 7 pm and 5 am.

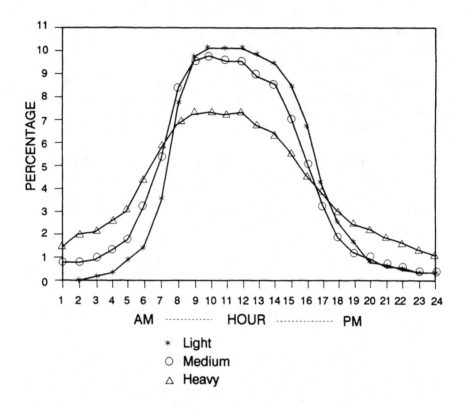

Figure 2.1 Hourly variations in truck traffic, Chicago, 1986

Source: Rawling (1989), p 117.

These are aggregate figures for a metropolitan area. Patterns for specific areas (e.g. central city, truck terminal area, industrial park) may be different, and patterns for particular land uses may also be quite different, depending upon the nature of truck travel demands.

The patterns of pickup operations across a day is different from that for delivery operations. A study conducted for the South Coast Air Quality Management District in Los Angeles (Lockheed Information Management Services, 1990) showed significant variations in the time distribution of shipments received and despatched, as well as between truck sizes. The results are shown in Table 2.7. Although activity continues throughout the working day, there is a tendency to receive in the morning and despatch in the afternoon. Night time activities are limited, although there is a greater tendency to ship at night than to receive, particularly for the smaller trucks.

Table 2.7
Average number of shipments received and despatched per week, by truck size and time of day, for businesses with at least one shipment, Los Angeles, 1990

Time of day	Received		Despatched	
	light	heavy	light	heavy
12–6 am	0.30	0.16	0.68	0.13
6–9 am	1.36	1.22	1.46	1.25
9–11 am	1.41	2.28	1.44	1.04
11 am–1 pm	1.04	1.41	1.37	0.95
1–4 pm	1.00	1.63	1.99	1.31
4–7 pm	0.22	0.30	0.53	0.53
7–12 pm	0.22	0.04	0.42	0.01

Source: Lockheed Information Management Services (1990), p 32 ff.

Trip generation by land use

Urban truck trips are generated by a wide variety of land uses. For example, Table 2.8 shows the distribution of trip destinations by land use in Chicago in 1986.

The overall picture presented by these figures is broadly comparable with earlier studies (e.g Smith, 1969; Ogden, 1977b), suggesting that the land uses associated with truck trips are perhaps more robust than some of the other variables such as trip length and distance travelled.

Trucks in the traffic stream

Possibly the best measure of trucks in the traffic stream is to consider vehicle kilometres (miles) of travel by trucks and other road vehicles.

There have been a number of studies of this parameter by various vehicle types, for example:

-   For Chicago in 1986, Rawling (1989, p 100) has reported that trucks represent 12.5 percent of vehicle equivalent miles of travel, where the equivalent comes from a weighting factor (unspecified) to account for the fact that a single truck has a greater influence on the traffic stream than a single car. After converting back to raw vehicle miles (or vehicle kilometres) using the proportion given by Reilly, Rosenbluh and Rawling (1987, p 41), it is estimated that trucks comprised 9.4 percent of Chicago's vehicle kilometres. Most of this travel was by small trucks and vans; it is estimated that trucks exceeding 8,000 lb (3.6 t) comprised 3.3 percent of vehicle kilometres of travel.

Table 2.8
Truck trip generation by land use, Chicago, 1986

Destination land use	Trips (percent)
retail	23
terminal/warehousing	21
residential	18
manufacturing	14
office, service	12
public, government	5
construction	2
in transit	1
agricultural	1
other, missing	2

Source: Reilly, Rosenbluh and Rawling (1987), p 43.

- In Australian capital cities in 1987–88, trucks (>4.5 t) travelled a total of 5.01 billion kilometres, which represented 5.8 percent of vehicle kilometres. As with Chicago, most of this was travel by small trucks; rigid trucks represented 4.8 percent of total capital city vehicle kilometres, and articulated trips represented 0.9 percent (Australian Bureau of Statistics, 1990, Table 11). Ogden (1988a) has noted that travel in Australian capital cities by heavy articulated trucks has grown rapidly, increasing by 12 percent per year between 1975–76 and 1984–85, compared with a rate of growth for all travel of about 4 percent per year.

- Analysis of the 1983 US National Truck Trip Information Survey (Blower and Campbell, 1988, Table 2) shows that 30.8 percent of all miles travelled by trucks (> 4.5 t (10,000 lb)) was undertaken in large urban areas, with 12.4 percent generated by rigid trucks and 18.5 percent by articulated trucks.

Usage patterns

Urban trucks serve a variety of industrial needs. Table 2.9 shows the distribution of vehicle kilometres by industry served and truck type for Melbourne, Australia in 1984–85. Overall, building construction, road transport (i.e. commercial or hire and reward trucking) and wholesale and retail trades were the main contributors, accounting together for nearly 70 percent of urban truck travel.

Movement of goods

The previous sections of this chapter have presented a profile of the urban freight truck fleet and trips made by that fleet. This may be thought of as the 'supply' side of urban freight (see Chapter 3). The 'demand' side of the picture involves an analysis of the movement of goods consignments.

The distinction between the movement of trucks and the movement of consignments is fundamental. A consignment is the movement of a single commodity from its point of loading to its point of unloading, and as such it may be associated with several distinct truck trips. Conversely, a truck trip may not be associated with a consignment if it involves the movement of an empty truck.

Table 2.9
Total annual kilometres by industry served and truck type,
Melbourne, Australia, 1984–85

| Industry | km (million) | | |
	Rigid Trucks	Artic Trucks	Total Trucks
agriculture	51.9	11.8	63.7
mining	6.7	7.2	14.0
manufacturing	125.6	33.7	159.3
building and construction	198.4	47.0	225.4
wholesale and retail	237.0	29.7	266.7
road transport	213.1	70.8	283.9
government	64.1	1.9	66.0
other and not stated	60.0	2.3	62.3
total	956.8	184.7	1141.2

Source: Australian Bureau of Statistics Survey of Motor Vehicle Usage, microfiche Table 8A (unpublished)

Unfortunately, in spite of the fundamental importance of commodity consignments in urban freight analysis, very few studies of goods movement (as distinct from truck movement) have been made. Those that have presented such information are reviewed below.

Demand per capita

The amount of freight demand movement generated within an urban area will depend to an extent upon the nature of the industrial and export base of that area. However, it is an interesting statistic, and House· (1979, p 26 ff) has outlined various ways in which it may be estimated.

36

Depending upon what is included, and the assumptions made, House estimated that 'the extent of urban goods movement activities in most cities would be between 45 and 73 tonnes per capita per year.' The breakdown of this amongst commodity groups in Canada is shown in Table 2.10.

Table 2.10
Per capita goods demand by commodity, Canada

Commodity	Tonnes per capita per year
food	2.0 - 3.6
beverages	0.5 - 0.7
paper	0.9 - 1.0
timber	1.0 - 1.2
garbage	1.1 - 1.6
mail, parcels, etc	0.2 - 0.3
construction	16.8 - 23.6
fuels	2.7 - 4.2
other	20.0 - 36.4

Source: House (1979), p 32.

These estimates include both internal movements, and goods delivered to an urban area from outside. Chicago data did not include this statistic directly, but an estimate based upon results published by Rawling (1989) would suggest about 80 tonnes per person per year for that urban area, including goods shipped out of the area. It would seem therefore that the Chicago results are close to Houses's upper bounds.

Hasell, Foulkes and Robertson (1978a) have published similar information for London, which seems somewhat at variance with House's conclusion. The London data showed an average road freight demand of about 27 tonnes per capita per annum, with food being greater (6.3 t) and building materials being much less (3.4 t). Perhaps this reflects different practices in different parts of the world, or perhaps it merely reflects different survey methodology.

Commodities moved

Rawling (1989) has presented data on commodity carried for Chicago in 1970 and 1986. Unfortunately, the commodity classifications are not identical across the two years, making time series analysis difficult. Moreover, as Rawling himself pointed out (op cit, p 100), 'structural differences in the survey techniques make it a case of comparing apples and pears.' Therefore, Table 2.11 shows only the 1986 results.

Table 2.11
Distribution of internal freight demand by commodity, Chicago, 1986

Commodity	Tonnes (percent)
waste and scrap	13.6
parcel post and express	13.4
food and kindred products	9.0
stone, clay, glass and concrete	7.6
loaded tankers and trailers	7.3
excavation	7.0
printed matter	6.6
non-metallic minerals	4.6
electrical machinery	4.0
petroleum and coal products	2.4
all other	24.5

Source: Rawling (1989), p 114–115.

Similar data are available for Australian capital cities as a whole. Table 2.12 shows the distribution of internal road freight tonnage by commodity for 1987–88.

Table 2.12
Distribution of freight moved within Australian capital cities by commodity, 1984–85

Commodity	Tonnes (percent)
sand, gravel and crushed rock	29.3
iron, steel and manufactures	12.0
other manufactures	10.1
processed food	8.2
cement, concrete and products	7.6
petroleum products	4.9
minerals	4.0
all other	23.9

Source: Australian Bureau of Statistics Survey of Motor Vehicle Usage, microfiche Table 49 (unpublished)

These results are broadly comparable with earlier results, e.g. in New York (Tri-State Transportation Commission, 1968), and Melbourne, Australia (Ogden, 1977c), with the exception that Chicago's results for parcel post and express, and for printed matter seem quite high, and petroleum products seem quite low (although this latter could be due to distribution patterns within the region, e.g. use of pipelines).

It is interesting to compare the distribution of freight demand (tonnes) by commodity with the distribution of truck trips by commodity. Ogden (1977c) has produced the following information for Melbourne, Australia in the 1960s:

- processed food and beverages accounted for 9 percent of tonnes and 6 percent of trips;

- tools and equipment accounted for 3 percent of tonnes and 12 percent of trips;

- petroleum products accounted for 6 percent of tonnes and 1 percent of trips;

- sand, rock, soil and gravel accounted for 15 percent of tonnes and 1 percent of trips, and

- waste products accounted for 12 percent of tonnes and 3 percent of trips.

Similar comparisons have been prepared in New York (Port Authority of New York and New Jersey, 1989, p 32). These comparisons emphasize the distinction that must be drawn between truck trips and commodity consignments.

Generation by land use

There is an absence of recent information on the generation of urban freight demand (in tonnes) by land use. Ogden (1977c) has presented data for Melbourne, Australia which showed that the main origin land uses were manufacturing industries, freight terminals and extractive industries, while the main destination land uses were again manufacturing industries and freight terminals, together with waste disposal, construction sites, retail and wholesale activities, and residential land uses.

A related statistic to land use is the industry served. For all Australian capital cities in 1984–85, the main industries served by road freight (in tonnes) were as shown in Table 2.13.

It can be seen that two industries, road transport (i.e. commercial or hire and reward trucking) and the construction industry together accounted for nearly half of urban freight tonnage. Of course, the commercial trucking industry in turn serves other industries, but it is interesting to note that over three-quarters of the total freight task does *not* use the services of the commercial trucking industry. Interestingly, this distribution is quite similar to that reported for the New York region in the 1960s; for-hire carriage (24.8 percent), wholesale and retail (22.0 percent), construction (18.3 percent), and manufacturing (16.5 percent) were the leading commodity groups (Wood and Leighton, 1969, p 331).

Miyamoto (1989) has presented summary data for Tokyo, Japan indicating that the main commodity groups moved within that metropolitan area are chemicals (27 percent of tonnes), metals and machinery

(16 percent), mineral products (15 percent), and waste and other goods (13 percent).

Table 2.13
Distribution of tonnes of freight carried within Australian capital cities, by industry served, 1984–85

Industry served	Tonnes (percent)
building and construction	24.7
road transport	23.0
wholesale and retail	15.6
manufacturing	11.7
government	10.6
all other	14.4

Source: Australian Bureau of Statistics Survey of Motor Vehicle Usage, microfiche Table 48 (unpublished)

It is interesting to compare the distribution of tonnes by land use with the distribution of trips by land use. Ogden (1977c) has noted that for Melbourne, Australia in the 1960s:

- residences accounted for 28 percent of truck trips, 4 percent of origin tonnes and 7 percent of destination tonnes;

- freight terminals accounted for 5 percent of truck trips, 15 percent of origin tonnes and 14 percent of destination tonnes;

- extractive industries accounted for 1 percent of truck trips, 1 percent of destination tonnes, but 12 percent of origin tonnes, and

- retail stores accounted for 20 percent of truck trips, 3 percent of origin tonnes and 8 percent of destination tonnes.

Similar comparisons have been made using data for London, by Hasell, Foulkes and Robertson (1978a). These comparisons emphasize the need to distinguish between the truck trip generating characteristics of land uses, and their freight generating characteristics. Some important freight generators have few truck trips associated with them, while on the other hand several important truck trip generators do not generate much commodity flow. In analysing truck trip characteristics, it is important to realize that a high proportion of urban goods movement is accommodated on a quite small proportion of urban truck trips. Although these comments are based on data that is quite old, these conclusions are almost certainly still valid.

Haul length

The average length of a haul is an interesting statistic, but one which is not often produced. However, if the estimate of total tonne kilometres is divided by the estimate of total tonnes, a measure of haul length can be obtained. For road freight in Australian capital cities in the four survey years 1975–76, 1978–79, 1981–82 and 1984–85, the average haul was 27 km (16.8 miles), 26 km (16.1 miles), 38 km (23.6 miles) and 35 km (21.8 miles) respectively (Ogden, 1988a). This would seem to suggest a trend towards increasing haul length, and this would be consistent with other statistics which reflect the changing pattern of industrial location and changing distribution patterns.

Freight moved by type of truck and operator

Although as noted above, the heavier trucks are a minority of the fleet, they carry a significant proportion of the freight task. In Australia, for all capital cities in 1984–85, articulated trucks carried 46 percent of urban tonne kilometres of freight. Moreover, the contribution of such vehicles to the urban freight task has increased quite markedly as truck operators seek to obtain the productivity gains that large trucks offer. Ogden (1988a) has noted that the contribution of heavy articulated trucks to the Australian urban road freight task increased at an average rate of 14 percent per year between 1975–76 and 1984–85, compared with an overall rate of increase in urban tonne kilometres of freight demand of about 6 percent per year over that period.

Similar trends have been observed in Tokyo, Japan. Miyamoto (1989, p 5) has shown that over 60 percent of tonne kilometres of freight moved is carried in larger commercial trucks, with some 25 percent being carried in larger non-commercial (ancillary or private) trucks. The balance is carried in smaller trucks.

Overview

As noted in the introduction to this chapter, recent comprehensive data on urban freight and urban trucking are very scarce. What data are available have been reviewed for what they reveal about the characteristics of urban freight, in terms of various parameters related to both trucks and commodities.

The information presented here is indicative only. Every urban area is unique, with its own pattern of industrial activity, imports and exports, land use patterns, industry structure, etc. This means that the urban freight activities associated with that urban area are unique, and therefore cannot be transfered to another place. In particular, the data presented here for Chicago (the only urban area with comprehensive recent data on freight activities) reflect the role and characteristics of that metropolis; they would not reflect the freight activities in another urban area with different characteristics.

That having been said, it is nevertheless the case that the overall general characteristics represented by Chicago and the other urban areas reviewed here may be of general interest. Such aspects as the economic significance of freight, the distribution of truck types and ownership, the distribution of trips by land use and commodity, the proportion of trucks in the traffic stream, freight generation by commodity and land use, and the difference between truck trip characteristics and freight flow characteristics are probably of general application, even though the specific features will vary from urban area to urban area.

Time series data are almost non-existent. Even though Chicago has undertaken two freight studies, one in 1970 and the other in 1986, comparisons between them are difficult because of survey methodology. However, it appears that some characteristics of urban freight are fairly robust over time, and perhaps even between cities. These include the distribution of trips generated by land uses, the number of trips per truck per day, the distribution of freight by broad commodity groups, distribution of freight by land use or industry served, and trucks as a proportion of total daily traffic.

On the other hand, several characteristics appear to have varied over time. Truck trips appear to have increased in length, mainly as a result of the suburbanisation of industry; distance travelled by a truck in a day has increased along with truck trip length (but total daily trips per truck do not appear to have changed much); some specific commodities have increased in significance (e.g. parcels); there has perhaps been a change in the distribution of truck trips across the day, with fewer trucks on the road in peak periods; and there is a greater preponderance of heavier trucks, both as a proportion of traffic and as a contributor to the urban freight task.

Notes

1. An overview of US data sources is presented in Rothbart (1988). Examples of aggregate national data sets are the *Highway Statistics*, published annually by the US Department of Transportation; the *Surveys of Motor Vehicle Usage*, undertaken tri-ennially by the Australian Bureau of Statistics; and the annual *Transport Statistics Great Britain*, in Britain.

2. Billion equals thousand million, or 10^9.

3. A useful glossary of terms used in trucking in the USA is contained in an appendix to Smith and Mason (1988).

3 The urban freight system

In Chapter 1, we emphasized the fact that urban freight transport is extremely complex and heterogeneous. There are many facets to it, many disparate and distinct activities, and many different persons and organisations with an interest or responsibility in one or other part of the process. Moreover, it is strongly inter-related with many other aspects of the urban system: the urban passenger system, the inter-urban freight system, the land use system, regional development, aspects of the physical and social environment, employment, and so on.

Therefore, it is necessary to devote some effort towards trying to understand the urban freight system, its role, and its complexities. In this chapter, we address three topics, firstly the physical distribution process of which goods movement, and urban goods movement in particular, is but part; secondly, the various participants in the overall urban goods movement process, and their often varying and conflicting perceptions and goals; and thirdly, the role and nature of urban freight, emphasising that it is essentially an economic activity and examining the supply and demand aspects of that activity.

The physical distribution process

Goods movement

A representation of the goods movement process, highlighting the various transport activities within it, is presented in Figure 3.1. This highlights the various phases through which a particular consignment may pass on its passage from a 'shipper' (i.e. the origin of that particular shipment) to a 'receiver' (the destination).

Usually the responsibility for the consignment is with the shipper. This is not always the case (e.g. a retailer may pick up goods from a market and bring them back to the shop in the firm's own truck). Also, in many cases the details of the distribution system, including delivery schedules, modes used, etc, may be the subject of negotiation and even contract between the shipper and receiver. However, usually it is the shipper who has day to day responsibility for arranging the transport of goods.

The shipper has three basic options. The first is to use the firm's own truck fleet to deliver goods, usually directly to the receiver. This is variously referred to as private trucking, ancillary operation, or own-account operation. There may be a number of reasons why a company may choose to use its own vehicles in preference to using a commercial carrier or freight forwarder, including reliability, control, customer relations, speed of delivery, flexibility and cost (Foster, 1979).

The second option is for the shipper to engage a commercial trucking firm to undertake the task. Trucking firms are of several types, as we will see shortly. The trucking firm will collect the consignment from the shipper and if it is a full truckload (FTL) deliver it directly to the receiver, i.e. literally a door-to-door operation. If it is less than a full truckload (LTL), the consignment may be first delivered to the trucking firm's terminal, where it may be consolidated with other shipments going to the same receiver or (more usually) to the same part of the urban area so that several shipments will be delivered on a delivery round. For intra-urban shipments, normally there would be only a single terminal operation involved (i.e. pick up to terminal to delivery), but if the consignment is to another urban area, there will probably be a terminal operation involved at the destination city (i.e. pick up to origin terminal to destination terminal to delivery). At the terminal at the destination end, the process is reversed; the incoming consignment is deconsolidated and the individual shipments are delivered to each receiver on a delivery round.

The movement from one urban area to another is referred to as line-haul, and may be undertaken by a variety of modes, including trucking, rail, ship or air. If trucking is used, usually the truck involved will be a combination vehicle (tractor semi-trailer, or twin or triple trailered truck, depending upon what the regulations allow); this is to take advantage of the obvious economies of scale of carrying freight in larger vehicles. Clearly, rail and shipping (if available) offer potentially even greater scale economies where freight flows are high enough to make them economic, though often at the

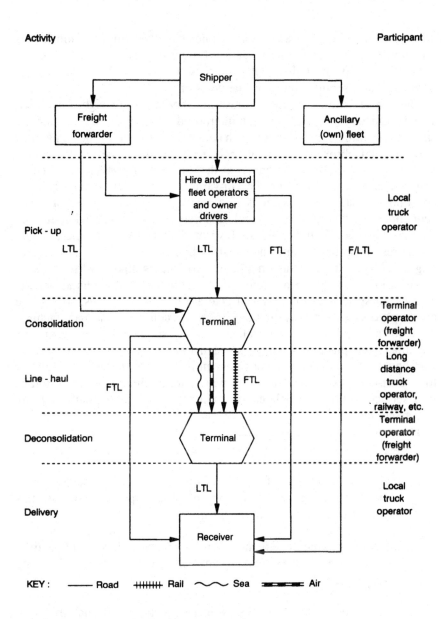

Figure 3.1 The goods movement process

Source: May, Mills and Scully (1984), p 15.

expense of level of service. Various studies have been made of the factors affecting mode choice for long distance freight (e.g. Harker, 1987; Young, et al, 1982; Jeffs and Hills, 1990) and these emphasize the importance of both price and service quality in the decision.

The shipper's third choice is to use the services of a freight forwarder. This is basically a service function interposed between the shipper and the carrier. Forwarders may or may not have their own fleet of trucks, i.e. they may be solely brokers arranging service on behalf of the client, or they may be virtually indistinguishable (at the intra-urban level) from trucking firms. The essential role of the forwarder, as we will see later, is to consolidate loads from various shippers to take advantage of scale economies. At the inter-urban level, this may be a multi-modal operation. At the urban level, the more sophisticated forwarders are increasingly taking responsibility for the whole distribution chain on behalf of a shipper (e.g. a manufacturer or a supermarket chain), not just transport (see below).

The above description has referred to shippers and receivers as generic entities. In specific terms they can take a multitude of forms, so that the above process may reflect anything from the delivery of a manufactured item to a retail store, the delivery of a sub-component from one manufacturing plant to another, the delivery of an item to (or from) a warehouse, the delivery of a consignment of sand or gravel from a quarry to a construction site, the delivery of petroleum products from bulk storage to a service station, the delivery of mail from a roadside mailbox to an addressee, etc.

There are several important implications of the above description from the viewpoint of urban freight planning and policy:

- there are a multitude of participants in the process, some concerned with demand, but most with one or other aspects of supply; this aspect is taken up later in this chapter;

- the ways in which goods move within, and to and from, urban areas can be quite complex, making analysis and (especially) modelling very difficult;

- a given consignment may be associated with several truck trips as it moves from one part of the system to the next;

48

- similarly, one tonne of inter-urban freight can lead to several tonnes of intra-urban freight since each separate urban delivery would constitute an additional tonne; and

- as products move from one part of the production to the next, they may increase in mass (e.g. addition of water as in beverage production) or decrease in mass (e.g chemical processes as in steel production, resulting in garbage, discharges into sewers or the atmosphere, etc) thus placing varying demands on the freight system.

Logistics management

The above description has briefly outlined the elements of an urban transport system. However, it is important to emphasize that the transport of goods is but one part of a chain of activities concerned with ensuring that those goods are at the right place at the right time. This overall activity is now usually referred to as logistics management (the term physical distribution management was previously used, but has now been supplanted).

Logistics management[1] has been defined by the Council of Logistics Management (quoted in Gilmour, 1987, p 4) as follows: 'the process of planning, implementing and controlling the efficient, cost effective flow and storage of raw materials, in-process inventory and finished goods, and related information from point of origin to point of consumption for the purpose of providing cost-effective customer service'.

More succinctly, Hutchinson (1987, p 2) defines it as 'the process of having the right quantity of the right item in the right place at the right time.' Button and Pearman (1981, p 141) emphasize that it is not concerned with demand creation, which is a marketing role, nor with the actual manufacture of goods, but it does make a positive contribution to the form, and hence value, of the product. As such it is an input, 'and can be traded off against product quality and cost, like many other inputs (and) should not be treated, as it often was in firms' accounting procedures, merely as an overhead cost.'

It is implicit in this that urban freight is but one part (albeit a key part) of a management process concerned with the transport, storage and handling of commodities. In the manufacturing sector, transport is increasingly seen as a variable item with costs and characteristics which are subject to management and control, rather than in its traditional terms as an 'overhead' which was a necessary, but essentially exogenous, cost item.

Gilmour (1987, p 5) has suggested the following reasons for the development of logistics management, and consequently for the changing perception of the goods transport task by manufacturing industry:

- the scope for logistics management to counter rapidly rising costs elsewhere in the manufacturing sector;

- the development and application of operations research techniques and computer technology to enable complex distribution problems to be analysed;

- the increasing size and complexity of business organisations;

- the expanded range of alternatives available in transport and distribution;

- changing markets and channels of distribution; and

- the growing tendency for retailers and wholesalers to shift the responsibility for inventory control back to the manufacturer.

In terms of its effects on the urban transport and traffic system, this broader level of consideration means that decisions about freight transport are made not just on the basis of transport variables per se (e.g. cost, reliability), etc, but also about how these variables affect the overall cost structure. Specific examples include:

- The 'just in time' (JIT) concept[2], whereby inventories are reduced or eliminated. This requires a transport system which is capable of delivering inputs to the manufacturing process with a very high level of regularity and reliability. This requires detailed cooperation between supplier, purchaser and transport operator, with implications for both transport technology (e.g. road rather than rail transport if there are reliability questions with the latter) and transport corporations (e.g. a large, well-managed firm is more likely to be able to offer the required service levels and back up than a smaller, owner-operated firm).

- The centralisation of warehousing activities, e.g. having one supply centre for the whole of a metropolis, a state, or even the whole of the nation, rather than a plethora of centres. This again requires the existence of transport capacity, and its ability to deliver goods with reliability at short notice. Its effects are felt in the balance between internal and external urban freight generated by the urban areas concerned, the use of various transport modes, the location of warehouses, and thus the location of traffic demand.

- The development of contract warehousing, or 'distribution centres', whereby the entire warehousing and distribution activity is carried out by specialists. This is particularly significant in the supermarket and food industries and is becoming more common with the petroleum industry. It has consequences for freight transport in terms of vehicle size, and location of traffic demand through the changing pattern of warehouse location.

Participants in the urban freight process

It is implicit in the above description of the physical distribution process that there are a large number of participants in urban freight activities. Further, the perceptions, objectives, constraints, and options which each group of participants has will be different. It is important to attempt to understand these disparate views because, as Noortman (1984, p 8) has succinctly put it, 'the urban goods movement problem seems to be to find an acceptable balance between these conflicting interests.'

Although the participating groups, or 'actors' may be categorized in several ways (e.g. Blaze and Raasch, 1970; Rimmer and Hicks, 1979; Meyburg, 1979; Wood, 1979; Tee, 1979a; Anon, 1989a), one useful categorisation is as follows:

shippers
receivers
forwarders
trucking firms
truck drivers
terminal operators and firms in other modes of transport
impactees
road and traffic authorities
government

In the discussion below, we attempt to paint a brief thumbnail sketch of each of these, examining the range of variants within each group, and exploring the disparate views each may have of the urban freight system. Such views must be something of a caricature, because in reality there will be considerable variation *within* each group, just as there is variation between groups.

Shippers

The term shipper is a generic one describing the person or organisation at the origin end of a consignment. Shippers thus cover almost the full spectrum of industrial, commercial and retail activities in the economy. As noted previously, the shipper usually arranges and pays for freight transport. It would be reasonable therefore to say that shippers are primarily interested in the total costs of distribution. To this end, they will typically seek to minimize total logistics costs, which may or may not equate to minimizing transport costs. That is, shippers may knowingly select a form of transport which is more costly than another, but do so because of savings elsewhere in the distribution (or manufacturing) chain.

However, if the distribution channel is a simple one so that there are no tradeoffs between components of logistics costs, or if the distribution is dominated by transport costs, it is reasonable to say that the goal of the shipper is to minimize transport costs, subject to the provision of an acceptable level of service to the receiver.

This goal will be pursued by such means as selection of transport mode and/or freight transport company (or use of private trucks). The shipper has an interest in installing adequate loading facilities at the despatch area, and having good industrial relations to permit the efficient outwards movement of products.

Receivers

The term receiver is also a generic one to denote the entity at the destination end of a consignment, and again this may cover almost every sector of the economy. Almost all firms are therefore both shippers and receivers. However, a firm may adopt a somewhat schizophrenic attitude towards freight, being very conscious of the costs of despatch, but being relatively indifferent to the costs of receival; because transport costs are usually paid by the shipper, the receiver is not directly conscious of the costs of inefficient receival facilities.

Thus receival areas in many instances can be poorly designed, inadequate, or poorly served. Even where the receiver is directly responsible, facilities may be poor, for the reasons outlined above. In other instances, the receival facilities may be the responsibility of a third party, e.g. a building owner in the case of an office building. In these cases, the tendency has been for the developer to regard delivery docks as 'dead space', and there is little incentive to provide adequate facilities; provision of the minimum required by government regulation is the norm. In use, many such facilities get utilized for purposes other than freight delivery, such as car parking.

The goal of the receiver is again probably to minimize transport costs within a broader logistics framework, but because, as mentioned, they do not usually pay directly for inwards goods transport, their attitude towards receival is more related to level of service (e.g. on time delivery and ensuring that there is the desired level of stock to keep the firm's employees occupied), industrial relations in the receival area, and efficient handling of goods once they arrive.

Forwarders

As mentioned above, a forwarder is a broker of transport services, who may be interposed between the shipper and one or other of the transport operators. Their essential role is to permit economies of operation by combining the shipments from two or more shippers, typically by mixing freight of varying densities to achieve optimum mass and volumetric loadings on line haul operations.

Forwarders come in many guises. They may be national or international in their operations, or concentrate on a specific route only. They may be uni-modal (e.g. shipping or trucking) or multi-modal; indeed, the wholesaling of rail freight services by a road freight operator has led several former trucking companies to become major freight forwarders, especially in Australia where the fact that interstate transport operation has been free of government regulation since the early 1950s has allowed a very efficient, highly competitive freight forwarding industry to evolve. Their is also a tendency for niche-marketing, with separate firms (often subsidiaries of a major parent) being established to serve, say, parcels express, computer deliveries, cut flowers, refrigerated products, etc.

Forwarders may operate their own fleet of trucks, rely solely on contractors, or have a mixture of both – this applies to both the line haul and the urban pick up and delivery operation.

The forwarder's objective is profit oriented, and so far as the urban freight task is concerned, this is reflected in attempts to minimize costs and maximize throughput. Forwarders are therefore typically commercially aggressive, employ trucking companies on a short term (daily or single load) basis, and can be highly footloose in their choice of terminal location.

In recent times, forwarders have evolved into contract warehousing, involving the management and operation of major 'distribution centres', whereby they carry out the entire warehousing and distribution activity on behalf of an industry client. This is particularly significant in the supermarket and food industries and is becoming more common in the petroleum industry.

Trucking firms

Trucking firms, or road freight operators, come in a large variety of forms, characterized by size, area of operations, and legal form.

Size. Trucking companies come in all sizes from single trucks (owner operators) to large national or multi-national fleets. However, truck fleets are typically of modest size, of perhaps 20 vehicles.

Owner-operators, or owner-drivers as they are known in some places, occupy an important role in the road freight industry in many countries. They are of several types, including those which are permanently on some form of contract to another company (which may be a trucking company or a freight forwarder, or a specific industry such as a truck carrying ready mixed concrete); they may be on a short term contract, such as hauling wheat or logs during a harvesting season; or they may be truly itinerant, operating on a trip by trip basis.

Owner-operators may get work through word of mouth, have an on-going relationship with a trucking company, freight forwarder, or shipper, or may be booked through a so-called 'loading agent', which is a broker between individual owner-operators and users of their service, usually on a single trip basis.

Forwarders and trucking companies use owner-operators for several reasons: they tend to be lower cost; as small business-persons in their own right they may be regarded as harder-working and more conscientious than employees on wages; the trucking firm's capital is not tied up in trucks and equipment; administrative costs are reduced; and there is possibly a better industrial relations climate.

For their part, owner-operators are attracted to the industry because of the lifestyle, the preference to be self-employed, and in some countries because of tax advantages, either because of the potential to income-split with a spouse, or to offset income and costs in an associated business such as a farm or a service station (see Wyckoff, 1979).

Area of operation. Although there are many national trucking firms in most western countries, there is also a very high degree of specialisation, especially in the urban trucking industry. Market segmentation is by specific industries (e.g. bricks, petroleum), market niches (e.g. the waterfront), or individual shippers (e.g. a retail store). In many countries, entry to the urban road freight industry is relatively free of government regulation, so this sector tends to be highly competitive. Rates may be on an hourly or a consignment basis.

Legal. In most countries and/or states within them, there are legal restrictions on the operation of the road freight industry, even in these days of so-called 'deregulation'. For example, in the US, there are four legal forms (Magee, Copacino and Rosenfeld, 1985, p 130):

-   Common carriers, which provide service according to a published tariff and often a published schedule, under close regulation. They may be authorized to operate within a specific geographical area, between specified terminal points, or for specified commodities only.

-   Contract carriers, which are limited to serving a specified shipper or limited number of shippers under contract; they have no service obligation to the general public and have freedom to negotiate rates.

-   Exempt carriers, which are those involved in the transport of products which are not subject to economic regulation; these may include agricultural products, lumber, etc. In most states, local delivery and urban cartage firms are exempt carriers, because of the administrative complexity of regulating such tasks.

-   Private carriers, which transport their own goods, as an ancillary function to the main line of the firm's business, such as retailing.

While the objectives of trucking firms, of whatever sort, are probably related to profit maximisation, this may be expressed as maximising the

55

vehicle's earnings. This can be pursued in the short term by varying the scheduling and routing of the vehicle, and the prices charged for its services. On a day to day basis, much depends on the skill of the vehicle despatcher, who may need to anticipate the likely pattern of demand for the firm's services in the course of the day, and attempt to have vehicles positioned to serve the expected demands.

In the longer run, the firm can modify the number and type of vehicles in its fleet (the increased contribution of large articulated trucks to the urban freight task noted in Chapter 2 is a reflection of the greater productivity which these vehicles can achieve), modify or lease specialized equipment, or reposition equipment. The firm also has the option in the longer term of relocating its terminal activities, and entering or exiting specific market segments in response to a marketing strategy or changing commercial opportunities.

Truck drivers

Although often overlooked in the discussion of urban freight, the truck driver occupies a key role. Driving a truck is a skilled occupation, and driving it in traffic, especially a large truck, is a stressful job. In many instances, the road and traffic system is poorly designed for large vehicles, while access to and use of many loading and delivery areas leaves much to be desired; the truck driver must confront all of this. There has been no formal research on urban truck drivers, and the most significant work on truck drivers generally (Wyckoff, 1979) specifically excluded urban operations.

The truck driver is responsible not only for the safety and security of the truck and its load, but also for ensuring that delivery schedules are met, and that the necessary documentation is completed. The driver also interfaces with many other people, and, particularly at the 'white collar' end of the market, may need to play an important public relations role on behalf of the carrier.

The driver's objective is probably not greatly different from that of the workforce in general, and may be expressed in terms perhaps of income, job security, and stress. In this latter regard, the significance of traffic congestion as a contributor to driver stress should not be overlooked; a study of the road freight industry in Sydney, Australia, found that the cost of stress-related illnesses amongst urban truck drivers was significant (Colston and Budd, 1984).

Terminal operators and firms in other modes of freight transport

Terminal operators are at the interface between the various modes of freight transport, e.g. seaports, airports, rail terminals, and truck terminals where urban pickup and delivery operations interface with line haul trucking operations.

Truck terminals may be part of an integrated system, where goods move on-line between a company's urban operations and its line haul operations. In this case, the terminal activities, while critical to the overall efficiency of the firm, are nevertheless seen in the context of the firm's total operation. With other truck terminals, as with the terminals operated by sea, air and rail transport firms, the activities and objectives of the terminal operator are probably very similar to those described above for the shipper and receiver (depending on whether the firm is despatching goods to the urban area or receiving goods for transport to another city).

In the case of seaports in particular, the terminal operator (i.e. the stevedoring company) occupies a key role, and has an important influence on the overall efficiency of water-borne freight and the costs of international transport of freight in particular; this is discussed in detail in Chapter 11.

Impactees

An impactee is one who is affected by the urban goods movement system while not being directly involved in it. In this sense, all urban residents are impactees[3], because all receive the benefits of the system (i.e. the goods which the system delivers). Conversely, since the costs of inefficiency, congestion etc are passed on, the customer ultimately pays for these.

However, most urban residents do not think of themself as impactees in this way, and the term is probably best used to apply to those who perceive a more immediate impact. These impacts, or externalities in economic jargon, are of several types. They include environmental effects such as noise, vibration and air pollution; safety effects through truck involvement in road crashes and incidents involving hazardous goods transport; effects on residential amenity (e.g. the visual effects of overnight truck parking, truck noise, etc) and effects on property values, which may be positive or negative.

In addition, the effect of trucks in the traffic stream should probably be regarded as an impact, to the extent that they are perceived by other motorists (fairly or unfairly) as contributing towards traffic congestion; this

57

includes not only moving trucks occupying road space, but also reduced sight distance and the perceived 'threat' of large trucks, and the effect of trucks parked (or double-parked) on the street to load and unload goods.

The impactee's objectives are probably quite simple: to reduce or eliminate the problem! This can and has led to quite draconian restraints on truck and freight activities, such as route or area truck bans, truck prohibitions by time of day, constraints on terminal location or operation, etc.

This tendency is exacerbated by three factors. First, elected politicians tend to pay more heed to a vocal group of voters than they do to an industry group. Second, the costs of imposing restraints of these sort are rarely if ever met by those insisting on them (goods delivery to an area with a truck size restriction costs more, for example, but traders in that area usually due not pay more, since delivery costs are averaged out over areas of the city and different receivers). Third, as a more general case of the second point, the costs of urban freight to the regional or national economy are rarely appreciated or included in decisions of this sort.

Undoubtedly the impacts of urban freight on some groups can be severe, and some form of government intervention is appropriate in many cases to protect impactees or minimize the extent of the impact. What is needed however is a framework within which these decisions can be made in the knowledge of all the likely consequences. Such a framework will be discussed in Chapters 4 and 5.

Road and traffic authorities

Road and traffic authorities include agencies at all levels of government that have responsibility for traffic control and road construction and maintenance. They occupy a key role because they provide the roads over which the trucks run, and thus the access conditions which influence the location of key generators, including freight terminals and major industrial areas.

These authorities' objectives may be expressed in terms of providing a service to road users, but as the previous point illustrated, there may be conflicts between different groups of road user – trucks, motor cars, pedestrians, cyclists, etc – which may not be easily reconciled.

Road authorities have a particular responsibility so far as heavy vehicles are concerned, since it is these that cause most wear and tear on road pavements. They thus seek to optimize their use of construction and maintenance resources over the lifetime of the pavement.

The role of these authorities, and the way in which they can contribute to urban freight objectives, is reviewed in detail in Part B.

Government

Finally, government, at all levels and in many guises, has a range of interests in urban freight. Responsibility for road and traffic aspects discussed in the previous section is of course one of these. However, more generally, government is concerned with the allocation of public resources to various sectors including transport, and the allocation of those resources within transport, including aspects that are related to urban freight. At another level, governments are concerned about economic development, and as we have seen in Chapter 2 that the costs of urban freight are significant in overall terms, governments have an interest in promoting more efficient and effective urban freight systems. Governments also regulate many of the activities of the transport sector, and the need for these regulations and their appropriateness should be reassessed from time to time to see that they are still achieving what they set out to achieve. Government is also concerned with environmental and road safety objectives, and the urban trucking industry has been the focus of some attention here, as discussed above. Finally, government must attempt to resolve concerns which are raised by residents and industry, and as we have seen both groups have complaints which they have placed at the door of government for resolution or attention.

Clearly, many of these objectives are conflicting and involve tradeoffs. We discuss the role of government in more detail in Chapter 4, and much of the discussion in Part B is about the role of the public sector in relation to urban freight objectives and strategies which may be used to achieve those objectives.

Nature and role of urban freight

The preceding sections of this chapter have highlighted the complexity of urban freight, the need to consider it in the context of a broader process of physical distribution, and fact that there are many participants in the urban freight system with a range of disparate and oft-conflicting goals.

The complex and multi-dimensioned nature of the system requires us to explore thoroughly the nature and role of urban freight. It is important that planning and policy for urban freight, which is the focus of this book, takes place in the context of a clear conceptual framework. In the absence of such a framework there is a danger that planning and policy might be less fruitful than desired, and even counter-productive.

In this section, we outline the basis of such a conceptual framework. The balance of the material in this book will be developed within this framework. Its essential features are:

- freight must be recognised as being essentially an economic activity;

- a clear distinction needs to be made between supply and demand aspects of urban freight; and

- while many of the problems of urban freight appear on the supply side, the key to understanding urban freight processes lies on the demand side.

Freight as an economic activity

The demand for freight transport does not arise from the transport system, nor do consumers demand freight services for their own sake. Rather, the demand for freight arises from the demand for goods; as Button and Pearman (1981, p 35) have put it, 'the demand for freight transport arises because firms use it as an input, either to their production processes (incoming raw materials), or to their distribution (taking their production to shops, customers or other firms), or both. In the formal language of economics, the demand for freight is a derived demand.'

Harper (1982, p 14) has suggested that freight transport adds 'utility' (which he defined as usefulness or the ability to give satisfaction) of four sorts:

- place utility: so that goods can be where they wanted;
- time utility: at a time that they can be used;
- form utility: in a useable form; and
- possession utility: in the possession of the person or firm that needs them.

The sole function therefore of the freight system is to move goods from one location to another to be consumed, processed, repaired, modified, stored, disposed of, or otherwise used or acted upon. It does not itself add value to the commodity being moved, but makes it possible for other sectors of the economy to add value. In essence, freight transport is the means by which goods are moved as part of the economic process of production and consumption.

It is necessary to take this fundamental view because it emphasises that freight is essentially an economic activity. The demand for freight is not for transport per se, but it is for a commodity or service which is presently at some other location. Nor do goods move for their own sake; they are moved only if they are greater value at some location other than their present one.

As with any other economic activity, freight transport has both a demand and a supply side. We now explore each of these: the nature of freight demand, and the relationship between demand and supply.

The demand for urban freight

Arising from the above discussion, we can say that:

> *the demand for freight arises from the economic process of production and consumption.*

In turn, freight demand must reflect the range of social and economic activities in the community. Consequently, freight transport allows the community to achieve a wider set of social and economic goals.

The goals of the community, and of individuals in the community, are many and varied. They may be inconsistent and conflicting. They are certainly not the same for all members of the community, and they change with time. Some goals are concerned with factors that are essential to life, such as the need for food, clothing or shelter. Other goals devolve from the norms of society since these have a significant influence on individual behaviour patterns.

These community goals have a number of direct and indirect effects on urban freight flow, as follows:

- They have a significant influence on the form and structure of urban areas, and thus of the location of trip ends. Individuals within the community make personal decisions regarding such factors as choice of home, job, shop, and so on. Although these choices may be circumscribed to an extent by factors such as zoning ordinances and travel costs, these factors in turn partially reflect community goals

61

and aspirations. The sum total of all of these location decisions and preferences has a dominant effect on urban form and structure.

- The influence of community goals affects the location of certain specific activities which are important freight generators. For example, the separation of residential and factory areas, the development of industrial and business parks and regional shopping centres, and other similar developments reflect the community's attitude and behaviour to the siting and use of these activities. But once having been thus located, the traffic patterns, and in particular the freight flow patterns, associated with them are determined.

- The generation of urban freight, and the mix of commodities which are transported, are a direct reflection of community goals. It would be possible to conceive of a community which had little if any demand for freight transport. It would be a community in which each family or small group was self-sufficient in terms of items such as food and clothing, and one in which there was little or no tendency to accumulate material possessions. Construction activity would also be minimal, and 'service industries' would not require materials like paper and furniture. Communities like that might exist, but modern western communities are not like that. Food and other essentials are grown or produced at distant places, the community places a high value on material possessions, building is essential and substantial, the manufacture of material items is a mainstay of the economic system, and service industries both consume and produce goods.

The implication of this is not that demand is a fragile thing, likely to collapse as community attitudes change. (Indeed, the nature of urban areas and the attitudes of their inhabitants are such that freight demands will continue to exist; the form and structure of existing cities and their industrial bases require that goods of all descriptions be transported to, from, and within them.) The implication is rather that the movement of goods is demand-oriented. Depending on the goals and aspirations of the community, different types and amounts of goods will be sought, and thus moved. As these goals change, so the type and amount of goods *produced* will change, and thus the freight task will change.

A further implication of these arguments is that the demand for freight movement within an urban area is largely inelastic with respect to the price of transport. These prices will have a marginal and sometimes significant influence on the location of specific activities, but generally the demand for urban freight movement will prescribe its supply.

The demand for freight is not totally inelastic of course. The demand for freight is directly dependant upon the demand for goods, and this is turn is partly related to the price of those goods. Thus only to the extent that the cost of transport affects the price of goods will it affect the demand for freight. Therefore, it is only where freight costs are a significant component of a product's value that the cost of freight will affect the demand for that product (Friedlaender, 1969). This situation is rare, because, as discussed in Chapter 2, transport costs can be quite a small proportion of the cost of production for manufactured items. The only products in the urban environment whose demand may be elastic with respect to the price of transport are bulk commodities such as sand, rock, pre-mixed concrete, etc.

The effect of transport cost on urban transport demand is more likely to be found in terms of ex-urban mode use (for those transport markets where there are competing modes), location of freight terminals, alternative sources of supply for a particular commodity if there are freight cost differentials, and decisions concerning the quality of freight service demanded.

Button and Pearman (1981, p 36) have outlined three hypotheses about demand elasticity for a derived input such as transport:

-   the elasticity of demand for transport varies directly with the elasticity of demand for the product transported;

-   the smaller the cost of transport as a proportion of the total cost of the product, the less elastic will be the demand for transport; and

-   the demand for transport will be the more elastic the easier it is to substitute some other factor for it; this might include another mode or replacement of transport with electronic communication (e.g. document delivery with the fax transmission).

There are in general only four ways in which the demand for urban freight can be reduced:

-   Freight movements can be replaced by passenger movements, e.g. by consuming food at a restaurant instead of taking it home. These situations are rare, and in any case may increase rather than decrease the total urban transport task.

- Freight may be replaced with freight substitutes – coal with electricity, letters with telephones, documents with fax, etc. Again, while these changes are important in themself, the overall effect on urban freight demand is marginal.

- The form and structure of urban areas could be altered to reduce the transport task by bringing shippers and receivers closer together. While this can and perhaps should be a goal of urban planning, it must be seen as but one of many goals, and to achieve success would mean reversing trends, which as we have seen in Chapter 2 has seen a substantial suburbanization of freight demand with consequent increases in trip length and average haul.

- The quantity of goods produced and consumed could be reduced. Consumer preferences or government policy may affect these changes. For example, if consumers prefer to purchase small cars instead of large cars, or if they decide to purchase expensive (but lightweight) electronic equipment instead of heavier consumer items like cars or electrical appliances, the mass of urban freight would be affected. However, changes of this nature do not arise from the transport system; if a consumer buys a personal computer instead of a refrigerator, it needs to be delivered just the same, and the cost of its delivery would have little to do with the choice. Government policy can be quite influential in the case of some specific commodities or industries, arising from such areas as the state of the national or local economy, support for specific industries (e.g. agriculture of building construction), tariffs or other barriers or incentives to trade, etc. The common feature of these policies is that they are *not* specifically directed at urban freight; increases or decreases in freight flow as a result of such policies are incidental outcomes of such a policy.

These arguments have practical as well as conceptual significance in the context of urban transport planning and policy. In analysing urban freight, the demand side must be looked at very carefully. There is little scope in the short term for transport policy or planning decisions to affect the quantity of urban freight flow, and any action on the part of the planner to restrict it would immediately have economic, social and political consequences. It may be possible in some cases to shift it around: move to another route, another time of day, even perhaps another mode, but hardly ever to eliminate the demand. This contrasts sharply with urban passenger transport, where it is sometimes an explicit policy objective to restrain demand, rather than increase the availability or efficiency on the supply side. This approach is sometimes feasible with passenger travel, where some of the demand is discretionary.

Relation of supply to demand

If it is accepted that the level of demand for urban freight is inelastic with respect to freight transport cost, as argued above, it follows that:

the function of the freight system is to provide the means of meeting a given level of demand.

The supply of an urban freight transport service thus arises fundamentally in response to the demand for goods by the urban community. The vehicles, terminals, labor force, etc are resource inputs to the supply of that transport service.

Hicks (1977, p 121) has succinctly described the relationship between supply and demand in urban goods movement:

Demand for goods transport stems from the decision-making involved in economic production and consumption. The central factors are the community's output of goods, the nature, value and utility of these goods, the community's consumption patterns and the economic, geographic and demographic relationship between consumers and producers. Supply of goods transport represents the response to this demand by commercial enterprises, government and individuals. The nature of this transport supply is determined by decisions affecting the size and description of the vehicle fleet, the road network and terminal facilities, and the operation, scheduling and routing of vehicles... It would be simplistic and economically improper to attempt to maintain a rigid distinction between the supply and demand sides of urban freight: their interrelatedness is total. Yet the distinction is useful.

The relationship of supply to demand in urban freight is rather different than it is in the case of urban person movement. In the latter, particularly with regard to travel by private car, the supply characteristics have been virtually prescribed once demand has been defined (Hicks, 1977, p 121). With urban freight, the relationship is not as strong. The shipper of a

65

particular consignment may be quite unconcerned about the details of the transport service by which the consignment is moved – the type of vehicle, its route, consolidation with other consignments, or (within limits) the time taken. There are two important consequences of this supply-demand dichotomy.

First, it implies that few, if any, persons or organisations are concerned with the total urban freight process. The shipper, receiver, truck operator, terminal operator, and each of the other participants described above have their own spectrum of interest, and do not concern themselves with other aspects of the total process. Some (shippers and receivers) are concerned with demand, most are concerned with one or other aspects of supply.

Second, it highlights the different ways in which supply and demand are manifested:

-   On the demand side, freight is manifested in terms of *consignments*: the movement of a particular commodity shipment from the shipper to the receiver. Demand on the transport system is thus measured in terms of *tonnes* or *tonne-kilometres* to be moved. In economic terms, it would be measured in terms of the value of freight moved, but this data is rarely available for urban goods movement.

-   Freight supply, i.e. the means by which such a consignment is moved, is manifested in terms of *vehicle movements*. In the case of road freight (which accounts for most intra-urban freight), these movements are measured as *vehicle trips*, i.e. the one-way movement of a truck from a trip origin to a trip destination.

The distinction between the two is emphasized on an urban pick-up and delivery round, where a consignment would be included in several trips, and a particular trip would incorporate several consignments. Conversely, a trip need not involve any consignment, if it is the movement of an empty truck.

In studying and analysing urban freight, both the demand for freight movements and the supply-side response to that demand are important. Demand is important because, as Simons, et al (1972) have put it 'analysis of the urban goods movement system and identification of desirable changes in it starts with assessment of demand.' The key to understanding urban freight clearly lies on the demand side. On the other hand, the supply side is important because many of the costs and impacts of urban freight are associated with he movement of trucks, and analysis of the efficiency and impact of the urban freight system must be concerned with the operation of transport facilities.

Moreover, the nature of freight demand and the industry (or supply-side) responses are dynamic and change over time. Possible future trends are discussed in Chapter 12.

Summary

In the development of planning and policy for urban freight systems, it is important that a clear perspective on the nature of urban freight be maintained. This perspective should recognise the following:

- Freight is essentially an economic activity. It has no function or value in itself; its sole function is in the movement of goods from one location to another where they are of greater value (or to be disposed of in the case of waste products). Goods transport is the means by which commodities are transfered as part of the economic process of production and consumption.

- A clear distinction needs to be made between demand and supply aspects of urban freight, while recognising their intimate interdependence. The freight system exists to cater for the demand for the movement of goods. Trucks, freight terminals, etc are resource inputs to the supply of a transport service.

- While many of the problems, costs and impacts of urban freight appear on the supply side, the key to understanding urban freight processes lies on the demand side.

Notes

1. The subject of logistics management is a distinct entity, and a significant and growing aspect of business management. Detailed discussion is beyond the scope of this book, but sources such as Gilmour (1987), Hutchinson (1987) and Magee, Copacino and Rosenfeld (1985) provide useful introductions.

2.   There is more to the 'just in time' concept than merely reducing inventories, although that is important. It is really a reflection of a different manufacturing production philosophy. The traditional production method is to 'push' material through the manufacturing process until it has been transformed into the finished product; material is manufactured into sub-assemblies and pushed on to the next stage of assembly or moved into stock. The alternative method, pioneered by Japanese industry, relies on a demand-pull system, whereby products are removed one at a time as they are completed, thus creating an opening within the manufacturing system that 'pulls' the exact amount of materials into production. The Japanese use a card-based system called *Kanban*, which ensures that materials can only be provided when needed as evidenced by a request from another work centre. A consequence of this is that production lines can be much more flexible in the variety of products that they produce, resulting in smaller production runs and hence higher quality and greater variety at lower cost (Hutchinson, 1987, p 122).

3.   This is well-illustrated in a bumper sticker once used by the American trucking industry: *If you got it, a truck brought it!*

4 Freight policy and planning

Previous chapters have reviewed the freight system, its components and functions, and presented an overview of the system as a whole. In this chapter, we begin to focus in upon the particular theme of this book, namely public sector policy and planning for urban freight.

We begin by postulating an overall goal, in a policy context, for urban freight planning and analysis. An analysis framework is then developed, which will enable us to structure and categorize freight issues and policy responses to those issues. Using this framework, the role of government in urban freight is discussed.

This material forms the basis for much of the balance of the book. In particular, the overall goal for urban freight postulated in this chapter is developed in detail in the next, in terms of a set of specific policy objectives covering the full spectrum of freight impacts. Means of achieving these objectives are then examined in Part B, and implementation of freight policy in Part C.

Goal of urban freight policy

It is helpful, even necessary, to begin our discussion on urban freight policy by attempting to articulate a set of explicit goals and objectives for urban freight. We distinguish goals from objectives, using the definitions of Stopher and Meyburg (1975):

-   *goals*, idealized end states towards which a plan might be expected to move: the desired eventual states of a planning process.

- *objectives*, operational statements of goals: measurable and attainable.

In Chapter 3, we argued that the role of the freight transport system is to supply a transport service to meet the demand for goods movement within an urban area. We emphasized that freight is a derived demand, of no value of itself, but only of value if it permits the transport of goods from one place to another place where they are of higher value (or the transport of waste products to disposal).

However, in supplying such as service, the freight transport system imposes a number of costs on the wider economic, social, and environmental system. Not all of these costs are internal to the transport system; some are recognized and met by that system but some are imposed on the community at large, in the form of externalities. (An externality is a cost imposed, as a result of urban freight movements, on a third party not directly involved in those movements (Button and Pearman, 1981, p 55)).

While, as the discussion in Chapter 3 has indicated, there are many legitimate objectives set by particular participants in the freight process, and while the public sector in particular has a multitude of roles, it is argued that the over-riding interest of a public policy in freight has to do with social costs. Hicks (1977, p 102) has asserted this in the following terms:

Demand for freight is a derived demand, the movement of goods being an input in the production and consumption process; it is a means, not and end. Thus the primary operative objective of the urban freight transport system becomes clear. The freight transport task should be performed at the lowest total social cost possible. The total amount of resources consumed and the disbenefits created in performing the freight task should be minimized.

From this, we can postulate an overall *goal* of urban freight policy and planning: again in the words of Hicks (op cit, p 102):

The discovery and effective implementation of measures which will reduce the total social cost of goods movement to the lowest possible level commensurate with the freight requirements and objectives of society.

In developing urban freight policy and analysing the urban freight system, the public sector is therefore concerned with the full range of costs and impacts of urban freight, the opportunities for and incidence of tradeoffs between the various cost elements, and the interaction between freight demand and freight supply.

It was noted in Chapter 3 that increasingly, in manufacturing especially, the movement of goods is being undertaken within a wider framework, often referred to as logistics management. The essence of this approach is that the whole distribution process, from the time a product leaves the supplier until the time it is received by the customer, is treated as a single management process, and the costs involved (including transport, warehousing, insurance, interest on the capital value of goods in transit, etc) are minimized as a whole. This implies that tradeoffs may occur between the various cost components, since the minimum total logistics cost is unlikely to be found with all individual cost components at a minimum. In particular, it may be that additional transport costs are knowingly and deliberately incurred in order to achieve efficiencies elsewhere in the distribution chain. However, this does not negate the validity of the overall goal as postulated above, that the freight transport system should operate at minimum resource cost. To the private sector, it merely implies a broader definition of the freight system (which is what is implied by the logistics management concept anyway). From a public policy perspective, the goal should still be to establish a framework within which overall social costs can be minimized, but acknowledging that certain users may not wish to minimize their own internal transport costs because they have a broader internal objective, and can trade those costs off against other internal costs.

For our purposes, it is helpful to identify six components of what we have called total social cost. Each of these readily translates into an *objective*, which are discussed in detail in Chapter 5. The six components of cost, or objectives, are:

- contribution to the regional, state and national economy;

- efficiency of operation (including traffic congestion);

- road safety;

- environmental impact;

71

- community costs (especially the cost of road construction and maintenance); and

- urban form.

A framework for analysis

In this section we develop a framework for analysis of urban freight issues. The essence of the framework is to define and specify the various components of the urban freight task in terms of supply-demand interactions (Ogden, 1984).

This leads into a discussion of the role of government, in the context of the overall goal of urban freight as discussed above, for each of these components. Problems and opportunities (i.e. the focus of urban freight policy) are then discussed in the context of this framework.

Building upon the material developed in Chapter 3, the analysis framework is based upon measures of urban freight demand and supply:

- Freight demand is expressed in terms of two variables - *commodities*, and the *land uses* which generate these commodity demands.

- The supply side can be represented by three basic variables: the transport network, the vehicle fleet, and vehicle movements. However, because of the importance and ubiquitous nature of the road network, it is useful to extract this as a special case, thus producing four supply variables: *road network, non-road network, vehicle fleet* and *vehicle movements*.

These six variables interact with each other. The interactions are shown in Figure 4.1.

The leading diagonal of this figure represents the characteristics of each of the six supply-demand variables as outlined above; these are defined and described in the balance of this section.

The remaining interactions represent particular manifestations of the freight task, each of which has a set of policy issues associated with it. These are discussed later in this chapter.

	VARIABLE	DEMAND		SUPPLY			
		Commodity	Land Use	Road Network	Non-Road Network	Vehicle	Vehicle Movement
D E M A N D	**Commodity**	Commodity	Freight generation	Commodity flow by road	Commodity flow (non-road)	Vehicle design	Vehicle loading
	Land Use		Land use	Location	Location	Building site design	Trip generation
S U P P L Y	**Road Network**			Road network	Modal transfer	Traffic design	Road traffic flow
	Non-Road Network				Non-road network	Right-of-way design	Non-road traffic flow
	Vehicle					Vehicle	Industry structure
	Vehicle Movement						Vehicle movement

Figure 4.1 Analysis framework

Source: Ogden (1984)

Commodity

As discussed in Chapter 3, the freight system is essentially concerned with the movement of goods, measured in terms of commodity consignments.

A complete description of a commodity consignment might include the following:

-   classification or description of the commodity (e.g. a commodity classification code such as the National Motor Freight Classification used by motor carriers in the US (Harper, 1982, p 198));

-   state (e.g. general freight, liquid, bulk, frozen, etc.);

-   mass of the shipment;

-   volume of the shipment;

-   value of the shipment;

-   number of pieces or individual items in the shipment;

-   the perishability, fragility, degree of hazard, and any other characteristics of the commodity that might mean that it needs special handling or care in transport;

-   the urgency of the shipment, its regularity or seasonality, or other characteristic of the shipment which may need special attention by those responsible for its transport; and

-   the frequency with which that despatch is made, which may have implications for the shipper, receiver or transport operator in terms of equipment, control, etc.

Some of these characteristics may interact. For example, the value of the product in relation to its bulk has a major effect upon the cost of transport as a function of product value, and will likely determine the characteristics of the transport system used to transport it (e.g. a million dollars worth of oil will move in very different manner than a million dollars worth of diamonds). Similarly, the bulk in relation to the mass is important, particularly to road freight operators who often attempt to configure their

74

loads so that they are full volumetrically and near to maximum load and axle limits. Further, truckload (or container load) shipments constitute a different type of demand than less than truckload (or less than container load) shipments, since the means by which they are transported might vary considerably.

Land use

The second element of demand is the land use pattern at the attraction and production ends of the commodity consignment. The elements of land use might include the following:

- the land use classification (e.g. manufacturing, retail, residential, etc); most urban planning authorities have designated land use classifications, and planning controls (including any which are directed at goods movement) usually depend upon them;

- the industry, which may or may not be synonymous with land use (e.g. the chemical industry and the auto component industry may both be classified as manufacturing land uses, but they could be very different in their freight needs);

- the type of building, such as single level, multi-level, etc;

- the availability and type of loading/unloading facilities;

- special storage features (e.g. frozen, bonded, etc.);

- access/egress conditions; and

- some measure of size (e.g. employment, floor area, site area, throughput, etc).

Road network

The road network is the first of the supply-side variables. It includes all the fixed infrastructure dedicated to the movement of goods by road, including the network itself, and the road freight depots or terminals associated with it.

The road network specification might include such factors as:

- road classification in both functional terms (e.g. arterial road, access street) and design terms (e.g. divided road, undivided road);

- road link distances;

- road link travel times;

- details of traffic control or equipment (e.g. speed limits, traffic signals);

- details of any restrictions or prohibitions directed at trucks, such as overhead clearances, load limits, truck bans;

- road link capacities (including both physical capacity and environmental capacity);

- road pavement strength;

- accident and incident record, including any information on truck involvement in these; and

- nature of abutting land use.

Also included as part of the fixed infrastructure of the road network would be details of freight terminals and depots; these are properly regarded as part of the supply side of the freight transport system, not as part of the demand side, which includes shippers and receivers of the commodity shipments. In practice, the distinction may become a little blurred.

The characteristics of the terminal might include similar information to that described above for land use. In addition, it would probably need to include details concerning:

- type of terminal (i.e. commodities handled, industries served), and any special needs thus arising, such as refrigeration, hazardous materials implications, etc;

- activities undertaken (e.g. on-line movements, inter-line movements; connections to other modes such as rail, pipeline or ship; break bulk; container stuffing and unstuffing, etc);

- materials handling equipment;

- ancillary operations, such as vehicle servicing, office functions;

- throughput capacity;

- hours of operation during the day; and

- factors having potential environmental impact, such as exterior lighting.

Non-road network

As mentioned in Chapter 2, most intra-urban freight movements are carried by truck. However, other modes are important because they may provide for external movements (those with an origin or destination outside the urban area concerned) and/or through movements (those with both origin and destination outside the urban area, but which pass through that area en-route). In addition, in some urban areas, non-truck modes, such as barges, contribute towards intra-urban freight.

In specifying and describing elements of the non-road network, the same or analogous factors to those listed for the road network apply.

Vehicle

As just mentioned, most of the vehicles relevant to urban freight are trucks. These may be broadly defined as any vehicle whose purchase is wholly or largely dictated by the need to carry goods. The definition of a truck is clearly somewhat arbitrary; the potential for joint carriage of both passengers and freight in one vehicle prevents any rigorous or exclusive delineation of passenger and freight tasks.

However, passenger cars and recreation vehicles should be excluded, as the carriage of goods is only rarely their prime function, and in any case it is hard to see how the inclusion of passenger cars could contribute towards freight planning or policy analysis.

The biggest problem probably lies with the service vehicle, defined by Staley (1978, p 654) as a vehicle 'configured as a truck and licensed as a truck, which is primarily used for any purpose other than the carriage of cargo or for strictly personal transportation.' Staley's examples included:

- utility repair and service, e.g. telephone, water, electricity, gas, etc;

- trades persons, e.g. painters, plumbers, heating and air conditioning services, electricians, interior decorators, locksmiths, carpenters, etc;

- industrial and commercial services, e.g. service and repair of computers and office equipment, vending machine service, industrial machinery service and repair, elevator service, janitorial and cleaning services, etc; and

- domestic services, e.g. laundries, dry cleaners, diaper services, radio, television and appliance service and repair, mobile lunch vehicles, etc.

In essence, the function of all of the above is to convey both the persons who are to perform the service together with their tools, equipment and materials. In many cases, the latter might be quite small in mass or volume (e.g. office equipment repair), while in other cases it might be quite significant (e.g. house builders). Moreover, in many cases the trucks used are light vehicles similar (even identical) to recreational vehicles.

In practice, a pragmatic approach is probably necessary, and a truck would be defined in terms of either size (e.g. any vehicle exceeding 4.5 t or 10,000 lb; the definition should correspond to a legal requirement, such as vehicle registration or the need for a heavy vehicle drivers licence), or description (the simplest of which is probably any vehicle with more than two axles or more than two wheels on the rear axle - excluding cars towing trailers!).

The characteristics of the truck might include the following:

- configuration (rigid (or straight) truck, tractor semi-trailer, twin, triple, etc.);

- body type (e.g. tray (or flat bed), tanker, refrigerated, tipper, concrete agitator, etc);

- mass (unladen and gross);

- dimensions (length, width, height);

- number of wheels and axles, and axle spacing (especially if pavement or bridge loading is an issue);

- load capacity, and volumetric capacity;

- type of ownership, especially distinguishing between trucks owned by firms within the road freight industry, private (or ancillary or own-account) trucks, and government owned trucks;

- operational control, especially whether the truck is controlled by its owner, or whether it is under contract to a third party; and

- any special features associated with the use of the truck, such as the need for permits to operate on particular roads.

For non-road vehicles, such as barges, ships or railway rolling stock, analogous specifications may apply, depending upon the need for such information.

Vehicle movements

The final variable is the movement of vehicles across the transport network. For trucks, this is measured in terms of trips, i.e. the one-way movement of a truck from one stop to the next. This definition needs careful attention in the case of a pick up and delivery round, where a truck might make literally dozens of stops in the course of a day, each of which, strictly speaking, corresponds to a trip. Careful attention must be given to trip definition and the use to which any data on trips is to be put in a policy or planning context.

In the case of truck trips within urban areas, key specifications include:

- truck trip purpose (e.g. pick up, delivery, pick up *and* delivery, return to base, empty return, maintenance or repair of vehicle, serve passenger, service function, etc);

- time of day; and

- trip origin and destination characteristics, including land use and/or industry, and location.

For other modes, and for long-distance trucking, additional information is involved, such as whether the movement is scheduled or on-demand, whether it is a unit-load or involves multiple shipments, and whether it is a single or a multiple origin-destination movement.

These broad outlines of each of the variables shown in Figure 4.1 are presented as indicators of what is meant by the terms used. Clearly, in any given application, the precise details of the information needed for the purposes of that application would need to be determined; it may be more or less detailed than that outlined above.

The role of government

The role of a public sector policy or planning agency in urban freight needs to be defined in the context of an urban freight sector which is essentially in the hands of private enterprise.

This sector in most western countries (including both the trucking industry and ancillary operators) is characterized by a large number of individual firms of varying size, free entry and exit, and an ability to serve its market. Many associated activities, including freight forwarders, terminal and market operators, long distance road freight companies and shipping companies, and perhaps airlines and railroads are also within the private sector. Ports and airports (and perhaps rail terminals) are operated by public corporations, which in their corporate objectives may have more in common with the private sector than the public service.

Planning and financial objectives within the private sector are, by their very nature, limited to those factors which are the direct concern and responsibility of the individual firms. It has been argued above that the goal of freight policy is to minimize the *total* social cost of goods movement. Thus it is important to note that the private sector will normally take account only of private, or internal, costs. Other costs (including those described above under contribution to regional and national economies, road safety, community costs, and urban structure) will rarely be taken into direct consideration.

Moreover, as Goettee and Cadotte (1977, p 40) have noted, 'the people most directly involved with freight movement (shippers, carriers and receivers) commonly accept the inefficiencies of the transportation system and either feel that they cannot influence the efficiency of the system or choose not to spend time influencing it.' Reasons for this include:

- problems to any one firm may be too small to worry about, although in aggregate, costs could be substantial;

- problems may be intermittent, and are accepted as a temporary inconvenience;

- delays and costs may be perceived as being small and less urgent than other day to day management concerns;

- businesses may be unaware that action can be taken; and

- trucking firms do not want to draw attention to themselves and their problems for fear of unfavourable publicity.

Most importantly, 'those in the private sector generally do not find it worthwhile to encourage any major improvements in system efficiency for freight because it would have no real effect on their profit margin. Since freight movement is quite competitive, any reductions in operating expenses would accrue directly to the consumer' (op cit, p 40).

For these reasons, decisions made in the private sector may not be optimal in a wider context. There is thus an important role for government to either remedy this, or attend to its consequences. Such intervention should minimize the extent to which there is outside interference in the day to day activities of private firms, since operating decisions should be left to the market, with competition between firms ensuring that an efficient outcome is achieved.

However, where there are external costs which are not the responsibility of the private sector (e.g. noise), or where there is a likelihood that problems would not be adequately dealt with if left to the market (e.g. safer vehicles), there is a case for government intervention.

As discussed above, an ideal role for government may be to attempt to 'internalize' as many of these external costs as possible. Indeed, Watson (1975, p 8) in discussing the role of government in relation to urban freight suggests that 'government has come to see its role as one of protecting the general public from negative externalities', and goes on to say that the primary strategy for doing this is to find policies which internalize the externalities, i.e. which transfer the costs back to the person or firm creating the problem. In this way, the costs of particular operating and investment decisions fall where they are due. Perhaps the best example of this is with controls on vehicle noise and safety equipment, where the additional costs which these requirements impose are in reality an internalization of some of the externalities. However, this principle is extendable to many of the policy issues discussed above, through such mechanisms as land use controls, regulations on vehicles, drivers and use of vehicles, etc. There is an extensive body of economic theory having to do with economic evaluation of proposals featuring externalities, and the criteria under which they are 'worthwhile'; these criteria are variously referred to as Pareto optima or Kaldor-Hicks criteria, which in essence say that a proposal is worthwhile 'if and only if the gainers from the project could (but not necessarily actually do) fully compensate the losers from the project without themselves becoming net losers' (Sudgen and Williams, 1978, p 8).

As times and circumstances change, the specific ways in which government may choose to participate in urban freight may change. However, it seems inevitable that government must continue to have roles to play in the urban freight field. As Hicks (1977, p 117) has said, 'it is difficult to separate almost any governmental decision from the realm of urban goods movement, because of its influence on economic activity and therefore on quantities of goods to be transported.'

Freight system descriptors and policy issues

With those general comments, we can now return to the analysis framework presented in Figure 4.1. As previously mentioned, each of the interactions within the matrix results in a particular manifestation of the urban freight task. In turn, associated with each of these is a particular set of policy issues, i.e. problems or opportunities in connection with the movement of freight within, or to and from, urban areas.

In the following discussion, we highlight therefore not only the various aspects of the freight task, but also the policy and planning implications arising therefrom.

There are fifteen supply-demand interactions shown in Figure 4.1, but the two commodity flows, the two locations and the two traffic flows may be discussed together, leaving twelve separate descriptors. These, and their policy implications, are reviewed below.

Demand-demand interaction

As Figure 4.1 shows, the single demand-demand interaction is freight generation, i.e. the generation of commodity flow by origin and destination land uses or economic activities.

Since, as discussed in Chapter 3, this activity is the whole function of the freight system (i.e. to move commodities), it is of fundamental importance in a policy context.

Policy issues related to the demand for freight include:

- the economic significance of the freight industry, in terms of such factors as employment, capital employed, investment, imports and exports, tax base, etc;

- the contribution which an efficient freight sector can make to the competitiveness of industry in the region concerned;

- conversely, the deleterious effect on a region if its industries are rendered uncompetitive due to poor freight services; and

- the effect of freight costs on the cost of commodities consumed in the region.

In short, since it is the demand for commodity movements which 'drives' the whole freight system, policy determination in urban freight must consider this aspect closely. Concomitantly, policy development elsewhere (i.e. on the supply side of urban freight) must take cognisance of possible spin-off effects on the demand side, which could in some cases have unwanted and undesirable effects; an example might be a regulatory policy which had the effect of making freight transport more expensive, with adverse consequences on an export industry.

Supply-demand interaction

There are six supply-demand interactions shown in Figure 4.1.

Commodity flow. This results from the interaction of the commodity and the two network variables. It is thus described as the flow of commodities over the transport network, by mode.

Policy issues in connection with commodity flow considerations include:

- the freight task (tonnes and tonne-kilometres) of freight movement, as an essential input to estimating, controlling or planning for other aspects of freight system supply;

- policies relating to mode use; and

- such broader policy questions as taxation policy (vehicle registration, fuel taxes, etc.) are closely related to this descriptor, since commodity flow is a measure of the extent of the freight task.

Vehicle design. This results from the interaction of commodity and vehicle variables, and involves the design of the vehicle to cater for particular commodity characteristics.

The main policy aspect here is consideration of the mass and dimension limits of the vehicle. Policy in this area has an important effect in two areas; the efficiency of the freight sector, and the design parameters (e.g. pavement strength) for transport system infrastructure.

Vehicle loading. This is the descriptor which results from the interaction of the commodity and vehicle movement variables: the mass, volume, etc of the load on each vehicle movement.

Policy interests here overlap with those for vehicle design, particularly so far as maximum vehicle loads are concerned. Other policy aspects include means of dealing with special loads, such as movements which exceed normal maximum mass and dimension limits, or treatment of hazardous goods movements, etc.

Location. This characteristic refers to the location within the urban area of the various freight generating land uses.

This is an important consideration from a planning and policy viewpoint, since one of the key ways in which public policy can be used to directly and deliberately affect urban commodity flow is by influencing the location of the land uses which generate that flow.

Building and site design. This descriptor results from the interaction of the land use and vehicle design variables. It refers to the compatibility (or lack thereof) between site or building design and the vehicles which service that site.

84

This again has important policy or planning implications, because of the ability of planning authorities to regulate to ensure that adequate facilities are provided. Particular aspects include:

- design of access roadways, ramps, etc;

- requirements for off-street loading/unloading facilities;

- requirements for off-street truck parking, and provision of truck parking facilities; and

- number, layout and design of parking bays, loading docks, etc, and their use (especially control of illegal use, such as for car parking, which prevents their use by trucks).

Trip generation. This is the result of the interaction between land use and vehicle movement variables, and refers to the number of truck trips generated by particular land use categories.

This variable leads directly to traffic demand. From a policy viewpoint, most of the consequences of the demand for truck flow are reflected elsewhere, particularly in the traffic flow descriptor (see below).

Supply-supply interaction

Notwithstanding the earlier observation that the freight system exists to serve the demand for the movement of goods, there are some important interactions between the various suppliers of these transport services.

Modal transfer. This results from the interaction between one mode and another, e.g. rail terminals, ports, airports, etc.

Policy interests here are related to various aspects of these terminal facilities. Publicly owned facilities such as ports or (in many countries) rail terminals have particular interest, since an agency of government has operational and investment interests. Thus, policy-makers are concerned with such aspects as location, investment, design, efficiency, and perhaps operational aspects.

Connection of the terminals to the urban road network is another interest, for both publicly and privately owned terminal facilities. Similarly, proposals to operate larger combination vehicles such as twins or triples in an urban area is a policy matter within this heading. Certain environmental aspects of terminal operations, such as noise, fall within this category also.

Traffic design and right-of-way design. These descriptors apply to the interaction between the vehicle variables and the respective network variables. They refer in particular to the design of transport infrastructure to cater for the physical dimensions, mass, etc. of the vehicles using transport facilities.

This is of particular concern to a road or traffic authority since there are policy and planning considerations in connection with the road network including design aspects (such as lane widths, pavement depths, overhead clearances, maximum road gradients, etc). Also relevant is the wider question of recovering from the road freight industry the costs of providing those elements of road infrastructure which are attributable to trucks.

While it is probably true that these factors are less of an issue in urban road infrastructure design than they are in non-urban situations, they are nevertheless of importance because they do have some effect upon the cost of providing and maintaining the urban road system. As such, they are the converse of the vehicle design policy issues discussed above.

Traffic flow. The movement of freight vehicles on the road network, or its equivalent for other networks, results from the interaction between vehicle movements and networks.

Policy and planning in this area is of considerable importance because it represents one of the main areas where public policy can influence the urban freight system to both minimize its deleterious effects and contribute to its efficiency. Particular aspects are:

- to facilitate the movement of trucks, or control the routes which trucks might take, mainly though the application of traffic management techniques;

- noise associated with truck or other freight vehicle movements, and its control;

- safety aspects of truck and freight movements; and

- in the case of publicly owned freight facilities, such as ports, policy-makers may be interested in the operating efficiency of the terminal concerned; this is particularly important in the case of seaports, since there is often competition between ports and an inefficient port can lead to the area served by it being less attractive for industrial growth, while in the case of rail freight (where government is responsible for it), these considerations are likely to be less relevant to urban freight movements than to long distance rail freight.

Industry structure. This is the term given to the interaction of the vehicle and the vehicle-movement variables, and refers to the recognition that vehicles are only supplied and their movement only occurs because there is a freight industry in place to supply those freight services.

From a transport policy viewpoint, the main concern is with the type and extent of government intervention in and regulation of the industry. Some pertinent considerations include:

- legal and constitutional constraints or requirements concerning freight industry regulation;

- extent and administration of regulation, including both quantity aspects and quality aspects, as defined above;

- processes of consultation between government, industry representatives and unions; and

- treatment for regulatory purposes of ancillary vehicles.

Summary

Although the above description has been in general terms and somewhat cursory, it has aimed to develop, within a systematic and consistent framework, a means of viewing and conceptualising policy issues in urban freight, and to describe what those issues are.

The resultant policy issues which have been discussed in relation to each of the components of the urban freight sector are of relevance in themselff, and since policy is essentially concerned with specific responses (or initiatives) in relation to specific problems or opportunities, discussion at the level of individual elements of the system is appropriate.

Many of the policy and planning instruments discussed in this chapter are reviewed in detail in Part B. This includes traffic management, planning and location, infrastructure, licensing and regulations, pricing policy, terminals and modal interchange, and the encouragement of more efficient or less intrusive operational practices by freight shippers, receivers or transport operators.

5 Objectives of urban freight

Introduction

In Chapter 4, we postulated an overall goal of urban freight for the purposes of policy and planning as being to minimize the total social costs of goods transport. Following the usual procedure whereby an overall goal (defined as a 'desired end state') leads to a number of more specific objectives which help to achieve that goal, we then suggested that there were six sets of objectives of urban freight, as follows:

- economic objectives;
- efficiency objectives;
- road safety objectives;
- environmental objectives;
- infrastructure objectives; and
- urban structure objectives.

Since the overall goal is expressed in terms of costs, it follows that each of these *objectives* can also be considered as *costs*, e.g. in talking about efficiency objectives, we are referring to ways of reducing the operating costs of urban goods movement. Further, these costs may be referred to or described as *problems*, e.g. where operating costs are excessive due to poor goods receival facilities, the operator might describe that as an operating problem. For our purposes here therefore, we consider objectives, costs and problems as essentially three ways of looking at the same thing.

There is much discussion in the literature about urban freight 'problems'. However, to base our discussion solely on a litany of problems does not achieve much; as House (1979, p 4) says, 'any industry presumably suffers from problems'. Rather, by basing our discussion on objectives, we implicitly acknowledge that in some areas there are costs of urban freight which may be excessive, either because of the operating environment (e.g. congestion), or as a result of externalities which are not reflected in the market place, such as noise or air pollution. Further, by referring to objectives rather than problems, we avoid the 'if it ain't broke, don't fix it' argument about urban freight: one that essentially denies the need to do anything.

This chapter therefore discusses each of the above six objectives in turn, describing what is meant be each of them, and discussing the ways in which they are experienced by the various participants in the urban freight process.

Economic objectives

An important objective of freight policy is to develop and improve the freight system towards an improvement in the regional, state or national economy. As the US National Association of Regional Councils (1984, p 2) expressed it,

> Goods movement flows within and between localities are linked both to the stability of regional economies and to the national economy. The collective result of separate goods movement inefficiencies and bottlenecks which occur from region to region have negative impacts on national productivity and growth. It follows therefore that improvements to regional goods movement networks will not only yield benefits to regions and their businesses and industries, but will ultimately bring forth benefits (either directly or indirectly) to the national economy.

Costa (1988, p 84) has outlined four economic effects of changes in freight transport costs:

-   an income effect, in which a change in freight system costs will have a multiplier effect which will raise or lower the level of production of other industries and their value added;

-   a price effect, which would be similar in its influence to an income effect if changes in costs led to changes in prices; this may not always be the case, as for example if the government chose to use

90

the benefits of a more efficient railway system to reduce its deficit, and in this case the benefits of transport efficiency improvements will be revealed elsewhere in the economy via a general lowering of taxes, ceteris paribus;

- market share effect, which would result from particular commodities or industries becoming (or ceasing to be) competitive in a given market area; and

- system-wide effects, which reflect the interaction between freight and passenger transport, and denote, for example, the effect of congested road networks on freight costs.

Whereas many efficiency gains are, in reality, transfers within the national economy, gains in the external account contribute real improvements to the national income. There are basically three ways in which this can occur:

- Where the world price of those goods is set by the market (i.e. increases or decreases in a country's exports have a negligible effect on world price), the net gain to the national economy is that world price minus the cost of production, transport and distribution. Thus, if the cost of domestic transport can be reduced, the net gain to the national economy is positive.

- Where a country's contribution to world production in a commodity is significant, a reduction in the cost of its exports may be able to affect a reduction in world market price. This may stimulate demand, resulting in a higher level of production and exports.

- Where transport system inputs are imported, any improvement in efficiency or productivity in the transport sector will reduce the level of such imports, for a given level of transport demand. The specific commodities here may vary from country to country, but could typically include petroleum products and trucks (including parts).

However, it is mainly in the trade exposed (i.e. exporting or import-competing) manufacturing sector that the urban transport system is critical for its contribution to regional and national economic performance. An important study of the inter-relation between transport efficiency and its effects on the national economy was conducted by Travers Morgan (1987) in Australia. It concluded that reduced urban freight costs, resulting from either more efficient operation or road improvements that led to travel time savings or more reliable delivery times, can directly effect the competitiveness of benefiting firms. If a firm used this cost reduction to increase export sales or squeeze out imported competition, there would be a direct benefit to the national balance of payments. This would then enable the national government 'to pursue expansionary economic policies, to the point where the increased imports that result from the stimulation equal the initial balance of payments gain flowing from the road improvement' (op cit, p 8).

The report went on to estimate the effect on the Australian gross domestic product (GDP) as a result of such a policy, and concluded that the multiplier was between 5 and 8, i.e. 'the ultimate increase in GDP flowing from this ... policy is about 5 to 8 times the value of the initial improvement in the balance of payments.' However, a multiplier of this magnitude would rarely be possible in practice because of other constraints on production, such as capital, labor, and the need for imported products generated by the trade-exposed sector itself. These factors reduced the multiplier to an estimated value of 1.5.

This work was related to another study in Australia (Road Construction Authority, 1987) which examined the economic benefits resulting from urban road investment, and in particular the benefits to regional or national economies resulting from reductions in domestic transport costs for trade exposed industries. It concluded that 'estimates of ultimate benefits to the national economy from major urban road improvements should involve increasing the benefits conventionally calculated for the freight sector (for time and cost savings) by about 50 percent.'

This is a very significant finding, for it implies that the benefits to the economy which result from certain freight-related road improvements are much higher than hitherto considered. A higher level of road investment, or a redirection of investment from person-oriented travel to freight travel is thus likely to be economically justified.

The critical importance of examining trade-exposed industries in any consideration of economic objectives in urban freight was also highlighted in a study undertaken in London, England. This study (Buchan, et al, 1985) examined the potential negative effects on the London economy of various types of ban on the operation of trucks within the London area, especially night-time bans. It concluded (op cit, p 33) that most industries served by trucks would not be driven out of business, but would be able to pass on any increase in freight costs. The ones at risk were 'firms based within London but competing with firms outside London for a regional, national, or international market ...' In this particular case, such firms were exempted from the provisions of the ban, but the general point is that in this study, as in the Melbourne study, the firms which were critical from the point of view of the effect of urban freight costs on the regional economy were those which were exposed to competition from outside the region.

The Southern California Association of Governments (1983) has addressed the question of international trade on the economy of the Los Angeles region. It concluded (op cit, p 30) that

Without doubt, the growing importance of international trade to the regional economy ... will continue to depend heavily upon the efficient movement of goods to and through the region's transportation systems. Disruption and delay in this movement can only serve to place the regional economy at a competitive disadvantage relative to other regional, national, and international economies.

A later study (Southern California Association of Governments, 1989a, p I-34) concluded that about 11 percent of jobs in the Los Angles area were export-related, with 6 percent in merchandise exports and 5 percent in the export of services. It went on to make a number of specific recommendations concerning the facilitation of export movements (op cit, p 15). Those relevant to our interests here included:

- improved access to ports and airports;

- including merchandise trade needs and status among the criteria for prioritizing transport infrastructure funding and construction;

- enhanced access and circulation at ports and inland markets and intermodal transfer terminals;

- eliminate where possible unnecessary delays and circuitous routeing of goods on the region's transport system;

- plan and provide for freight routes which minimize impacts on residential neighbourhoods and heavy commuter routes;

- support freight consolidation and improvement of intermodal facilities, and construction of on-dock and near-dock container transfer facilities; and

- provide for efficient freight movements at locations where passenger movement dominates, especially at airports.

Finally, other analysts have also shown that strategic road investments give rise to substantial benefits over and above the transport cost savings accruing to users (Hussain, 1990; Quarmby, 1989). In particular, Quarmby, based upon an analysis of retail distribution in Britain, concluded that 'benefits to commercial vehicles of road improvements ... could exceed the benefits of straight time savings by 30-50 percent. It is important that the 'business potential' released in this and other industries by (road) network improvements should be better understood.'

In summary, an efficient urban freight system can contribute towards regional or national economic development and employment, especially to the extent that it assists trade-competitive firms or sectors of the economy to be more competitive.

Efficiency objectives

Efficiency objectives relate to minimizing, or at least reducing, transport operation costs. These are the costs incurred by the shipper, receiver and transport operator, and include such components as drivers' wages, vehicle operating costs, vehicle depreciation and registration charges, as well as the terminal costs of packaging, storing, loading, unloading, recording and insuring the goods (Hicks, 1977, p 103).

As discussed in Chapter 2, the costs associated with transporting goods represent a significant proportion of the total cost of production for some commodities. Moreover, they are the only costs usually identified and attributed to the transport sector in, for example, national account statistics, though even here, only those costs incurred by the freight transport industry would normally be included, since freight costs incurred in private trucking (otherwise known as ancillary or own-account trucking) would normally be assigned to the industry served, e.g. retailing or agriculture. Needless to say, such externalities as the cost of crashes, environmental impacts, or the provision of roads and road facilities are not considered as part of the freight sector for accounting purposes.

Operation costs may be reduced by the more efficient use of labor and plant, and conversely anything which tends to reduce the utilisation of labor and plant will increase transport operation costs.

The economic gains referred to in the previous section were real net gains, in that they enhanced the national economy. Improvements in internal efficiency resulting from savings in transport operation costs are merely transfers between different sectors of the economy, i.e. there is no direct net national gain to the economy as a whole. These effects are nonetheless important, for two reasons.

First, as discussed in Chapter 3, since freight transport is a derived demand, there is no value whatever in it consuming more resources than the minimum necessary to move goods in the most efficient manner. Any resources thus freed are available for use in other sectors. (This assumes, of course, that other sectors can utilize additional resources.) Second, transfers within the national economy are important from an equity viewpoint, in that national goals related to income redistribution can be pursued (or negated) through over or under allocation of resources to particular sectors.

Urban freight involves a great variety of activities and vehicle operations, ranging from full truckload to individual parcels and letters and from large combination vehicles to small passenger type vehicles. Inevitably, there are enormous variations in efficiency and productivity across different tasks and activities. Nevertheless, there is evidence that some important activities, particularly those involving pick up and delivery rounds, are characterized by low levels of productivity, as measured by, say, capacity utilisation, average truck speed, average shipment size, etc (Crowley, et al, 1980, p 6). This does not necessarily imply low levels of efficiency, as the particular firm may be utilizing its resources to the maximum extent possible given the operating environment, but it does imply that there is potential for productivity gains.

This raises the question of the role of policy and planning functions in contributing to urban freight efficiency. As Hicks (1977, p 105) points out, 'if firms could be relied upon to minimize (operating costs) in the pursuit of their commercial interest, policy attention could be focussed on (other freight objectives) in the knowledge that transport operation costs could be minimized at all times.' However, there is evidence that this is not the case. For example:

- poor management skills, especially in small trucking firms, or in firms with ancillary fleets where the management attention is directed towards the firm's main area of activity;

- lack of concern with freight costs by shippers, due to these being only a small proportion of product cost; and

- acceptance by the trucking industry of current levels of congestion, since there is no competitive advantage to any one firm as a result of a lower level of congestion.

In the following discussion therefore, we consider three aspects of transport operation costs as they contribute towards freight efficiency. These are:

- costs incurred by a truck en-route from an origin to a destination, (particularly noting congestion effects);

- costs incurred at end points where trucks are loaded and unloaded; and

- energy considerations.

En-route costs

En-route costs are of two types: traffic congestion and road network deficiencies. Although obviously related, it is helpful to consider these separately.

Traffic congestion. Goods and passenger traffic, including vehicles and pedestrians, may interact with each other on any way or terminal that they share. In most cases this interaction is detrimental. Interaction between goods and passenger vehicles occurs on arterial roads where trucks, cars, buses and pedestrians compete for space and priority. Congestion is thus a double-edged sword: trucks are responsible for delay to other road users, and other road users delay trucks.

Trucks, being larger in most cases than passenger vehicles, effectively reduce the capacity of the streets to handle passenger traffic. In addition, trucks may accelerate more slowly than cars, and are frequently involved in curbside loading and unloading. Both of these characteristics have the effect of retarding the flow of passenger traffic, or blocking it entirely. Conversely, generally high levels of traffic flow on such roads will lead to delays to trucks, and to stop-start operation which is costly to all vehicles, but particularly to large vehicles.

The degree to which goods and passenger traffic interact depends upon a number of factors, including the layout, width and capacity of streets and footpaths and the size and performance of goods vehicles. Other factors such as the purpose of the goods journey, the duration and frequency of stops for each type of goods journey, and the facilities for goods handling provided at the pick-up and discharge points may also be relevant.

Effects of congestion. Congestion due to trucks moving in the traffic stream is due firstly to their physical presence on the road. As noted in Chapter 2, trucks typically comprise around 6-10 percent of urban traffic flow. The contribution of trucks to traffic congestion may be magnified by their greater size and slower acceleration; it is common for example in capacity and traffic flow analyses to consider that each truck is equivalent to a given number of passenger cars. However, as Currie (1981, p 21) has noted, urban truck movement is spread throughout the day and therefore its impact during the peak hours is not as pronounced as is that of private car commuter traffic. Moreover, in many urban areas, truck traffic is more prevalent on certain specific routes such as that serving a port or terminal area, tending again to reduce the overall metropolitan-wide impact of truck traffic on congestion.

Trucks also contribute to congestion when stationary - parked trucks, trucks being loaded or unloaded at the roadside (including trucks which are double-parked) and trucks moving in and out of the traffic stream from rest. This is a particular problem in the central areas of older cities, where there are insufficient or non-existent off-street loading facilities. Habib (1981, p 44) has modelled the effect of downtown urban pick up and delivery operations, and has estimated that even a minimal level of such activity will reduce the effective throughput capacity of the street by about 12 percent.

Kearney (1975, p III-19) has estimated the effect of truck induced congestion on US urban roads, and concluded that on heavily trafficked urban roads and streets, a typical pick up and delivery stop of 12 minutes duration which blocked a single lane of traffic could cause as much as 17 vehicle hours of delay to other vehicles. While this is a hypothetical result (presumably if the potential for delay was so great, it would not be

97

permitted), it nevertheless serves to underline the critical importance of pick up and delivery operations on city streets.

The reverse side of the coin - delays experienced by trucks due to other vehicles - is also very real. For example, Hasell, Foulkes and Robertson (1978b) quoted the results of a study undertaken in London, England which showed that for trucks engaged on urban distribution:

-   brakes were applied on average every 137 m (450 ft);

-   the engine was running for only 25 percent of the time, and for one-quarter of that time, the engine was idling;

-   gear changing took place every 82 m (268 ft), and 45 percent of the time the truck was in second or third gear; top gear was engaged for an average of only 25 s; and

-   the full steering lock was applied every 820 m (2690 ft) on average.

Similarly, TTM Consulting (1989, p 2) reported the results of a study undertaken in Melbourne, Australia, in which a fully laden, diesel-engined tractor semi-trailer took 2 hours to make a 60 km (37 mile) trip, used 35 litres (9.2 US gal) of fuel, had 280 gear shifts, and spent a total of 17 minutes under brakes.

While these data no doubt reflect the particular traffic and road conditions applying in London and Melbourne respectively, they nevertheless indicate some of the conditions under which urban trucks operate. US data quoted by the Urban Consortium for Technology Initiatives (1980, p 4) suggest that about half the time spent by trucks in central business districts is spent parked.

Cost of congestion. Congestion has a significant effect upon truck operating costs, either directly through its effects of vehicle productivity and fuel consumption, or indirectly through its effects on operations.

In a study of freight flows associated with major transfer terminals in Sydney, Australia, Plant Location International (1983, p 47) noted the following effects:

Road congestion was seen as a major problem by all the people approached in the field interviews... Where possible, freight forwarders have tried to ensure that others carry the cost of increased road congestion by either paying drivers on a trip basis rather than a time basis or in the case of long term contracts with firms, charging major clients on a time basis..

(Another) effect of increased congestion has been to force terminals to operate longer hours and incur overtime costs. In many cases pick up and delivery trucks will be loaded in the evening and taken home by the driver so that delivery operations can be commenced as early as possible the next day.

Heavy traffic flows in the near vicinity of some terminals severely limit the movement of heavy vehicles during peak periods. (In some areas) heavy vehicles ... will normally delay departure for up to two hours to avoid afternoon peak congestion.

It is important to note this report's general conclusion on the effects of congestion on trucking operations, that 'it is clear that practice of evaluating the benefits of road improvements to commercial operators by simply looking at reductions in journey times, overlooks the significant costs that are incurred by the freight transport industry in trying to avoid the use of roads during periods of peak congestion.'

Similar comments have been made by May and Patterson (1984) for inner city firms in England, and by Travers Morgan (1987, p 42) for Melbourne, Australia.

There have been a number of efforts made to quantify the costs of traffic congestion, and especially to estimate the costs of congestion to truck operators.

In the Los Angeles area, the Southern California Association of Governments (1988, p 8) estimated the daily recurrent congestion costs (i.e. that due to traffic flow, not to accidents or incidents) in the Los Angeles metropolitan areas at $7.1 million per day in 1984. Over one-third of this was incurred by business travellers, but the truck component of this was not isolated. The study went on to forecast the 2001 cost of congestion under various scenarios; under the worst scenario (no action), the 2001 cost of congestion (in 1987 dollars) rose to $104.1 million per day, while even under the best scenario (extensive demand management plus facility construction), it more than doubled in real terms from the 1984 level. The proportion of the overall cost due to business travel did not vary greatly between scenarios or over time (remaining at between 34 and 38 percent).

Although the amount of this incurred by trucks was not separately identified, it would be significant.

The reverse side of the coin - the effect of congestion on truck operators, has been estimated in a few instances. An early study in Toronto, Canada (Barnstead, 1970) highlighted the costs of operating a truck in different environments. Relative to suburban operations, inner suburban operations cost 25 percent more, central city fringe operations cost 46 percent more, and city centre operations cost 2.6 times as much. Similarly, in a review of the costs of congestion in US cities, Mele (1988, p 62) cited an industry consultant who suggested that it takes twice as long to make deliveries in inner cities as in suburbs. The variation between these various environments is primarily due to congestion; Barnstead (1970) noted that 'stops and starts attributable to congestion were about three times as high in the city centre as in the fringe. Forty percent of all traffic stops in the city centre were caused by congestion.'

In a study in Sydney, Australia, Colston and Budd (1984, p 5) identified the major costs of congestion to the urban trucking industry in four groups:

- time costs, especially wages;

- vehicle operating costs, principally fuel, tyres, repair and maintenance, vehicle capital costs;

- accident costs; and

- hidden costs, including the cost of stress-related illnesses, cost increases due to unreliability of delivery schedules, and cost of damage to goods resulting from breakages in transit.

The report concluded (op cit, p 76) that more effort 'should be made in future to clearly identify, in the evaluation of major road projects, those indirect benefits and costs which would accrue to the road freight industry.' A recent study by Bowyer and Ogden (1988) found that any increased productivity of vehicles and drivers resulting from reductions in travel time are almost always used by the industry, and thus this increased productivity should be valued at the overtime rate of pay. The question of the economic evaluation of road proposals, and the inclusion of benefits to trucks in such evaluation, is taken up in Chapter 8.

Road network deficiencies. Delays and costs can be increased by deficiencies in the road network. These include both local (spot) deficiencies and problems covering a wider area. While obviously these will be unique for any given urban area, some general comments can be made.

Among the spot deficiencies which exist in many locations to the detriment of the movement of heavier, larger and slower vehicles are the following (Ogden and Richardson, 1978, p 264; Rimmer, 1978, p 30; Anon, 1989a):

- lanes which are too narrow;

- absence of pavement markings or lane markings;

- poor maintenance of road pavement, perhaps because of the institutional factors which do not allow sufficient finance for the upkeep of roads in commercial or industrial areas;

- poor road geometry (left and right turns at intersections) resulting in turning trucks having to encroach into another lane or back up in order to complete the turn;

- sharp bends, which may have effects similar to those at intersections;

- excessive or incorrect road camber and superelevation, which poses problems for high vehicles especially, and can result in damage to the vehicle and/or roadside furniture such as poles or shop awnings;

- poor visibility at level crossings, and in some cases inadequate vertical alignment at level crossings which can in the worst case cause the truck to become stranded on the crossing;

- sub-standard clearances on overhead bridges, which not only lead to more circuitous truck routing, but also have the potential to cause trucks to become jammed under the bridge, perhaps damaging it (see Figure 6.11 in Chapter 6);

- poles, signs, hydrants, shop awnings, etc. which are too close to the kerb, resulting in damage to the fitting and/or the truck;

- overhanging trees, which if not trimmed periodically can damage vehicles and/or their loads; and

- pedestrian malls, which all too often are introduced where there is inadequate access to the rear of premises facing such malls, so that truck drivers are required to trolley goods in by handcart to the receiver.

Network deficiencies applying over a wider area are in general of two types: those resulting from local area traffic management schemes, and those resulting from the configuration and capacity of the arterial network.

Local area traffic management schemes can create particular problems for truck access. These schemes often involve the installation of traffic control devices such as roundabouts, chicanes, road humps etc for the purpose of discouraging through traffic or reducing traffic speed. In some cases, the traffic management scheme may be specifically directed at discouraging trucks, or even making it impossible for large vehicles to enter. Whether directed specifically at trucks or not, these devices have the effect of making access by trucks difficult or impossible. While the discouragement of extraneous truck traffic in a residential area is quite understandable, nevertheless there are many instances where truck access is legitimate (garbage collection, furniture removal, fire services, building construction, service utilities, etc), and the legitimate access needs of these vehicles should be preserved.

In some urban areas, there may be network deficiencies at the arterial road level, i.e. the arterial road network serving a particular locality may be inadequate. Obviously, no general comments can be made here since each urban area is unique, but perhaps it is relevant to note that existing road investment appraisal techniques may not take sufficient account of the benefits which accrue to truck traffic on urban arterial roads (see below); to the extent that this is true, adoption of different evaluation procedures could maybe see a higher priority given to roads carrying high volumes of truck traffic.

Policy implications. One important characteristic of congestion is that it forms part of the operating environment for trucking firms, and because it affects all firms operating in that environment in the same way, these costs are passed on in the form of higher prices. For example, a study in Melbourne, Australia (Travers Morgan, 1987, p 52) found that 'the attitude of most transport companies is to accept traffic conditions as given, and to plan as far as possible to avoid the worst aspects of the road network through scheduling of deliveries to avoid the peaks, time restrictions, route restrictions, and congested areas.' Ogden (1977d, p 46) found similar responses in Toronto, Canada, including examples where the firm had relocated its terminal to get away from congestion.

This is an important observation from a policy or planning viewpoint; congestion is a cost which affects the whole community, and the transport industry is not likely to complain unduly about it since no one firm can gain a competitive advantage or disadvantage; as Goettee and Cadotte (1977, p 420) have noted, trucking firms 'perceive no profit incentive because greater efficiency in freight movement would force the delivered price to be lower because of competition'.

Similarly, shippers (or receivers) are only likely to notice the effects of traffic congestion on their freight costs if they compare such costs between urban areas which have different levels of urban congestion, but their response here is more likely to be to move their facility since there is nothing that a single firm can do to reduce area-wide traffic congestion in a large city. The conclusion therefore is that the problem of congestion affects the whole community, and is thus a policy and planning issue, since costs are passed on.

Attention to road network deficiencies is probably one of the most important areas where the public sector can contribute towards freight efficiency. Many of the local deficiencies are relatively easily and cheaply dealt with, and often require no more than a recognition on the part of the traffic engineer that heavy, large vehicles have different requirements than passenger cars and that there are important community benefits in catering for trucks explicitly. Ways of doing this are discussed in detail in Chapter 6.

Road investment planning procedures, to the extent that they depend upon the results of formal economic evaluation techniques, may under-value the benefits to the economy from a more efficient freight sector; as noted above, one study concluded that benefits as usually calculated should be increased by 50 percent to derive the full economic benefits. From a policy or planning viewpoint, it is relevant to note that urban road investment can play an important role in freight efficiency; this aspect is discussed in Chapter 8.

End-point costs

All freight consignments have to be loaded and unloaded at some point, and may also have to be transfered from one vehicle to another or one mode to another. In many cases, these operations are efficiently conducted; loading and unloading operations within freight terminals and deliveries of a repetitive nature (e.g. bulk deliveries, deliveries to large retailers, etc) are probably not major issues from a policy or planning viewpoint.

However, there are other operations which are not so efficiently carried out, such as deliveries to central city areas where there are no off-street facilities, or deliveries to sites where access is difficult or loading and unloading facilities are inadequate. Moreover, the few data which are available on truck usage all reveal that urban trucks spend most of their time at rest (see Chapter 2), and it follows that there is potential to improve the productivity of urban road freight operations by improving operations at the end points of trips or shipments.

End-point costs, as we have defined them here, may be categorized into five areas: loading and unloading delays; truck parking; costs and delays at freight terminals; hours available for delivery; and site access and egress. While these are obviously related, it is helpful to consider them separately, as they tend to be revealed and experienced in different ways.

Central city loading and unloading. Delays due to parking, loading and unloading are commonly associated with poor receiving and despatch facilities at older buildings in the central city. In many cases, these buildings do not have off-street facilities; this results in traffic congestion, and often means that extra time is taken to find a parking place and complete the pick up or delivery. The problem is aggravated when it is necessary to pick up from or deliver to a tenant on a specific office in a building, especially in a multi-storey building. In congested streets, drivers may return to their trucks, only to find that they are blocked in by other trucks which have double parked beside them. Security against theft is a concomitant issue whenever a truck driver has to leave the truck. Hedges (1985) has asserted that 'improvements at shipping/receiving points are regarded frequently as the most desperately needed urban goods movement strategy, at least with respect to trucks.'

A report of the American Society of Civil Engineers (Anon, 1989a) listed four areas of concern with central city loading and unloading: lack of off-street loading zones, lack of curbside loading zones, misuse of loading zones, and time restrictions for trucks at loading zones

Most city planning or building ordinances today require that off-street loading and unloading facilities be provided (see Chapter 9). However, these are not always adequate for the eventual end use of the building, access to them may be difficult with the result that truck drivers prefer to park on the street, or the loading spaces may be misused, e.g. used for car parking or trash dumpsters (Walters, 1989a). Off street facilities are however most desirable, and effort should continue to be made to ensure that their numbers, layout and access is satisfactory.

It should be noted however that not all pick up and delivery operations will utilise such facilities even where they are provided; courier operations, and delivery of other small items such as mail, newspapers, etc are unlikely to go to the time and expense of accessing a truck loading area (Urban Consortium for Technology Initiatives, 1980, p 4). Finally, such ordinances are of course only valid for new buildings; many central cities have large numbers of buildings which pre-date the requirements for off-street loading facilities, and in many of these cases there are no facilities at all for goods receival or despatch; trucks serving these buildings must park on the street.

Most central cities (and suburban areas too for that matter) have regulations governing the use of curb space. These typically include loading zones as well as other zones, especially car parking. City authorities typically try to minimize the amount of space devoted to loading, because other uses (especially car parking) is regarded as more important; from the viewpoint of shopkeepers, it is preferable to maximize the opportunity for potential customers to use the shops.

Another freight problem which is felt particularly keenly in central cities is that of delivery of construction materials to major building sites. Very often, these materials are delivered essentially to the curbside, and lifted into position by crane. The need to accommodate these vehicles (especially structural steel and ready-mixed concrete deliveries) creates potential congestion, safety and environmental problems for other road traffic and pedestrians. In some cities, such deliveries are restricted to evenings and weekends. A related problem may be that of concrete batching plants which need to be located fairly close to the central city area, often for only a comparatively short period of time; the traffic flows which these plants create, and the environmental problems associated with them can cause headaches for city planning and traffic officials.

Habib and Crowley (1976a, b) examined the economics of providing curbside loading spaces in New York City, in terms of such costs as car parking, freight delivery, cost of off-street facilities, congestion cost, energy costs, and environmental costs (air pollution). While obviously the results are dependent upon the valuation of each of these costs, they nevertheless concluded (op cit, 1976a) that 'for roads with high volume/capacity ratios, the least cost solution shows that ensuring no double parking on travel lanes by pick up and delivery vehicles can be justified, and on low volume streets, the installation of loading zones by removing on-street automobile space is a questionable practice.'

A similar analysis was performed by Walters (1989a) in Dallas, Texas. Walters considered the costs to four groups - the public, building owners, tenants and carriers - and compared both planned and unplanned curb use, and various configurations of off-street facility. The off-street facilities were lowest cost ($14,700 to $17,800 per space per year), but not that much lower than the planned curb use ($18,800). However, unplanned curb use was by far the highest cost alternative ($43,300).

Providing loading zones is one problem; ensuring that they are not misused is quite another. All too often, zones intended for use for freight pick up and delivery operations are used for car parking, or by service vehicles. This is both an enforcement issue (especially for illegal car parking), and a question of how the ordinance is framed; in particular the question of whether service vehicles associated with such activities as building or equipment maintenance, telephone installation, etc are appropriate users of loading spaces is controversial (Anon, 1989a).

Travers Morgan (1987, p 53) have listed the following courses of action available to a truck driver who cannot find a vacant curbside loading space:

-   park further away from the delivery point;

-   drive around until a space becomes available;

-   use a driver's assistant to deliver the shipment while the driver circulates in the traffic;

-   request that the shipper or receiver makes someone available at the curb to hand over or accept the shipment;

-   violate a parking or traffic ordinance (e.g. double park, park in a no parking area, park on the footpath); or

-   return at another time, or another day.

The report noted that 'each of these add to delivery costs and usually impede traffic flow'.

Finally, time restrictions on the use of curbside loading areas for the duration of the peak period (known in some areas as 'clearways') is common in many cities. By making the curb lane available for traffic flow a greater road capacity is provided. It also reduces the risk of accidents between parked vehicles and through traffic. As far as moving or through traffic is concerned, clearways can be said to benefit both passenger and freight movement. However, the same cannot be said of trucks which have to service frontages along the clearway. Unless off-street loading and unloading space is available, those frontages can only be served by trucks in non-clearway periods. These periods may be quite short in that clearway restrictions may often continue till 9.30 am for the morning peak and recommence at 3.30 pm for the evening peak. Thus the effective working day for deliveries is reduced to six hours. This disruption is particularly acute for those frontages which absolutely require truck servicing during the peak periods. Examples of outlets requiring peak period servicing are shops selling baked goods which require deliveries in the morning period, and mail and courier services which are keyed to late afternoon and evening peak periods.

Non-central city loading and unloading. Problems of a similar nature to those listed above may exist in suburban areas, especially in the denser inner suburban areas with heavily trafficked streets. In inner city areas in England for example, on-street loading was one of the main problems cited by firms located in London (May and Patterson, 1984). Shortage of loading space, poor access and egress facilities, physical deficiencies in the road system, and restricted arterial road space are common problems.

One particular feature worthy of note for non-central city locations is that of truck size. In the central city, few deliveries involve tractor semi-trailers, with most freight activity involving a rigid truck. In suburban truck operations, especially those serving industrial sites and freight terminals, larger vehicles are more common. The implication here is that for planning and design of roads and terminals in suburban areas, explicit consideration needs to be given to the needs of freight vehicles for movement and access. This is particularly so in new developments, where it is so much easier to insert appropriately designed facilities at the beginning than to retro-fit them later (Anon, 1989a).

At the site level, the main issue relates to building or planning regulations governing the provision of off-street loading or unloading bays for industrial, residential or commercial establishments. It is acknowledged that the development of such regulations is difficult, since different industrial activities may have very different freight requirements, and also since needs change over time. (For example, the increase in the use of containerization for both domestic and overseas transport results in many instances in containers having to be delivered to and picked up from premises which were never designed to accept or accommodate them.) However, guidelines are available; these are discussed in Chapter 6.

Truck parking. Truck parking is emerging as a significant issue, in response to both environmental and safety concerns. It affects both trucks used for intra-urban purposes and those used for line-haul or intercity operations.

Many municipalities have banned overnight parking of trucks on residential streets, and the practice is likely to spread (though to be effective, appropriate levels of enforcement must be instituted). Where this restriction applies, it means that trucks must be parked elsewhere. While many companies have sufficient space at their depot to accommodate overnight parking of trucks, many do not. Various alternative arrangements may be available, including the use of private or public truck parking areas. It is likely that as more cities restrict overnight truck parking for environmental reasons, there will be an increasing need and opportunity for such facilities to be provided. In London, England, for example, the Greater London Council provided public off-street truck parks as a concomitant of its trial ban on overnight truck parking; the experiment was described as 'very successful' and has subsequently been extended to other areas (Hasell, Foulkes and Robertson, 1978c).

Apart from any explicit price paid for overnight truck parking, another cost implication is that the trucking company may lose some of the advantage of loading the truck the previous evening for early start of the following day's morning delivery operations. Also, it may mean that the truck driver has to now use an automobile to get to work instead of driving the truck, resulting in extra cost and perhaps congestion (Hasell, Foulkes and Robertson, 1978c).

Terminal delays and costs. Many urban freight shipments pass through a terminal at some point in their delivery. Most shipments coming from or going to another urban area pass through a truck, rail, sea or air terminal, while passage through a terminal for intra-urban shipments may occur with, say, parcels or courier operations.

There can be a number of inefficiencies associated with terminals, resulting from their design, location or operation. For example, Currie (1981, p 29) noted the following sources of delay in terminals:

Detention at the actual load/unload point is common. The customer or depot operator wishes to make maximum use of staff and equipment, and a line of waiting trucks is a guarantee of continuous employment...

Loading and unloading itself is often slow, using outdated equipment and methods, and docks themselves can be inadequate for large trucks ...

Paperwork and checking for freight security are also causes of delay at a loading dock. There are no uniform methods of documentation, and it may take some time to ensure that all receipts and dockets are correct.

With high value freight it may take some time to see that all is in order, the load may have to be depalletized and each box checked individually.

Terminal efficiency and operations are discussed in Chapter 11. It might be noted here however that operators of road freight terminals in particular may see terminal efficiency as of key importance in a competitive environment. As noted above, traffic congestion affects all operators in a particular market to the same extent, and so terminal efficiency may be one way of at least partially overcoming the costs of congestion. Plant Location International (1983, p 48) has emphasized this point, noting that 'the major effect of traffic congestion has been to force operators to improve terminal operations so that trucks can be turned around more rapidly and as a consequence have more time to cope with road congestion'.

Hours available for delivery. The number of hours which a truck and its driver are able to spend in productive employment in a day is a key factor affecting urban freight efficiency.

As transport is a service industry, the span of hours a truck is employable is dependent on the customer's work schedule. In general, the road freight industry is quite flexible, being prepared to start as early as necessary and work into the evening if that is the customers wish. Most operators, particularly those having large trucks, are prepared to make extra use of their expensive equipment by paying their drivers overtime if the work is available.

One of the factors tending to reduce truck productivity is the mis-match of working hours of different employment groups. In an Australian study, Currie (1981, p 21) commented that 'the multiplicity of awards under which customers, depots and terminals operate, ensures that someone is always having lunch, a tea break or changing shift. Some large dispatchers and receivers employ extra staff to work through breaks, but the practice is not universal.'

There are conflicting tendencies at work in this area. On the one hand, work hours in many countries are becoming more flexible, with less rigid hours of work even in areas like the waterfront where opposition to changes in traditional work practices is notorious. This means that shippers and receivers, as they become more aware of the importance of logistics management and the benefits of more efficient freight operations, are likely to want to make their receival and despatch operations more efficient. Similarly, a consequence of the increasing length of the daily peak periods is that truck operators are going to be increasingly seeking opportunities to use their equipment in less congested evening hours; in some urban areas such as Los Angeles, there are increasing restrictions on peak hour truck operations (see Chapter 15), with consequent pressure for more evening deliveries. On the other hand, the same trend towards flexibility of work hours is seeing some industries or firms work nine days in two weeks, have one day a month off, or something similar. In some cases these practices may result from government pressure directed at workplace-oriented travel demand management. The effect however is that it is becoming increasingly common for urban truck drivers to be unable to effect a freight delivery because there is no-one at the receival end to accept it. This has obvious effects of efficiency, since a return visit has to made at a later date or time.

The general question of evening delivery and other operational practices aimed at improving the efficiency of urban goods movement is taken up in Chapter 12.

Site access and egress. Finally, one of the important factors affecting efficient urban freight operation may be the relative ease of gaining access to a specific site. It is difficult to generalize about this, since obviously each site and each locality is unique, but some of the features of truck access include the following (Plant Location International, 1983, p 5; Travers Morgan, 1987, p 55; Ogden, 1991):

- sites within industrial and commercial areas can be a problem, especially for tractor semi-trailers, unless they have direct access off wide streets which carry comparatively light traffic;

- sites on major arterial highways with a median can be a problem since it may be necessary for a truck to either perform a U-turn or access the site via a more circuitous route through local streets; not every site can have a median opening directly opposite;

- there is an inevitable contradiction between the objective of preventing direct access to arterial or main roads and the twin objectives of discouraging heavy vehicles from using local roads (especially residential streets) and minimizing the cost of maintenance of local roads; this conflict of objectives can be more readily resolved in new industrial zones where internal roads can be constructed to a suitable standard, with signalized intersections with the arterial road system, and without direct linkage to residential areas;

- access routes on the site itself, including their width, geometric layout, and approach to the loading dock, are all too often designed without real regard to the needs of the trucks using them; examples include poor horizontal and vertical alignment, inadequate overhead clearance, steep ramps, direct access to a ramp adjacent to a footpath (with sight distance and safety implications), and insufficient space for a truck to turn around so that it must reverse back onto the road;

- delivery points located at a distance from the contact point, so that once a truck is parked at the loading dock the driver must walk a long distance to report in;

- loading areas or doors of inadequate height; and

- inadequate manoeuvring areas and difficult access due to car parking arrangements at shopping centres.

Policy implications. Since trucks spend a considerable proportion of their time at rest, and since terminal operations and activities involving the actual pick up and delivery of goods is costly, policy and planning considerations in urban freight need to consider truck loading, unloading, and parking, and terminal operations.

The causes of excess cost at pick up and delivery points can probably be attributed to three factors:

First, high costs may be considered acceptable by some shippers and receivers. For example, a retail store which runs a small fleet of trucks may not be unduly concerned about inefficient loading or unloading facilities, since the costs may be small in relation to the firm's overall costs. There is probably not much that a planning or policy agency could or should do about this; if it is critical then the firm will either suffer a competitive disadvantage, or it will realise the necessity to do something to make its operations more efficient.

Second, costs may arise because of inadequate building, planning, or traffic codes at the local level. Although most cities have some form of ordinance covering (for example) the number of loading docks, these often leave much flexibility in their interpretation; this is probably necessary because of the need to encompass a wide range of specific land uses, site conditions, etc. Moreover, such ordinances cannot cover every eventuality, and the uses to which buildings are put may change markedly over time. However, there is probably scope for considerable improvement in the design, layout and specification of freight shipping and receival facilities in many cases.

Third, to the extent that costs of despatching and (especially) receiving goods are excessive, this may be regarded as a consequence of an unsatisfactory pricing mechanism. Since the pricing structure is usually arranged such that a receiver with poor or inefficient goods receival facilities is not required to pay directly for the cost of deliveries, there is little incentive to improve the facilities. Facilities cost money, and these must be passed on to tenants in the form of higher rent. This puts the building with facilities at a competitive disadvantage to the building without facilities. Since present trucking rates do not reflect the quality of the shipping and receiving facilities, there is no incentive on building owners to include goods facilities (Lea, 1971). There may be policy implications here in terms of attempting to make rates more reflective of costs, but this is probably impractical. A more practical measure is to insist, through some form of planning or building ordinance, upon the provision of adequate facilities. It is helpful nevertheless to recognise the breakdown in the pricing mechanism for what it really is.

Energy

The movement of freight in urban areas represents a small but significant proportion of total energy use in transport. Kearney (1975, p III-23) using US data from the early 1970s estimated that fuel consumption by urban pick up and delivery trucks accounted for 3.2 percent of transport fuel, or 4.5 percent of road transport fuel. A later study (Anon, 1982c, p 52) suggested that its significance was even lower than that - about 2 percent of energy used in transport in the US.

Direct energy use is affected by the following factors (Southworth, et al, 1981; Southworth, 1983):

- operating speed;
- loaded vehicle weight;
- fuel type (gasoline or diesel);
- idling time;
- truck body type (panel, pickup, trailer);
- roadway conditions (lane number and width, grade, surface, curves);
- traffic conditions (number of stops due to congestion);
- truck age;
- ambient air temperature;
- distance travelled;
- terminal base location;
- truck routing;
- time of day of operation; and
- carrier type (for hire, private).

Of these, truck speed is particularly important, especially in urban conditions. For example, the Federal Highway Administration (1980) has noted that at 16 km/h (10 mph), medium truck fuel consumption is nearly three times that at 56 km/h (35 mph); curves showing the relationship between fuel consumption and operating speed for various truck types are presented in Southworth et al (1981, 1982).

The type of commodity moved affects direct energy consumption through both its physical attributes (notably volume to weight ratio and perishability) and the type of delivery schedule it requires. Southworth et al (1981) present data for Chicago which shows a variation in fuel efficiency (megajoules per tonne kilometre) for different commodity groups ranging from a low of 1.07 MJ/t.km for non-metallic minerals to a high of 6.21 MJ/t.km for retail and wholesale products.

113

The energy efficiency also varies with both vehicle type (size and fuel used) and the carrier type (private, commercial) with diesel being more energy efficient than gasoline, and commercial operators being slightly more energy efficient than private operators, on a megajoule per vehicle kilometre basis (Southworth, et al, 1981; Christiansen, 1979, p III-28).

Policy implications. Except in the case of contingency planning for short-term fuel shortages, it is doubtful that energy conservation is an objective in its own right; it is properly regarded as one of the costs of transport operation, and as such can be traded off against other costs to achieve a price-service outcome which satisfies customer needs.

Provided that the price signals are correct, government has little direct role to play; the market will determine the appropriate price-service outcome and the importance of energy in this. However, the proviso (that price signals are correct) is important, as is government's concern about contingency planning for energy shortages. The policy implications of this include the following (Southworth, et al, 1981, 1982; Anon, 1982c, p 59; Maring and Politano, 1982, p 319; Bixby and Reno, 1982, p 329; Schuster, 1982, p 351; Goddard, 1980):

- more energy-efficient truck size and fuel combinations can be encouraged through taxation policies;

- more direct truck routing can be encouraged through truck terminal location decisions;

- consolidation of shipments to increase load factors can be encouraged through pricing, taxation and regulatory practices;

- more efficient operating conditions can be facilitated through road investment, traffic control, and demand restraint policies;

- more fuel efficient driving practices can be encouraged through improved driver training;

- there is potential for the development of more fuel efficient vehicles, and research towards this end can be encouraged or funded; and

- any regulatory measures which tend to discourage or prohibit more energy-efficient operating practices by carriers should be reviewed, especially with the aim of reducing the number of pick up and delivery calls.

Road safety objectives

Safety is a fundamental humanitarian concern. Everyone would agree that the urban road freight sector should operate in a way which produces a minimum of deaths, injuries and property damage crashes.

Trucks, because of their greater mass, tend to produce serious consequences when involved in collisions with passenger cars or pedestrians. In the US in 1988 for example, 75 percent of persons killed in fatal crashes involving heavy trucks were not occupants of the truck. For medium trucks, the corresponding figure was 73 percent (National Highway Traffic Safety Administration, 1989, p 6.27 and 6.34).

A number of studies have recently examined truck involvement in road crashes, although only a few have focussed upon crashes in urban areas.

In the US in 1988, 31.1 percent of vehicles involved in fatal road crashes were trucks. However most of these were light trucks, having many characteristics similar to those of a private car. Medium and heavy trucks accounted for 2.1 and 7.3 percent respectively of vehicles involved in fatal crashes. Unfortunately, data on truck involvement in urban crashes is not published (National Highway Traffic Safety Administration, 1989, Table 6.1).

Ogden and Tan (1989) examined the characteristics of fatal crashes involving trucks in capital cities (i.e. the major urban centres) in Australia in 1981. Their main observations were:

- about 13 percent of all fatal crashes in Australian capital cities involved trucks;

- 5 percent of such crashes involved only a single truck; 95 percent involved another vehicle or a pedestrian;

- the most common fatal accident type for rigid trucks was striking a pedestrian on the roadway (28 percent of such crashes; for urban fatal crashes as a whole, 45 percent were of this type);

115

- other significant fatal crashes involving rigid trucks were right angle or right-turn collisions at intersections (equivalent to US left-turn collisions);

- fatal crashes involving articulated trucks were fewer in number than those involving rigid trucks, and again occurred mostly at intersections; and

- expressed as a rate per vehicle kilometre, articulated trucks were significantly over-involved in fatal crashes in Australian capital cities; their involvement rate was 8.0 fatal crashes per 100 million vehicle kilometres (13 per 100 million vehicle miles), compared with a rate for rigid trucks of 3.4 (5.5), and a rate for cars of 2.3 (3.7).

O'Day and Kostyniuk (1985) have presented analyses of fatal truck crashes in urban areas in the US. Their results revealed that:

- the problem was again primarily a multi-vehicle problem (only 25 percent of urban fatal crashes involving a truck were single-vehicle);

- the truck was more often struck in urban areas (whereas in rural areas it was more often the striker); and

- about 28 percent of all fatal crashes involving a tractor-trailer combination occurred in urban areas; the corresponding figure for rigid trucks was 38 percent.

These data, although reported here in overview form only, serve to illustrate that fatal urban truck crashes are significant, and a cause of concern. However, it should be pointed out that the truck is not necessarily the cause of the problem; while they may be over-involved relative to distance travelled in some categories of crash, particularly fatal crashes, the truck is not necessarily the vehicle responsible. The problem is more often than not an error of judgement on the part of another road user, but, because of the energy associated with a heavy truck, the consequences for that other road user are often severe. For example, Smist and Ranney (1983, p 20) have analysed data for truck crashes in the US in the early 1980s, and found that for multi-vehicle crashes involving an articulated truck, the truck driver was primarily responsible in 39 percent of cases, and contributed in a further 21 percent. For straight (rigid) trucks, the corresponding figures were 33 percent and 20 percent.

Apart from collisions, the other major concern related to truck safety is its effect upon road operations, particularly accidents and incidents on freeways which cause significant delays to other traffic (Recker, et al, 1988; Teal, 1988; Bowman and Lum, 1990).

For example, in Los Angeles County in 1983-1985, a major freeway incident (one which closed at least two lanes and lasted at least two hours) involving a truck occurred on average every 2.6 days, and there were 20-25 truck incidents per day of lesser severity. Some 90 percent of these incidents occurred on weekdays, and 56 percent during peak periods. The most common incident type was an overturned truck (32 percent), followed by an overturn and spill (21 percent) and a collision (17 percent) (Recker, et al, 1988, p 4-5). Trucks were involved in about 70 percent of all major incidents, and the delay associated with such incidents tended to be longer, especially if it involved hazardous materials (Southern California Association of Governments, 1989b, p 127).

The economic cost of these incidents and accidents is considerable. The Los Angeles study considered four categories of cost:

-   delay cost, based upon modelling the total vehicle hours of delay on the freeways caused by the incidents, and multiplying this by an imputed time cost for various vehicle types;

-   accident cost, based upon estimates of property damage, injury-related costs (medical expenses, lost wages, etc), and fatality costs, based upon imputed values of human life);

-   increased vehicle operating costs, based upon a model of traffic operating conditions which led to an estimate of the cost of operating vehicles in the more congested flow conditions caused by the incidents; and

-   clean-up costs, which were the costs to the public agencies and private organisations of removing material from the roadway and returning it to a serviceable condition.

The total annual economic cost of truck incidents on Los Angeles freeways in 1986 was estimated to be in the range $107 - $189 million (Teal, 1988, p 41). Delay costs were the largest component of total economic cost, accounting for around 60-75 percent of the total, depending upon the valuation placed upon the cost components. Teal also found that a relatively small proportion of incidents were responsible for the bulk of the costs; major incidents and fatal crashes comprised 27 percent of the incidents but accounted for 60 percent of the costs.

Bowman and Lum (1990) undertook a similar exercise, based upon an examination of freeway segments in Detroit and Seattle. They too found that delay costs were the largest component, accounting for 70 percent of the total cost. They estimated the cost of truck-related incidents on urban freeways at $US393,000/km ($634,000/mile) per year, which converts to a total of $US1.6 billion per year, for all US urban freeways carrying more than 100,000 vehicles per day.

These findings relate to urban freeways, and may not be transferable to other urban roads. It would be reasonable to suppose that the delay costs and the increased vehicle operating costs of incidents and accidents on other roads would be a smaller proportion of the total economic cost. In Australia, for example, the InterState Commission (1990) concluded that the 'amount of insurance premium required of participants in the trucking industry ... is large and may in fact cover their crash cost responsibility'. However, this conclusion, even if valid, would apply only to the accident costs, not the other cost components identified in the US freeway studies. Nevertheless, to the extent that costs of crashes are internalized through insurance premiums, they are reflected in vehicle operating costs and thus passed on to the industry's customers.

In passing, we should note that accident cost evaluation is a difficult exercise, comprising both fairly quantifiable components (e.g. cost of property damage), and components whose valuation is controversial. In the latter category are included the valuation of travel time (and hence delay costs) and the valuation of human life (and thus accident costs). This is not the place to discuss these, but suffice it to say that there is considerable controversy about both the methodology for evaluating both of these, and the resulting dollar values used in analysis. (For a discussion of the issues here, see Scodari and Fisher, 1988; Meyer and Miller, 1984, p 389; Hensher, 1988).

Policy implications

A high level of attention to road safety within the urban road freight sector is justified, for both humanitarian reasons (death, pain and suffering) and economic reasons. Road trauma is a politically sensitive issue, and the community expects that policy will continue to be directed towards providing safer roads. Crashes involving trucks are often spectacular, and trucks are perceived (rightly or wrongly) to be over-involved in crashes.

There are a range of strategies which may be pursued to reduce the number of urban truck-involved crashes, and/or their consequences. These may be directed at areas as diverse as traffic management, road design, driver licensing and training, vehicle design and operation, loading practices, and land use planning. Many of these are taken up in Part B.

Environmental objectives

Urban trucking affects the physical and social environment in a number of ways, some measurable and some not. The measurable ones include noise, exhaust emissions, and vibration. The non-measurable impact may be described as truck intrusion, either as a perceived threat to people, or as truck intrusion into residential areas.

Intrusion

In Hindu mythology, Juggernaut, an idol of Krishna, was annually drawn through the streets on a giant vehicle, under the wheels of which devotees threw themselves to be crushed. Today, in some countries, especially Britain, the term juggernaut is applied to large trucks!

The word is emotional, yet reflects the reaction of those who feel adversely affected by heavy vehicles. As Hicks (1977, p 107) has pointed out, 'their dislike can be based upon a factual assessment of the external costs or on vaguer but no less real notions of the 'visual intrusion' of trucks or of a dislike of truck operators appearing to profit out of being a nuisance'. Hicks goes on to argue that the increased use of larger trucks and the more widespread use of containers 'can evoke the primordial and quite human fear of things which are big.'

These psycho-social disturbances, Hicks argues, 'can be a very significant external cost of the presence of trucks on the roads; they cannot be dismissed as mere foibles.' To planners and engineers, used to working with more quantifiable problems, these concepts can be difficult to come to grips with. It is important however to realise that the basic motivation for antagonism to trucks may stem from a dislike of the presence of the vehicles as such, and not necessarily from their undesirable features like noise and emissions.

119

This factor of truck presence per se, and truck size as a compounding factor was implicitly reflected in a measure of 'goods vehicle nuisance' developed in Swindon, England (Christie, 1977). This study noted that while the addition of trucks added a negligible amount to the measured noise level, noise 'does not appear to represent adequately the total nuisance caused by (trucks)'. The study went on to develop an index 'which would take into account implicitly additional factors such as fumes, vibration, and apparent threat'; this index took account of traffic flow, but weighted heavy vehicles by their gross vehicle mass.

Many municipalities, reflecting their citizen's concerns, have restricted truck access to residential streets, or truck parking on them, except for legitimate access needs. Some cities (e.g. London, England) have instituted quite extensive controls on truck movement and access for environmental reasons (Hasell, Foulkes and Robertson, 1978 a,b,c). Although noise and emissions were specifically mentioned as examples of an environmental problem, the essential problem was that 'London can only survive if it is an attractive place to live in, and this makes the environmental issues (associated with trucks) important in economic as well as social terms' (op cit, 1978a). Restrictions on truck access and use must be seen for what they are: a reaction to truck intrusion, which may result from a dislike or fear of trucks per se, and not just a response to measurable (and perhaps controllable) factors like noise.

Noise

A significant cause of concern about the environmental effect of urban freight is truck noise. Although truck drivers may be exposed to some risk of loss of hearing ability, the more cogent question is usually one of the annoyance caused to residents and pedestrians, especially at night-time and on routes which have a high proportion of trucks.

Traffic noise is more or less continuous noise, and may thus be measured on the A-weighted decibel scale (dBA) where the different frequencies of sound energy are weighted in rough proportion to the sensitivity of the human ear (Lay, 1986, p 622; American Association of State Highway and Transportation Officials, 1987, p 4).

There are a number of ways of measuring and expressing noise, the most common of which for road traffic is the so-called L_{10}. This denotes the noise level (in dBA) exceed for 10 percent of the time. Measurements are taken at, say, 10 second intervals, and the resulting distribution is analysed. A variation on this is the L_{10} (18 hours); this is calculated and measured in the same way, but for less than a full day. It is commonly used to express the noise exposure between 6 am and midnight.

The major factors contributing to traffic noise levels are as follows (Stopher and Meyburg, 1976, p 125; Lay, 1986, p 625; American Association of State Highway and Transportation Officials, 1987, p 7; Christiansen, 1979, p III-28):

Vehicle speed. Noise increases with speed. Traffic at 100 km/h (62 mph) registers about 15 dBA more than traffic at 50 km/h (31 mph). (A 10 dBA increase means a doubling of noise levels.) At low speeds, engine and exhaust noises are the main factors, while at higher speeds tyre noise and aerodynamic noise are of more significance.

Traffic flow. This has a diminishing effect upon noise. For example (Stopher and Meyburg, 1976, p 125) at 48 km/h (30 mph):

250 veh/h - 60 dBA
800 veh/h - 70 dBA
3000 veh/h -73 dBA.

Traffic operations. Stop-start conditions produce higher noise levels because of the noise (energy) associated with acceleration.

Road surface. Smoother roads produce lower noise levels. Asphalt is typically quieter than concrete.

Weather. Wet roads produce more tyre noise than dry roads.

Vehicle type and condition. Heavy vehicles (trucks and buses) produce more noise than cars because of the greater energy exchanges involved. There is however potential for engineering design modifications aimed at producing a quieter truck. Research has been undertaken on this, especially in Britain (Nelson and Underwood, 1982; Cooper, 1990).

Noise nuisance is primarily a function of the difference in intensity of a noise source and the ambient (or background) noise level, plus the distance between the receiver of noise and its source. As a general rule, 3-5 dB of noise over the ambient or background noise level is considered annoying (Kearney, 1975, p III-30; Christie, 1977, p 36).

Trucks, because of their size and more powerful engines, produce noise level as much as 15 dBA higher than passenger cars at a distance of 15 m (50 ft). The principal components of truck noise are exhaust, gears, fan, air intake and tyres. Engine exhaust noise tends to dominate for most operating conditions, particularly during acceleration. Also, the height of the exhaust stack can be 3 m (10 ft) or more above the ground (in order to disperse exhaust gases), and this makes it more difficult to shield, e.g. with noise barriers (American Association of State Highway and Transportation Officials, 1987, p 7; Christiansen, 1979, p III-31).

Trucks may be significant contributors to traffic noise if they are a high proportion of the traffic stream. Kearney (1975, p III-31) modelled their effects in US cities and concluded that:

> Heavier trucks have a disproportionally larger impact on noise pollution than lighter trucks. Further, stopping and starting, which results in acceleration and deceleration, tends to generate more noise than free flow of traffic at moderate speeds...

> As trucks approach 5 percent to 15 percent of the vehicles in the traffic stream ... noise levels are raised from 5 dB to 15 dB above those for auto traffic alone. Since a 5 dB increment is considered annoying, adding trucks to the traffic stream does, indeed, increase the overall noise levels.

These estimates are corroborated by field measurements. For example, Arrow, Coyle and Ketcham (1974) in a study in New York City concluded that while 'it is difficult to quantify the effects of trucks on ambient noise levels ... some data indicate that, whereas average noise levels on the busier city streets range from 70 to 75 dBA, trucks cause peaks of 88 to 97 dBA.'

However, because noise annoyance is not a linear function, adding trucks to an already noisy street adds only a little to its noise level. For example, Hasell, Foulkes and Robertson (1978c) have shown that reducing traffic flow in a lightly trafficked street from 500 veh/h to 200 veh/h reduces the L_{10} noise level by 4 dBA, which is probably a detectable difference to residents in that street. However, if that 300 veh/h is added to an arterial road carrying 3,000 veh/h, the additional noise created is an undetectable 0.5 dBA. This is very important characteristic, and gives strong support to the value of local area traffic management schemes which attempt to reduce traffic on local streets by diverting it arterial roads (This assumes of course that the arterial roads have some surplus capacity; intersection and other treatments to increase capacity are thus often an important component of local area traffic management schemes).

The disturbance caused by trucks (or any other noise source for that matter) is greater at night, because it may disturb people relaxing or sleeping. For this reason, truck operations may be prohibited or restricted during evening hours. For example, in London, the movement of trucks in excess of 16.5 t (36,300 lb) is heavily restricted between the hours of 9 pm and 7 am (Buchan, et al, 1985, p 16; Cooper, 1983). Similarly, in Los Angeles, two-thirds of local jurisdictions have comprehensive noise ordinances that include decibel-based limits on night time noise in residential areas, and 19 percent of jurisdictions explicitly prohibit night time loading and unloading activities in such areas (Southern California Association of Governments, 1989b, p 107); these ordinances are considered one of the greatest barriers to increased night time truck operations (see Chapter 15).

In summary then, while light trucks, whose noise emissions may not differ appreciably from automobiles, comprise the majority of trucks on urban roads and streets, medium and heavy trucks produce much greater noise levels and can cause a high, even excessive, level of traffic noise. These effects are greater in stop-start traffic, due to acceleration and braking, than in smooth flowing traffic. Night-time traffic noise is especially annoying, and this has led to prohibitions on truck use at night in some urban areas.

Emissions

There are several distinct types of pollutant emitted by road vehicles. Each has its own set of deleterious effects, and each is produced under different conditions. The major air pollutants are (Meyer and Miller, 1984, p 53; Lay, 1986, p 630; Southern California Association of Governments, 1989b, p 1-4):

Carbon monoxide. This is formed by incomplete combustion of fossil fuels, and is attributable almost entirely to motor vehicles. It is a poisonous gas which absorbs oxygen from the blood stream. A high concentration can kill. Lower concentrations (e.g. at the roadside) can cause dizziness, headache, fatigue and a slowing of reaction time. Because of problems with high concentrations, enclosed spaces such as tunnels, garages, and even downtown streets are particular problem areas.

Carbon dioxide. This is formed as a result of the combustion of fossil fuels. It is of concern since it is one of the principal 'greenhouse gases' which contributes to global warming.

Oxides of nitrogen. Nitrogen dioxide and nitric oxide are formed as a result of fuel combustion under high temperature and pressure. They are contributors to other air pollution problems, including high concentrations of fine particulate matter, poor visibility, and acid deposition. Nitrogen dioxide can cause respiratory problems and may reduce resistance to infection.

Hydrocarbons. These are unburnt fuel particles which can react with the air to cause smog. They may be carcinogenous.

Particulates. These are solid or liquid particles such as smoke, dust or fumes. They may settle (and can then damage plant life and property) or stay suspended in the air (and may irritate the lungs).

Lead. Lead is an anti-knock agent in gasoline. It has a cumulative effect in the body to those exposed to it over a long period. Unleaded gasoline is being introduced and will eventually become universal. However, this is not so much because of lead per se, but because lead destroys the catalyst in catalytic converters which are installed to remove carbon monoxide.

Photochemical smog. This is a mixture of gases and particles oxidized by the sun from the products of gasoline and other fuels. It irritates the eyes, nose and throat, makes breathing difficult, and damages vegetation and materials.

Ozone. This is formed by photochemical reactions between directly emitted nitrous oxides and reactive organic gases (ROG); ROG is formed from combustion of fuels and the evaporation of organic solvents. High concentrations of ozone result in reduced lung functions, particularly during vigorous physical activity. This health problem is particularly acute in children.

PM10. This refers to small suspended particulate matter, 10 microns or less in diameter, which can enter the lungs. Nitrates, sulphates and dust particles are major components of PM10. They can be directly emitted into the atmosphere as a by-product of fuel combustion, through abrasion, such as wear on tyres or brake linings, through wind erosion of soil, or as a result of chemical reactions in the atmosphere. They may carry carcinogens and other toxic compounds which adhere to the particle surfaces and can enter the lungs.

The contribution of trucks to overall vehicle emissions is significant. For example, trucks in total have been estimated to contribute 17 percent of domestic greenhouse gases (carbon dioxide) emitted by the transport sector in Australia, which translates to 4.4 percent of total Australian carbon dioxide emissions (Bureau of Transport and Communication Economics, 1990, 1991).

At the urban level, Nelson et al (1991) have estimated that for the California South Coast Air Basin (Los Angeles), heavy trucks (>8,500 lb, 3.9 t) contributed 4.2 percent of ROG, 18.2 percent of oxides of nitrogen, 12 percent of carbon monoxide and 2.8 percent of PM10 in 1987. Similar figures were quoted for other Californian air basins. A number of measures explicitly aimed at reducing the emissions from trucks in the Los Angeles basin have been proposed (see Chapter 9). Interestingly however, after all currently proposed measures have been into effect, the Southern California Association of Government (1989b, p 6) expects the total of ROG emissions to reduce by 37 percent, but the proportion of this due to trucks will increase, from 41 percent to 43 percent. This indicates that there are potentially greater gains to be made in tackling the air quality issue by focussing on other sources, especially the automobile.

The contribution of urban trucks to total emissions varies with the type of truck (light vs heavy), its engine type (gasoline vs diesel), the conditions under which it operates (free flow vs stop-start), the load carried, the mechanical condition of the engine, brakes, tyres, etc, and the total distance travelled.

Attention to these problems primarily focuses upon the source (the vehicle), but traffic management (to keep vehicles moving freely), land use planning, and time of day restrictions may be applicable also.

Finally, the Australian Bureau of Transport and Communication Economics (1991, p 45) has shown that tractor semi-trailers emit much less carbon dioxide greenhouse gases than other trucks for a given freight task (118 grams per tonne kilometre, compared with 290 for rigid trucks and 1168 for light commercial vehicles). As a result, while tractor semi-trailers carried 49 percent of Australian urban tonne kilometres in 1987-88, they contributed only 21 percent of the truck-related carbon dioxide emissions.

However, the report concluded (op cit, p 44) that 'given the variation in the types of products carried in urban areas ... it appears unlikely that the task could be efficiently performed with a very different vehicle mix. Even if some substitution of articulated for rigid trucks were possible, this would have only a marginal impact on total transport emissions given the relatively small level of emissions from urban freight.'

Vibration

Vibration is partly linked to noise, and may result from either movement of the ground or movement of the air. Complaints about vibration are less common than complaints about noise, but the former is inherently more difficult to deal with (Department of Transport, UK, 1979).

Levels of ground-borne vibration depend primarily upon the condition of the road, and can be controlled by reasonable standards of road construction and maintenance. Ensuring that vehicle loads are properly secured is important also.

Air-borne vibration is a greater problem to control. It is partly related to engine noise, but quietening the engine will not necessarily remove the probiem of low-frequency air-borne vibrations (Department of Transport, op cit, para 5.35).

Policy implications

The community is increasingly concerned about environmental matters, whether on a local scale (large trucks in a local street) or a global scale (greenhouse effects). The political process will respond to these pressures. They have implications at all levels of government; some strategies are essentially local (e.g. traffic restrictions), while others need to be national or even international in scope (e.g. emission or noise standards for new vehicles).

The Australian Bureau of Transport and Communication Economics (1990) has suggested four basic policy options in relation to emission reduction: regulatory devices, economic measures based on taxes or charges, infrastructure development, and public education. These are probably applicable, to a greater or lesser extent, to most environmental issues.

These measures may in turn be directed at a range of targets (Johnson, Joyce and Williams, 1977), including:

- land use (e.g. location of generators; double glazing of houses);

- the freight system (e.g. mode use, operational practices);

- the vehicle (e.g. emission and noise standards); or

- the traffic system (e.g. truck restrictions, road construction, traffic management).

Many of these strategies are considered in detail in Part B.

It must be recognised that most of these measures have a cost associated with them. However, any transport cost increases which occur as a result of the implementation of environmental policy are in effect an 'internalization' of the environmental costs, which are of course passed on to the eventual consumer of the goods. It is a form of tradeoff between efficiency and environmental objectives. Ultimately, attempting to work through internalizing the costs is likely to be more efficacious and efficient than other strategies because the market essentially takes over much of the detail of implementation, given that enforcement levels are adequate. Conversely, because of the cost and efficiency implications of environmental regulations and policies, it is incumbent upon those developing such policies to see that they are realistic and effective, and achieve their aims in a cost-effective manner.

The cost to the community of noise and emissions due to trucks is difficult if not impossible to quantify. However, a recent report of the InterState Commission (1990, p 96) in Australia estimated the cost to the community of excess truck noise as equivalent to 1 percent of total truck operating costs, and that due to emissions to 0.2 percent of vehicle operating costs. While this did not distinguish between urban and non-urban operations, it would be reasonable to suppose that they would be predominantly urban, especially the noise component. These costs are not internalized; i.e. they are true external costs imposed on the community by the road freight industry on behalf of its users. There are also costs to the road freight industry arising from compliance with regulations (e.g. fitting of mufflers and catalytic converters, cost of operations due to truck restrictions, etc), but because these are met by the industry they are in effect a method of internalizing some of the costs.

Infrastructure and management objectives

These objectives are related to the responsibility which the community as a whole, through government agencies, has for various elements of the urban freight task.

Governments have a significant influence on goods transport through such mechanisms as regulations, pricing controls and taxation policies. This control is more significant in the case of inter-regional, interstate and international transport, where there is scope for inter-modal competition and substantial economies of scale. However, in urban areas, controls on such factors as vehicle mass and dimensions, land use zoning, traffic regulations, and vehicle registration all have a direct bearing on urban goods transport. The application of these devices is discussed further in Chapter 9.

Road construction and maintenance

The major community cost associated with urban freight is the provision of capital works, such as roads, ports, airports and (in some countries) railway terminals. All of these can have a significant effect on the private costs of freight transport by providing the means to improve efficiency within the freight industry.

In the case of roads, a significant contribution to the total cost is directly attributable to freight through the need to provide for the passage of trucks. To the extent that the cost of road maintenance and construction is increased by this requirement, these costs are directly attributable to goods transport. The factors include pavement depth, lane width, ruling grades, curve radii and bridge clearances. Governments, of course, attempt to recover these costs to some extent through registration and licence fees, and road user charges generally.

The subject of cost-causality in the provision of roadspace has been much-researched in recent years, mostly in the context of attempting to achieve what is regarded as equitable recovery of road construction and maintenance costs from various road user groups. Trucks are critical in this, because, as mentioned above, there are certain costs of road construction and maintenance which would not be incurred if trucks were not present.

To go beyond this broad statement however, and in particular to attempt to quantify the costs incurred by various user groups is fraught with difficulty. Ogden (1988b) has indicated that there are four key issues:

- *objectives*: whether the concern is with economic objectives (i.e. a rational road pricing policy) or financial objectives (raising revenue to pay for roads);

- *cost attribution*: the determination of the costs that are relevant, including the treatment of capital and maintenance costs and externalities;

- *cost allocation*: the allocation of costs across user or beneficiary groups, often using vehicle classes as a proxy; and

- *revenue*: the determination of what taxes may validly be considered as 'user charges' to offset against costs.

The methods which have been used to undertake cost allocation or cost recovery studies have varied considerably. However, all have used, implicitly or explicitly, an approach which attempts to separate three categories of cost (Ogden, 1988b):

- *avoidable costs*: costs which are explicitly caused by a particular vehicle class (e.g. bridge strength);

- *common costs*: costs which are shared between vehicle classes in a measurable way (e.g. number of lanes); and

- *joint costs*: costs which are shared between vehicle classes in non-determinable proportions (e.g. roadside maintenance or land purchase).

Sometimes the avoidable costs for a vehicle class plus its share of the common costs are referred to as *attributable costs* for that vehicle class.

A major problem is that the third category of cost - joint costs - is usually found to dominate. Since the allocation of joint costs across vehicle classes is essentially arbitrary, the result is that 'the separate costs of each ... user group cannot be determined on any technical engineering basis' (Lawlor, 1982, p 6). Ogden (op cit) however argues that it is in fact unnecessary for the analyst to perform any allocation of joint costs: 'The analyst is on strong theoretical grounds to argue that each vehicle class should provide revenue to meet its attributable costs. But since any distribution of joint costs is essentially arbitrary, the analyst's contribution may end by determining the total amount of the joint costs and arguing that these should be recovered from road users as a whole. How that recovery is distributed amongst particular vehicle classes is ... a political decision.' In short, the result of any cost allocation or cost recovery study is always 'assumption sensitive' (Lay, 1984).

Moreover, those studies which have been undertaken in this field (e.g. InterState Commission, 1990; Federal Highway Administration, 1982, 1987; California Department of Transportation, 1987) have been concerned either with the total road system, or the non-urban component of the road system. Some have included only arterial roads, others have considered both local and arterial roads. The question of determining cost allocation and attribution in the case of *urban* roads is more difficult. Urban road pavements are almost invariably built to a higher standard, because of the need to reduce the costs of subsequent maintenance (either because of the potential to disrupt traffic in the case of arterial roads, or because local authorities insist that developers build local roads to a high standard to reduce the authority's subsequent maintenance responsibilities). Much of the cost of urban road construction and reconstruction involves service utility relocation - a joint cost, as defined above - meaning that there is a smaller proportion which can be allocated on a cost-causal basis. Road capacity (e.g. design standard, number of lanes) is related to peak period demand, and as we have seen, there is a much smaller proportion of trucks on the road at peak periods than at other times of the day. On the revenue side, if one was wanting to determine the cost recovery from heavy vehicles, it is not at all clear how one could estimate the proportion of revenues (after having decided what revenues to include - see above) accountable to urban and non-urban sources. For reasons such as these, any attempt to attribute a proportion of the costs of urban road construction and maintenance would be fraught with even more difficulty than is the case with non-urban roads.

However, Southworth et al (1981) has quoted a study which estimated that trucks were accountable for 50 percent of Chicago's freeway plus arterial maintenance costs and 38.4 percent of new roadway construction costs. Ogden (1976, p 113) using data based on Haritos (1973) has estimated that in the case of Toronto, Canada, 41-44 percent of maintenance cost and around 40 percent of construction cost is attributable to trucks. However, it is important to understand that estimates such as these are critically dependent upon the assumptions made to arrive at them. Different assumptions about cost allocation and cost attribution would produce quite different results.

Nevertheless, irrespective of what method is used or what assumptions are made, the resources devoted to road construction and maintenance in urban areas are significant, and truck usage must be responsible for a sizeable proportion of such costs.

Government freight services

A second category of community cost associated with urban freight is the operation of freight services by or on behalf of government agencies. As noted in Chapter 2, some 6 percent of the truck fleet is typically government owned, and around 10 percent of the goods movement task is undertaken on government trucks. These figures reflect a significant direct involvement by government in the urban movement of goods. Specific responsibilities include such disparate activities as mail, garbage collection, road maintenance, and national defence.

Other community costs

There are a range of other costs incurred by the community in association with urban freight. While no estimate can be made as to their dollar value, they include such aspects as (Hicks, 1977, p 106):

- the cost of government regulation and planning associated with various aspects of urban freight;

- the enactment and enforcement of legislation and planning strategies;

- the cost of police enforcement of traffic laws and regulations related to vehicles and truck loading; and

- the costs of research and development on aspects of freight, to the extent that government interests itself in these activities.

Policy implications

If nothing else, these factors indicate that government cannot completely ignore urban freight. As we have seen in Chapter 4, the interest of government in planning and policy areas concerned with urban freight has been at a low ebb in the 1980s. However, because government is responsible for a key component of the urban freight infrastructure -

namely the road network - and because it has other regulatory or operational responsibilities, government must retain an interest in freight efficiency, effectiveness, and its impacts. This is of course only the bottom line; beyond this, government can play, if it wishes, a much more activist role by using its powers and responsibilities for road investment, regulations, taxes, etc to actively pursue other urban freight objectives related to efficiency, environmental protection, safety, etc.

Urban structure objectives

The final set of objectives for urban freight policy relate to the interaction between freight facilities and urban structure. Costs in this area are very difficult to enumerate and allocate, but clearly goods transport does have an effect upon the structure of urban regions. Goods movement is an integral component of urban society. A city could not exist that did not allow for the inflow of food, energy and raw materials, the outflow of industrial products and waste, and the movement of commodities within the urban area. As such, goods movement is an essential part of the urban planning and urban development process.

Moreover, there are costs associated with a poor integration of land use and freight transport facilities. Once installed, new urban development and related transport facilities will usually remain in place for many years. Consequently, as Simons, et al (1972) have pointed out, 'whatever transport inefficiencies and negative externalities are built-in initially may be promulgated for decades'. Many of today's freight problems and inefficiencies stem directly from poor location and design decisions made in years past.

Urban structure objectives in the context of freight transport have three aspects: the interaction between freight and urban structure, city size and its effects of freight costs, and freight as a user of urban land.

Freight and urban structure

In a dynamic urban area, physical changes continually take place as the structure of the region responds to social, economic and technological change. Some of these changes which have a direct bearing on freight include the suburbanization of residential, commercial and industrial activities; the development of regional shopping centres, the rapid rise in the economic importance of service industries, the rise in the use of road transport for line haul freight (with typically suburban terminals) at the expense of rail (with typically near-central city terminals) and the tendency towards development of integrated 'parks' for industry, offices, etc.

The effects of these sorts of changes on urban freight are felt in such areas as the commodities which are moved, the location of origins and destinations of trips, traffic flow on urban roads, the urgency and frequency of deliveries, time of day of freight movements, and the productivity of the urban truck fleet (Button and Pearman, 1981, p 77).

Conversely, urban structure is at least partially affected by the freight system. The relationship here is straightforward; when a firm purchases land, it also purchases location, which 'will influence the costs of labor and raw materials as well as the delivered cost of its output (and thus) freight transport considerations may play an important part in determining the nature of the urban area, industrial (and consequently residential) location, the extent of urban sprawl and the vitality of the central business district' (Hicks, 1977, p 107-108).

In turn, location decisions have an important influence on urban freight costs. In particular, the location of both terminals and freight generating land uses affects truck trip length and shipment haul length; as noted in Chapter 2 for example, truck trips have increased in length over the years, but the number of trips (deliveries) made per day has not increased because trip lengths have increased as shippers and receivers have changed location.

At the macro-level, the location of freight facilities is influenced by a number of factors. One of the factors affecting industry and freight depot location is the ease and cost of truck access (Travers Morgan, 1987, p 34). Therefore, provision (or non-provision) of road facilities may be used as a tool to influence industry location. Young, Ritchie and Ogden (1980, p 71) in a study of freight facility location in Melbourne, Australia found that the location of firms in the freight transport sector was influenced by transport system characteristics. These characteristics included closeness to customers and other trucking firms, and closeness to arterial roads and freeways. This finding is supported by the empirical observation that in the US, many urban areas have a major freight terminal located near the point where inter-urban freeways meet urban 'beltway' routes.

For activities other than those in the freight sector, it is clear that the land use patterns which result from location decisions have a significant effect upon urban freight, since they are the direct determinant of trip origins and destinations. Land use planning policy in most western industrial cities has been to separate different types of activity: residential, retailing, light industry, heavy industry, extractive industry, warehousing,

133

etc. While there have been sound environmental reasons for doing this, it is important to realise that the separation of complementary industrial activities which results from this policy has the effect of building into cities the need for massive and sustained freight flows. The costs associated with this cannot be estimated, but are probably very significant; Kearney (1975, p III-33) for example has noted that 'a city which is organised into separate residential and manufacturing areas tends to generate a higher density of stops for each kind of goods movement than cities where these two functions are intermingled'. Similarly, Kearney argues (op cit, p III-34) that 'since the magnitude of goods movement transportation tends to relate to the demand for service, more affluent economic areas, which may demand higher levels of service, may require more urban goods movement than do less affluent areas'.

At a micro level, new urban development projects offer an opportunity to install facilities which are inherently more efficient or have fewer adverse effects. For example, the installation of adequate off-street loading and despatch facilities and the provision of good access conditions at new industrial sites, freight terminals, shopping centres and office developments will avoid creating the problems and costs which are endemic at older sites.

Freight as a user of urban land

Freight facilities occupy large areas of land in many urban areas, for ports, rail yards, truck terminals, etc. In many cases, this is no coincidence: one of the principal historical reasons for the siting and growth of urban areas is their location at the focus of rail and water transport routes, and their role as a freight interchange point.

In many urban areas, these facilities (especially rail yards and seaports) occupy prime real estate, and it could be argued that it deserves a higher use than that of a freight terminal. Not surprisingly therefore, there are several examples of massive urban redevelopment programs involving conversion of undeveloped, even derelict, urban land previously used as freight terminals into residential, commercial, or other uses. The London Docklands is probably the most striking example, but there are many others.

In the case of seaports in particular, the changing technology of waterfront activities is causing changes in land use patterns. Many seaports are moving their activities onto land reclaimed from the sea; this has occurred as river ports have moved their activities towards and outside the river mouth as ships have become bigger, and also because modern container technology requires that there be very substantial areas of flat land immediately adjacent to the berth. As a result, land uses in the vicinity of ports are changing, but too often the land-side transport system is not changing with them; the development of the Intermodal Container Transfer Facility to serve the ports of Long Beach and Los Angeles is a case where an opportunity to develop a modern land side facility was taken (see Chapter 11).

More generally, Kearney (1975, p III-35) has made crude estimates of the amount of space devoted to trucking facilities in US cities. They estimate that shipping and receiving facilities accommodate about one-tenth of one percent of urban land, truck parking requires about one-half of one-percent, and road facilities to accommodate truck movements require about 2-4 percent of urban land. If we accept these estimates, we could say that perhaps 3-5 percent of urban land is devoted to trucking purposes.

City size and density

There is evidence to suggest that freight costs increase with the size of the urban area. In Chapter 2, we presented some Canadian data which indicated that the cost of intra-urban freight rose rapidly with the size of the urban area. Larger cities mean that the distance travelled to complete a delivery is increased, and that stem time (the time between leaving the terminal and arriving at the first delivery point) is greater. Denser cities generate greater congestion and hence higher costs, ceteris paribus; this is reflected in some US data from the early 1970s (Department of Transportation, US, 1973) which indicated that if it cost $1 to deliver a 45 kg parcel in a small city like Nashville, TN, it cost $3 in Washington DC and $5.70 in New York City. While the actual numbers don't mean anything today, their relativities do.

However, Button and Pearman (1981, p 12) have suggested that there may be economies of scale in larger urban areas. There are two reasons suggested for this, firstly that larger, more efficient vehicles can be used, and secondly that a larger urban area generates more of its need for freight internally, at the expense of more costly movements to and from another urban area.

Policy implications

Poor location decisions and inadequate transport networks cause urban problems and increase the costs of urban freight. As the National

Association of Regional Councils (1984, p 2) noted, 'governments are gradually realising that business and industrial location decisions are not only based on access to raw materials but also on dependable transportation networks that ease goods distribution.'

It follows therefore that if freight transport facilities can and do affect urban development, it is possible to use those facilities as a tool to help shape urban form. Similarly, the development of urban plans, and the consideration of alternative urban futures presupposes that there are some futures which are more desirable than others. This in turn implies that there are criteria by which alternatives can be evaluated. Perhaps one such criterion is the efficiency of urban goods movement. The cost of transport is a component of almost all goods and services which are produced in an industrial economy, and if some urban strategies are more efficient, or have a smaller effect on the environment, then the community will tend to be better off with those strategies.

PART B

PLANNING: STRATEGIES FOR IMPROVEMENT

6 Traffic management

Introduction

Trucks have always been recognised as part of the traffic stream, and thus to an extent their needs have been included in aspects of traffic engineering practice. However, this recognition has been limited, and has only recently extended beyond such basic parameters as vehicle size and the use of passenger car equivalents (e.g. 1 truck equals 2 cars) in roadway capacity calculations.

It is now increasingly recognised that, on the one hand, trucks have special needs and problems that can and should be recognised by the traffic engineer, while on the other hand, there are real and unique benefits which can accrue from truck-oriented traffic management. These benefits relate to many of the objectives outlined in Chapter 5, including regional economic development, land use, road safety, environmental protection, and traffic flow.

Traffic management is a very important strategy in urban freight policy and planning. Indeed, management of truck traffic is one of the most powerful and direct ways in which the public sector can influence urban trucking efficiency and safety. Traffic management strategies are of four general types (Ogden, 1991):

- measures at a network level;
- measures at a site level;
- measures directed at parking and loading; and
- the removal of physical impediments to truck movement.

Network strategies

Truck routes

Strategies for application at the network level involve the nomination of specific routes for use by trucks. Various applications are possible (Gordon, Aitken and Clark, 1982), but the two principal applications are an advisory system and a statutory system.

An advisory truck route system involves making particular routes attractive to trucks, with the aim of attracting trucks to it away from 'protected' routes. There are obvious enforcement advantages with this approach.

In practice, this feature is very common, whether intended or not, in that certain routes are more attractive for trucks. In urban areas this would include most if not all roads forming the arterial road network. Many urban areas are content to leave it at that, being concerned that if a formal advisory truck route network was promulgated they would need to upgrade it to make it unambiguously the best route rather than just one of a number of suitable routes (Hall, 1982, p 11).

An advisory truck route network would usually include all freeways and major arterial roads in an urban area, and may encompass other road types where they extend into industrial areas or truck terminal locations. The network must be free of barriers to truck travel, such as sub-standard overhead clearances.

A designated advisory truck route network assists route selection, particularly by out-of-town drivers; it reassures truck drivers that the route is suitable for large vehicles and is reasonably continuous and connected to other routes; and, by helping remove traffic from other routes, assists in reducing the environmental impact of trucks in sensitive areas. From a traffic engineering viewpoint, designating an advisory truck route network helps to focus attention on traffic improvements to assist truck travel. As an advisory system, the enforcement costs and implementation costs are minimal, but on the other hand, it's usefulness may be susceptible to truck driver preferences (Loder and Bayly, 1981, p 30).

A statutory truck route system is one which legally prohibits trucks from using routes other than designated routes. In implementation, this approach tends to rely more on its corollary, i.e. particular areas (e.g. a local street network) are protected by an entry ban ('no entry except for access'); this type of control is discussed below under Area Bans. This was carried one stage further in Britain in the 1970s, where there was a proposal for a nationwide truck route network. Legislation in 1973 (the so-called 'Dykes Act') required local authorities to carry our truck surveys, formulate control proposals and publish draft orders for truck control. The prime response to this was a concentration on truck routing, and from this the proposal for a national network. However, for several reasons, mainly having to do with central government funding and desire for local autonomy, the proposal was abandoned in 1977 (Ogden, 1980; Cooper, 1990).

If a truck route network, whether advisory or statutory, is to be introduced, there are a number of factors to be taken into account in designating and promulgating it (Hasell, Foulkes and Robertson, 1978a; Christiansen, 1979, p IV-27; Institution of Highway Engineers, 1981; Gordon, Aitken and Clark, 1982):

- agreement must be reached between the various local governments in the urban area encompassing the network;

- the network should serve the major generators of truck traffic in as convenient and direct a manner as possible;

- it should comprise most if not all freeways and main arterial roads, with connecting and access links as necessary;

- the roads themselves should be in good condition, having adequate structural strength and geometric layout to accommodate larger, heavier vehicles, and should be reasonably smooth to minimize vibration;

- structures on the network should have adequate strength, and overhead clearances should be at least equal to the legal height limit for trucks in that state or nation;

- traffic lanes should be of adequate width, which may vary with the maximum permitted width of trucks in that state or nation; generally a lane width of around 3.6 m (12 ft) is appropriate;

- steep grades should be avoided, especially in localities where noise is a problem; perhaps a 4 percent grade would be a desirable maximum;

- the network should be selected with consideration for abutting land uses; residential and retail land uses and areas with high pedestrian activity should be avoided as much as possible;

- consideration should be given to present traffic volumes on the roads, and the capacities of intersections to accommodate extra truck traffic;

- roads used as part of the network must be through roads, with reasonable connection to other roads comprising the network, and with as few sharp turns as possible; this may mean that some reconstruction of intersections is necessary, e.g. to provide turn lanes;

- similarly, traffic control on all roads on the network should be adequate, with STOP or GIVE WAY control on all minor side streets, and signals or grade separations at all major intersections; roundabouts with small central islands should be avoided;

- driver and vehicle facilities should be provided along the route, and provision made for easy access to them and easy re-entry back on to the through route; these facilities include fuel, parking, toilets, telephones, food, etc;

- the network should be developed in close cooperation with the road freight industry, unions, and other affected parties such as public transport operators;

- in implementation, careful attention must be given to signing (Figure 6.1), and the distribution of maps and other publicity advising of the network and its conditions;

- further to the previous two points, the definition of vehicle to be affected by the route needs careful attention (e.g. mass, length, number of axles); this determines both the effectiveness of the network and its impacts on operators, and also the extent of enforcement in the case of a statutory truck route; and

- in the case of a statutory network, route designation must comply with relevant legislation.

Figure 6.1 Advisory truck route sign, Australia

Routes for designated vehicles

Truck routes may be designated only for specific classes of vehicle, of which the following examples are most common.

Overdimensional truck routes. These involve the nomination of specific routes for vehicles which exceed statutory mass, height, width, or length limits. Since such vehicles, by definition, would be operating illegally if they were used in the traffic stream in the usual way, all movements of such vehicles require a permit and possibly also an escort.

The designation of a specific set of routes for over-dimensional vehicles simplifies route specification, issue of permits, and traffic control for the movement of large indivisible loads. Routes should be selected to cover the majority of truck movements involving large loads, to ensure that overhead clearances are adequate, turn radii at intersections are suitable, and that impact on other traffic is minimized. In some cases (e.g. a route providing access to a power station which requires transport of large indivisible generating equipment) the route may have stronger structures to accommodate the heavier vehicles. By ensuring adequate clearances and restricting large vehicles to these routes, the potential for disruption due to collisions with overhead power lines, overbridges, etc is minimized.

143

Overdimensional truck routes cannot however cater for the every movement of large indivisible loads in an urban area, and there will still need to be individual route assessment for occasional movement of such loads on other routes, at least until they access the designated overdimensional network. Routes for overdimensional vehicles should be clearly signed.

Hazardous load routes. These involve the designation of specific routes for vehicles carrying hazardous loads (e.g. highly volatile, flammable or explosive goods, toxic wastes, etc), especially where the movement is frequent, e.g. between chemical plants, storage or disposal sites, etc.

The designation of truck routes and the development of management plans for the transport of hazardous materials should be based upon a risk assessment procedure. Risk may be broadly defined as 'the product of the probability of a hazardous materials accident and the consequences of that accident' (Scanlon and Cantilli, 1985). More comprehensively, the Organisation for Economic Cooperation and Development (1988, p 6) asserted that 'risk assessment analyses involve a chain of probability calculations in order to estimate the dangers particular transport movements may pose to people, goods, property and the environment.' This report goes on to outline three potential uses of risk assessment calculations:

- assist in the classification of goods for regulatory purposes;
- aid in route selection; and
- evaluate the effects of alternative risk management strategies.

Risk assessment may attempt to calculate the absolute risk of a given situation, but such calculations are severely limited by the quality and quantity of data available. Alternatively, as in the case of deciding between alternative routes, relative risk assessment is appropriate. For example, Harris, Roodbool and Ale (1986, p 47) describe a model developed in Britain for assessing the relative risk of hazardous goods movement by alternative modes of transport, while Saccomanno and Chan (1985) describe a model developed in Canada which assesses urban truck routes according to three criteria: minimum truck operating costs, minimum accident likelihood, and minimum objective risk assessment. The US Federal Highway Administration (Barber and Hildebrand, 1980) has developed a set of guidelines for the evaluation of alternative routes; Kessler (1986) has described the application of this methodology in Dallas, Texas (see Chapter 15). Pijawka, Foote and Soesilo (1985) have discussed the use of a similar model in Arizona. Other models and approaches are described in Rowe (1983).

In general, these models reveal that roads which are preferred for the transport of hazardous materials in urban areas have the following characteristics:

- all freeways and controlled access facilities are likely to be suitable;

- routes should be as direct as possible, all else being equal;

- where there is no direct freeway to freeway connection, a suitable route to facilitate such travel should be sought;

- routes should be less densely populated than alternatives;

- routes should avoid centres of concentrated population, such as shopping centres, schools, hospitals, cinemas, etc;

- routes should be largely free of physical characteristics likely to contribute to crashes, e.g. steep grades, narrow lanes, low overhead clearance bridges, sharp bends or ramps, poor shoulders, etc;

- rail level crossings should be avoided;

- crossings over open water supply aqueducts should be avoided; and

- the choice of route should take into account relative levels of exposure to risk, as measured by travel distance, persons exposed to risk, time of day, etc.

Signing of designated routes should be comprehensive, and maps showing the network distributed to all relevant parties. Unfortunately, there is no uniform international practice in route signing, although there are international conventions covering this (Organisation for Economic Cooperation and Development, 1988, p 67).

Emergency procedures involving fire, police, local government, etc should be in place for all areas through which the routes pass. In addition to traffic control, these should incorporate the following responses (Pijawka, Foote and Soesilo, 1985):

- contain or suppress the release of hazardous materials or their manifestations (fire, toxic fumes, etc);

- protect the public from the released material through warnings, evacuations, etc;

- monitor and assess secondary and long term impacts to health and the environment; and

- clean up any spilled material.

The specific materials covered by any such route designation should be carefully specified. In particular, there is rarely much advantage in prescribing such ubiquitous products as gasoline, since these need to move on virtually the entire arterial road network to access service stations, etc.

A hazardous load network has advantages and disadvantages. Among the former are the potential for increased public safety, reduced truck driver stress, attention to specific road and traffic measures to increase safety, and the focussing of emergency services onto a smaller part of the network.

On the other hand, there are some major disadvantages, primarily a strong negative reaction from among those people who live and work along the routes. An attempt to develop and implement a hazardous truck route network must therefore devote much time and effort to community consultation (Kessler, 1986, p 86). In addition, transport costs are increased and operating freedom is reduced, and enforcement needs are increased.

For these reasons, and particularly that relating to adverse community reaction, many cities do not designate an explicit network for vehicles carrying hazardous loads. More common are lower profile schemes such as those which prohibit hazardous loads in certain locations (e.g. tunnels), focus on specific commodities (e.g. LP gas), or rely on an informal understanding between local officials and transport operators that trucks carrying such loads will not travel past schools or through shopping centres.

High productivity vehicle routes. Regulations may prevent the use of certain classes of vehicle because they are not considered suitable for general, system-wide use. Examples include height limits, mass limits, or particular vehicle combinations such as double or triple trailered trucks.

However, in the interests of economic efficiency, it may be appropriate to designate a limited number of routes upon which high productivity vehicles may be allowed. An example might be the introduction of a limited network of roads near a port having higher axle load limits to accommodate shipping containers, many of which are of such a mass that they cause trucks to exceed usual load limits (see Chapter 11).

Perhaps the best example is the need for US States and cities to provide 'reasonable access' to Interstate and Federal-aid primary routes for the larger vehicles which are permitted on such routes by Federal law (Transportation Research Board, 1986b, p 50). Figure 6.2 shows a sign indicating that a freeway exit may be used by so-called STAA[1] vehicles for the purposes of access to services (S) and terminals (T).

The general question of the use of long combination vehicles on urban streets needs to be mentioned here in the context of the need to provide access for such vehicles (i.e. twins, triples, and trucks with longer and wider trailers). A number of studies have shown that these vehicles have performance characteristics which are significantly different than other tractor semi-trailers (Hutchinson, 1988; Hansen, Palmer and Khan, 1988; Hutchinson and Parker, 1989; DeCabooter and Solberg, 1990; Transportation Research Board, 1989). These differences include turn radius, braking, performance on grades, acceleration in traffic, trailer swing and lateral amplification, splash and spray, and their effects on vehicle overtaking. A case study involving an assessment of a possible route for large combination vehicles in Perth, Australia is described in Chapter 15.

Local or site strategies

Traffic management strategies at a local or site level include various types of truck ban, and design features such as traffic signal control and intersection geometry. These are reviewed below as follows:

- route bans;
- local area bans;
- regional area bans;
- truck lanes;
- traffic signal settings;
- linked signals;
- intersection geometry; and
- vertical geometry.

Figure 6.2 STAA truck route sign, USA

Route bans

This measure involves a prohibition on trucks using a particular route. It is applied only to trucks which exceed a certain mass or length limit, and may be applicable only at certain hours of the day (Figure 6.3).

This type of prohibition is particularly applicable to roads which appear to form part of the arterial road network, but which are considered to be sensitive to truck intrusion, such as scenic boulevards, seaside esplanades, 'parkways' etc (Christiansen, 1979, p IV-29). Figure 6.4 shows the truck ban on the Pasadena Freeway in Los Angeles, a scenic route of low geometric standard connecting central Los Angeles with suburban Pasadena. (This is claimed to be the world's first freeway, opened in 1930). However a route ban may be applied in some cases to retail or even office precincts also. Occasionally a route ban may be applied because the pavement strength or structural strength of bridges along the route is inadequate. It is rarely applicable to a single residential street; protection of such streets would normally be on an area-wide basis, as discussed below.

Figure 6.3 Truck entry prohibition sign, USA

Alternative routes must be available; Loder and Bayly (1981, p 31) suggest a diversion of not more than 4 km (6.5 miles), or more than 150 percent extra travel time if the journey is less than 8 km (13 miles).

Disadvantages of a route ban are that it needs enforcement; it may impose extra costs on deliveries, e.g. if a trucking company has to use smaller vehicles to access the area; and there may be a negative reaction from people living on roads onto which the truck traffic is diverted. There will probably need to be provision for certain exemptions, and this adds to enforcement difficulties and may create inequities.

An interesting variation on the theme of banning vehicle from particular streets was the introduction of a *passenger vehicle* ban on streets in the New York Garment Center in order to facilitate truck loading and access (New York City, 1976, p VIII-8; Hedges, 1985).

Figure 6.4 Truck prohibition on Pasadena Freeway, Los Angeles

Figure 6.5 Entry ban specified by vehicle length, Britain

Local area bans

This measure involves a prohibition on specific categories of truck entering a designated local area ('no entry except for access'). Trucks may be designated by length, mass, number of axles, or a combination of these (see Figures 6.5 and 6.6).

The most common application of this ban is to prohibit the through movement of heavy vehicles in residential areas, with the aim of improving residential amenity through reduction in noise, visual intrusion, vibration and hazard, and also because most residential street pavements are not designed to carry large volumes of heavy traffic. However, it is important to note that truck drivers generally choose to stay on the arterial road system, and if they are using residential streets it is probably because of deficiencies in the arterial network (Urban Consortium for Technology Initiatives, 1980, p 6).

Enforcement in this case can be a problem, particularly if there are a significant number of trucks which need to access the area. For this reason, the area covered by the ban should have few (preferably no) land uses which generate truck trips; in this case the only trucks with legitimate access needs are trucks serving residential premises, such as waste collection vehicles, furniture removalists, builders trucks, service vehicles, etc.

In some cases, physical devices are installed to deter or actually prevent trucks entering. Examples of the former are road humps, chicanes, and roundabouts; in this case (especially with roundabouts) some provision must be made for access by legitimate vehicles, e.g. by having a mountable curb on the central island. In Britain, it is common to install bollards or overhead beams which prevent access by wide or high vehicles. Hasell, Foulkes and Robertson (1978c, p 182) note that bollards 2.1 m (7 ft) apart are common in London, especially in instances where several streets are served by a single 'gateway', so a widespread area can be protected by the installation of one or two width restrictions. Provision needs to be made for access by emergency vehicles. (See Figure 6.7.)

If this measure was to be introduced for a number of local areas across a municipality, or for several municipalities in a metropolitan area, it is very desirable that there be consistency between municipalities, particularly in respect of the width, length or mass of vehicle to which the ban applied.

Figure 6.6 Entry ban specified by vehicle mass and length, USA

Regional area bans

In some cases, area bans apply to a whole town, region, or locality within a city, with the aim of restricting trucks to a limited network of arterial roads. Figure 6.8 shows a sign on a State Highway approach to a city in California.

Cundill (1976) has reported the effect of a range of possible 'no entry except for access' provisions for the city of Swindon, England. These were assessed according to several criteria, of which the two most important were reduction in nuisance from trucks, and total annual costs. The study concluded (op cit, p 51) that bans applicable to the whole town would give 'modest reductions in nuisances specific to heavy goods vehicles', at low cost to the community from additional freight costs.

Figure 6.7 Width restriction using bollards, Britain

A regional area truck ban inevitably produces a response from the trucking industry and its customers. For example, Cooper (1983) has suggested that a truck ban proposed for London, England would leave a company with five options: to use smaller vehicles; to continue to use large vehicles up to the urban boundary, and then break bulk to smaller vehicles; to use 'demountable bodies' to facilitate the use of smaller vehicles within the urban area; to cease trading; or to relocate.

At the intra-urban level, a proposal to restrict truck use of Los Angeles freeways at peak periods was examined by Cambridge Systematics (1988a,b). They analysed a similar set of responses, as follows (op cit, 1988a, Technical Memorandum 3.7): diversion of truck movements off the freeways onto surface arterials; shift of movements to off-peak periods; use of smaller trucks not subject to restrictions; and relocation of operations. They concluded (Grenzeback, et al, 1990) that the last two would be unlikely, and that peak period trips would be split 80 percent to arterial roads and 20 percent to off-peak periods. The effect of this would be to shift commuter traffic from the shoulders of the peak period to the peak, thus shortening queues at the bottleneck locations slightly, so that 'most of the congestion relief from a peak period freeway ban would likely be lost within 6 weeks to 6 months.' They concluded that there would be a net economic loss resulting from this proposal.

153

Figure 6.8 Truck entry restriction sign, USA

Perhaps for this reason (but probably more because of doubts about the legality of banning trucks from freeways (Grenzeback, 1990)), the proposal to prohibit trucks on freeways at peak periods has subsequently been modified to a proposal to restrict trucks on all surface streets in the City of Los Angeles at peak periods, with the aim of reducing truck traffic by 50 percent. This proposal is reviewed in Chapter 15.

Regional area bans need to be introduced with a great deal of caution and thorough analysis of the likely consequences, because it is not certain that they will have an overall beneficial effect. For example, Noortman (1984, p 50) noted that they 'likely increase the costs for the community and would not greatly reduce the nuisance caused by heavy vehicles'. Cooper (1983) made a similar comment: 'while the cost impacts of a lorry ban are real, the benefits may be illusory.' Smith (1976) went so far as to say that 'the disadvantages (of eliminating large vehicles from town centres) would seem to outweigh the benefits'. Kirby, Tagell and Ogden (1986) in a study in Manila, The Philippines concluded that the introduction of an area wide ban on large trucks had led to the introduction of a large number of smaller trucks (not covered by the ban), and 'any action which causes a single peak period truck to be replaced by more than two (light vehicle) trips will worsen traffic congestion, all other things being equal.'

Truck lanes

This measure involves the allocation of a traffic lane (or lanes) for the exclusive use of trucks, or for exclusive use by trucks, buses and perhaps other high occupancy vehicles. It has the potential to reduce delay, and aims specifically to benefit truck traffic, especially on a short section of congested road carrying heavy truck volumes (Organisation for Economic Cooperation and Development, 1977, p 24; Christiansen, 1979, p IV-25; Anon, 1978b, p 162).

While combined truck-bus lanes have been proposed (e.g. trucks being permitted to use exclusive bus lanes), there would likely be some operational and design challenges in combining bus and truck flow in a single lane (Loder and Bayly, 1981, p 41).

The application of exclusive truck lanes is likely to be extremely limited, since the advantages are few. Where truck volumes are very heavy, they establish their dominance in some lanes by sheer weight of numbers; compulsorily excluding other vehicles would seem to offer little extra benefit. Moreover, it may produce confusion, as presumably trucks would have to leave the lane at some point, e.g. to make a turn.

A variation on this theme is to provide trucks with an exclusive lane on freeway on-ramps, as is commonly done for high occupancy vehicles (buses and car pool vehicles) (Ross, 1978; Christiansen, 1979, p IV-33). This is again a measure aimed specifically at providing a benefit to trucks and the movement of goods, but it is not likely to be popular with other motorists.

Another practice under this general heading is that of restricting trucks to certain lanes on a roadway. For example, in California, trucks are required to use the two outer (right hand) lanes on a freeway and are not permitted to use other lanes unless specifically permitted to do so, e.g. at freeway-freeway interchange areas where several right-hand lanes form a connector to another freeway. Garber and Gadiraju (1990) have examined the capacity and safety effects of this practice, and found that headways were increased in the right hand lane (thus effectively reducing its capacity), and that there was a potential for increasing the accident rate. Grenzeback et al (1990) noted that a high proportion of trucks in the right hand lane 'creates a psychological, and sometimes a physical, barrier for drivers trying to merge, and contributes to sideswipes and rear end collisions'. To mitigate these effects, they proposed the construction of an additional continuous-merge right hand lane from which trucks would be prohibited except at entrances and exits.

Traffic signal settings

This measure involves taking explicit account of the needs of trucks in signal timing plans where truck flows are significant. Present signal design practices do not take explicit account of the needs of heavy vehicles, in terms of such factors as braking and acceleration capability and costs of stops. Moreover, current signal design practice concentrates on capacity maximization in the peak direction (usually radial), and this reduces the capacity in counter-peak and cross-town directions, which are the directions more likely to be used by trucks at peak hours.

Trucks are currently accommodated in traffic signal design mainly through the use of passenger car equivalents in capacity calculations. Recent research (Kimber, McDonald and Hounsell, 1986; Molina, 1987; Brown and Ogden, 1988) has confirmed the use of the values in current use for heavy vehicles as a whole, but has shown that larger trucks have a higher through car equivalent value, and where a large number of heavy trucks use the intersection, existing design practices will overestimate the capacity of the intersection. Brown and Ogden's results are shown in Table 6.1. Recent work by Fisk (1990) has suggested that the passenger car equivalent value may also vary with traffic flow, with the effect of trucks on capacity being greater at higher volumes.

The potential exists to do more, especially if signal equipment was modified to identify specific classes of vehicle (e.g. by number of axles) through a system of advance detectors, instead of (or in addition to) stop line detectors (Christiansen, 1979, p IV-22; Hutchinson, 1988; TTM Consulting, 1987, p D6). Potential changes might include:

- longer clearance times or all-red times, to allow for lower speed and poorer braking for through vehicles, and slower acceleration of turning vehicles;

- dynamic truck detection and green phase extension so that signals do not turn yellow as a truck is approaching;

Table 6.1
Through car equivalents for various vehicle types

Movement and vehicle type	Current values (Akcelik, 1981)	Survey results	
		aggregate	disaggregate
(a) Through movements			
car	1.00	1.00	
passenger car			1.00
light commercial			1.39
heavy vehicle	2.00	2.08	
rigid truck			1.79
articulated truck			2.46
(b) Unopposed left turn movements*			
car	1.25	1.27	
passenger car			1.27
light commercial			1.43
heavy vehicle	2.50	2.44	
rigid truck			2.13
articulated truck			2.67
(c) Unopposed right turn movements			
car	1.25	1.11	
passenger car			1.11
light commercial			1.00
heavy vehicle	2.50	2.47	
rigid truck			2.16
articulated truck			2.87

* for vehicles driving on the left side of the road

Source: Brown and Ogden (1988)

157

- longer minimum phase times (to allow for slower acceleration);

- adjustment of the gap and waste timers to allow for longer headways between vehicles (caused by slower truck acceleration);

- turning phase warrants to take particular account of truck turning volumes; and

- adjustment of passenger car equivalent factors where there is a high proportion of trucks, as discussed above.

An extreme case would be the detection of trucks fitted with transponders, so as to actually over-ride the normal operation of the signal controller to give priority to such vehicles. This is often done with buses, and in principle could be done with certain classes of truck. Examples may be a twin or triple trailered vehicle, where the sudden application of brakes is considered to be a potential hazard, but where for economic or other reasons it was desirable to have such trucks using the road; waste collection vehicles exiting disposal sites; trucks delivering newspapers; service vehicles such as fire engines, etc.

A specific example of this type of approach (albeit not using transponders) is in the town of Auburn in California. A signalized intersection is located at the crest of a 8 percent upgrade, with that road having significant use by heavy trucks, particularly associated with the timber industry. Tandem loop detectors have been placed in the right lane, 9 m (30 ft) apart, 293 m (960 ft) in advance of the signal. The signal controller is set so that trucks approaching at a speed of 24-32 km/h (15-20 mph) can expect to face a green phase. The pre-emption cycle is limited to once every two minutes, and the detector spacing ensures that it is only activated by long trucks. If a truck will not make the green phase, a warning flashes, advising the driver to prepare to stop. It is estimated that about 90 percent of long trucks are able to pass through the signal without stopping. The approach sign for this installation is shown in Figure 6.9.

Linked signals

Linking traffic signals to provide progression along a route improves the performance of the traffic system in terms of such parameters as reduced number of stops, reduced fuel consumption, reduced travel time and reduced accidents.

However, trucks can be disadvantaged by linked signal systems if the time offset between the commencement of the green at successive signals is set on the basis of car times, which trucks, because of their slower acceleration, cannot match. Sometimes the settings are such that trucks in fact face a 'red wave' rather than a 'green wave', being stopped at perhaps every signal along a route (Ogden, 1990).

TTM Consulting (1987, p D6) have suggested the following ways in which the design of linked signal networks may be modified to take explicit account of trucks:

- linking based on truck speeds;

- link high volume truck turning movements;

- link on the basis on counter-peak travel times when congestion in the peak direction precludes linking;

- minimize the density of signals (signals per kilometre or mile); and

- reduce cycle times as far as possible.

Intersection geometry

The critical points on a road network from a capacity, congestion and safety viewpoint are intersections. Therefore, considerable improvement can result from attention to the layout of intersections.

Provisions for right turn movements (for countries which drive on the right) and left turn movements (for those which drive on the left) in particular vary considerably due to such factors as road formation and road reserve widths, number of lanes, type of abutting development, etc. Some, but by no means all, such intersections of arterial roads in urban areas have slip lanes with islands. Many arterial road intersections, and virtually all local street intersections, use a simple curb return with no islands.

Figure 6.10 shows the relationship between approach lane width, departure lane width, and curb radius for three classes of truck in Australia: light rigid (straight) trucks, heavy rigid trucks, and articulated trucks (tractor semi-trailers).[2]

159

Figure 6.9 Truck preemption at traffic signals, Auburn, California

Figure 6.10 is based upon templates prepared using a computer package which generates wheel paths for vehicles of these configurations and dimensions (TTM Consulting, 1989). A similar approach has been used by Hummer, Zegeer and Hanscom (1989) for US trucks; although the Australian study used rather different design parameters than the US study, the results shown in Figure 6.10 (at least for tractor semi-trailers) appear to be quite comparable.

As mentioned above under local area bans, it may sometimes be a deliberate decision to retain, or even install, an intersection which a truck has difficulty in negotiating, in order to discourage extraneous trucks from entering (say) a residential area.

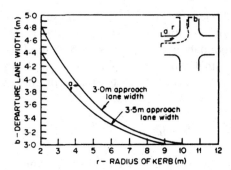

Light Rigid Truck

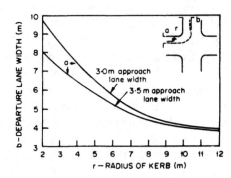

Heavy Rigid Truck

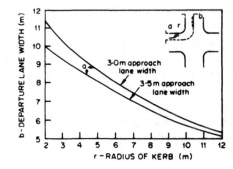

Articulated Truck

Source: TTM Consulting (1989)
Note: This is based upon vehicles driving on the *left* side of the road

Figure 6.10 Left turn geometry for trucks

161

However, as noted, even in these cases, it is necessary to ensure that trucks with legitimate business in the area can gain access; in the case of roundabouts for example, the central island should have a mountable curb so that a design vehicle (perhaps a large rigid truck) can get through the intersection; use of templates or computer packages, as described above, may be helpful here.

Vertical geometry

There are a number of ways in which trucks can or should influence the design of vertical geometry of a road.

The most obvious is overhead clearance; clearance at bridges, entrances to buildings, within loading areas, etc, should allow for the legal height of trucks (Christiansen, 1978). While this varies somewhat from jurisdiction to jurisdiction, a minimum height of 4.3 to 4.6 m (14-15 ft) is common. Bridges with clearances less than this should be clearly signed, although as Figure 6.11 shows, this is not always effective!

Another aspect is the height and offset of street furniture and awnings. Trucks predominantly use the curb lane, but the ability to do so may be restricted if roadside objects are too low or too close to curb line, after allowing for the crossfall on the road. Table 6.2 shows the relationship between lateral and vertical clearances and pavement crossfall.

Vertical alignment can also have a critical effect upon sight distances. A truck entering a premises by making a turn across the centre line of an undivided road (e.g. US left turn or British right turn) needs to have clear sight distance for opposing traffic, and if there is a crest immediately ahead, this may not be available, resulting in a potentially hazardous situation. Similar considerations apply to a truck leaving premises, and making a turn over the centre line (US left turn, British right turn); indeed this may be even worse, as the truck driver in this case is having to look in both directions of traffic.

Finally, as with intersection design, it may be a conscious decision to leave sub-standard bridges in place, where they restrict undesirable truck movements (Chatterjee, et al, 1979).

Figure 6.11 Low overhead clearance bridge, Australia

Table 6.2
Minimum lateral and vertical clearances

Pavement crossfall	Minimum vertical clearance		Minimum lateral clearance	
percent	m	(ft)	m	(in)
0	4.4	14.4	0.30	12
3	4.5	14.8	0.45	18
6	4.6	15.1	0.60	24
10	4.7	15.4	0.75	30

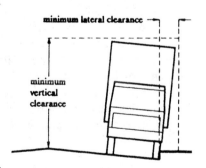

Source: TTM Consulting (1989)

163

Other treatments

There may be other traffic management techniques which, while not directed exclusively or even mainly at trucks, may nevertheless be given particular cogency by the presence of significant truck volumes. They may include:

- one way streets;
- reversible traffic lanes;
- intersection channelization;
- improved direction signs;
- variable message signs (e.g. crashes, queues, speed restriction);
- speed limits;
- advisory speed signs (e.g. freeway ramps);
- realignment of sub-standard curves, ramps, etc
- street lighting; and
- median barriers.

Grenzeback et al (1990) examined the effect of an 'aggressive' traffic management program on congestion on Californian freeways, including several of the above features. They concluded that it could produce a 15 percent reduction in vehicle hours of delay.

Parking or loading strategies

Strategies for loading, unloading and parking can be difficult to develop since they involve a host of individual planning and traffic management decisions (House, 1979, p 63). Examples include decisions about the provision of on-street loading areas; who may use them; time constraints applying to them; enforcement issues; requirements for the provision of off-street facilities; and the relationship of any or all of these to the various freight objectives outlined in Chapter 5, such as efficiency, environmental amenity, road safety, and industrial viability.

Strategies under this heading are of three types: curbside use, off-street facilities, and truck parking facilities.

Curbside use

Vehicles used in the delivery of goods and services require space near to the pick up or delivery point, often for only a short time. Where this is not provided off-street, a section of curb can be set aside for these activities. This is especially necessary in retail and commercial areas, where the curbside is also in demand for other uses, such as car parking, passenger pickup, bus stops, taxi stands, fire zones, etc (Christiansen, 1979, p IV-11). The absence of a loading zone in these areas may lead to double-parking of delivery vehicles, long access hauls, etc.

Arrangements include the provision of loading zones at selected locations, in which only commercial vehicles involved in pick up and delivery operations are permitted (Figure 6.12), or the provision of loading zones for certain times of the day only, either to encourage delivery operations at those times or because other demands (e.g. clearway operations or exclusive bus lanes) take precedence at other times (Figure 6.13).

In determining curbside loading arrangements, various factors need to be considered, including (Christiansen, 1979; Habib, 1981, 1983, 1985; TTM Consulting, 1987; Walters, 1982, 1989a):

- the variety of needs that have to be met, including short term pick up and delivery operations (e.g. parcel delivery), longer term requirements (e.g. truck load deliveries), and service vehicle needs (telephone, repair vans, etc);

- the need to protect buildings and vehicles from damage (see Table 6.2 above);

- the need for enforcement, in particular to designate the kinds of vehicles permitted to use the loading zone, and ensuring that other vehicles and non-delivery activities (especially car parking) are prevented; and

- there may be scope to consider alternative arrangements, such as the use of parking meters at loading zones, more explicit identification of vehicles which may legally use them, allowing trucks free use of metered car parking spaces, allocating space to loading for some times of the day and to parking for other times, etc. (Figure 6.14 shows a sign used in San Francisco, which allows delivery trucks to use car parking spaces at certain times of the day.)

Figure 6.12 Loading zone, Australia

Figure 6.13 'Clearway' sign (no standing in peak hours), Australia

Figure 6.14 Truck use of car parking space, San Francisco

It is important that explicit consideration is given to these issues in urban areas, and particularly in central cities and older areas where off-street facilities are less common. An explicit and well-developed curbside management plan, developed in consultation with local officials, shippers and receivers of goods, and the road freight industry should lead to more efficient use of a limited resource (curbside space), reduced on-street congestion from double-parking, improved aesthetics of retail and commercial areas, and development of off-street parking policies.

Specific guidelines for the provision of curbside loading zones have to be determined for each individual location. It always involves a tradeoff between this use and other uses (especially car parking and, in peak periods, moving traffic), and from the viewpoint of the trucking industry, it is rarely considered adequate. However, it is appropriate to note that limiting downtown car parking availability is often regarded as an important tool of urban transport demand management, on the grounds that supply of parking creates its own demand and reduces the demand for public transport. On the other hand, as Hicks (1977, p 114) has noted, lack of adequate loading facilities for trucks increases the costs of freight while having little effect on the numbers of trucks using the road system.

In operation on a day to day basis, much depends on a reasonable attitude of cooperation and assistance on the part of enforcement agencies. If this can be developed it will usually mean that pick up and delivery operations can proceed without too much difficulty, while ensuring that the curbside is used for its designated purpose.

As an example, Habib (1981, p 57) determined the need for curbside facilities in Manhattan depending upon the interference which *double-parked* trucks had on through traffic. He concluded that once traffic volumes exceeded about 900 veh/h and truck pick up and delivery operations exceeded about 50 per hour, double parking was unacceptable, and curbside loading zones were necessary. These arrangements probably reflect traffic conditions in New York, and what is tolerated there; other cities may have quite different expectations. For example, in the central business district of Melbourne, Australia, 60 percent of all curbside space is devoted to loading or commercial purposes at off-peak periods (Road Traffic Authority, 1988, p 17). In general however, any action taken to encourage delivery trucks to park at mid-block will tend to reduce vehicular delay caused by the double parking of such delivery trucks (Christiansen, 1979, p IV-15).

Another management issue on some downtown streets is the need to eliminate conflicts between the needs of bus operators and those of pick up and delivery operations. This may involve such factors as location of bus stops, location of loading zones, one way streets, and bus routing (Habib, 1981; JHK and Associates, 1983).

Finally, it may be expedient to impose time limits on truck parking, as a 'means of rationing scarce curb space' (Christiansen, 1979, p IV-16). This includes both the hours in the day during which truck parking is permitted (with perhaps car parking or clearway conditions applying at other times) and the time limit for any one stop. The latter is to prevent the mis-use of loading spaces (e.g. extended service calls, use for non-delivery purposes such as lunch breaks, etc). A typical time limit is 20-30 minutes, and, as mentioned above, may be policed either with parking officers or by the use of parking meters. An alternative form of control is one which limits the use of loading zones to commercially registered vehicles actually engaged in the pick up and delivery of goods (see Figure 6.12 above); this practice requires parking officers for enforcement.

Off-street facilities

Major new commercial, industrial and retail developments should have adequate off-street loading and unloading facilities for trucks servicing the development. In some cases, it is possible to coordinate the loading docks for several developments, with a common central facility (see Walters, 1982, 1989a for a description of a facility in Dallas, Texas, and Habib, 1982, 1983, 1985 for a description of this facility and others in Rochester and Brooklyn, New York State).

Since loading space is usually non-leasable, it is necessary for a public authority to prescribe its provision, usually through the planning approval process. The benefits of adequate off-street loading facilities include:

- reduced costs of deliveries, and higher truck productivity;
- increased service quality to building occupiers;
- improved security for vehicles and goods;
- curbside loading zones are freed for other uses;
- car parking spaces are not used by delivery vehicles;
- reduced on-street congestion (especially double-parking); and
- improved aesthetics of retail and commercial areas.

However, it must be noted that truck drivers show little willingness to use such facilities voluntarily unless they save time; this means both that the access and egress conditions and the layout of the off-street facility itself must be well-designed, and that enforcement of on-street parking and loading must be maintained. In New York City for example, Habib and Crowley (1978) have reported that only 70-90 percent of trucks servicing office buildings used an off-street facility when available; the compliance was higher at industrial sites (80-90 percent) and department stores (90 percent). This is especially the case with courier deliveries (TTM Consulting, 1987), and it is suggested that large developments should have limited space at the curb to allow these courier vehicles to stop for a short time (3-5 minutes).

It is also important to note that in some cases, the use of an off-street facility is a costly imposition, both because it is non-leasable (and therefore an extra cost burden on the developer), and also because the use of the building may change over time, meaning that the amount of space may be inappropriate (either too much or too little) (Habib, 1975, p 50).

Also, as noted previously, if off-street facilities are to achieve their objectives, it is necessary to ensure that they are not used for other purposes, such as car parking or trash dumpsters (Walters, 1989a; Anon, 1989a, p 5).

Requirements. The need for off-street loading facilities varies widely both between and within land uses, and planning for major new developments should be based upon experience or surveys of similar developments elsewhere. Moreover, as Habib and Crowley (1978) rightly point out, the amount of space devoted to loading facilities should bear some relationship to land price or rent, which is a measure of its value for alternative uses.

As examples[3], some recently developed guidelines for the number and size of loading spaces for various land uses will be cited.

- Table 6.3 shows typical requirements for various kinds of development for Australian conditions.[4] Courier and taxi requirements are additional to these and Table 6.4 shows typical Australian parking requirements for this class of delivery vehicle.

- Table 6.5 shows the requirements for Dallas in the US (Walters, 1989a, p 56; see also Walters, 1982 and Christiansen, 1978).

- In Chicago, Rawling (1989, p 110) has reported that office building require one space per 100,000 ft^2 (9,300 m^2) of occupancy, plus one additional space per additional 100,000 ft^2 of floor area.

While there is no particular reason why these disparate sets of requirements should line up, in general it is interesting to note that the Australian guidelines call for fewer spaces at smaller centres compared with the American guidelines, but more at larger centres. The recommended mix of vehicle types is fairly similar.

170

Design. The design of loading bays is an important but often neglected aspect of building and site design. Some aspects of good design include the following (Anon, 1978b; TTM Consulting, 1989; Walters, 1989a, p 59; Wood, 1979, p 231 ff; Stover, 1988, p 204 ff):

- rear loading and unloading is more efficient and convenient than side loading;

- where trucks are required to reverse into a loading dock, the design should be such that the driver uses a right hand lock on a right hand drive vehicle (or a left hand lock on a left hand drive vehicle), so that the driver is on the inside of the turning manoeuvre; this ensures that the driver's view is not obscured by the vehicle or its load;

- loading docks should be designed for the largest vehicle servicing a development; Table 6.6 shows suggested dimensions of loading bays for the three Australian truck categories defined above; US practice has been documented by Stover (1988, p 208) and is quite similar to this, as would be expected given that the size of trucks used in urban pick up and delivery operations does not vary greatly;

- the design should allow sufficient space for vehicles to easily manoeuvre into the loading docks; this may require the use of templates (Hummer, Zegeer and Hanscom, 1989). Figure 6.15 shows the manoeuvring areas necessary for truck movements to and from loading bays, again for the three Australian truck categories defined above;

- driveways and access roads should allow easy and convenient access to the dock area, and ideally should not be not used for car parking; suggested widths of access roads for one-way and two-way operation are shown in Table 6.7;

- horizontal curve geometry needs to take account of the turning requirements of various configurations of truck; refer to Figure 6.10 above;

Table 6.3
Typical loading bay requirements for development

Development type of	Floor area* m²	Minimum number bays
office	General	1/5000 m²
	Minimum	1 LR
	e.g. 5000 m²	1 HR
	e.g. 20000 m²	4 HR
shop	General	1/2000 m²
	Minimum	1 LR
	e.g. 2000 m²	1 HR
	e.g. 10000 m²	2HR + 3 LR
supermarket	General	1/1000 m²
	Minimum	1 HR
	e.g. 1000 m²	1 HR
	e.g. 2000 m²	1 A + 1 HR
	e.g. 4000 m²	2 A + 2 HR
department store	General	1/1000 m²
	Minimum	1 HR
	e.g. 2000 m²	2 HR or 1 HR + 1 A
	e.g. 4000 m²	1 A + 3 HR
showrooms	General	1/2000 m²
	Minimum	1 HR
	e.g. 5000 m²	3 HR
	e.g. 10000 m²	4 HR + 1 A

warehouse & Industry	General	$1/4000$ m^2
	Minimum	1 A
	e.g. 5000 m^2	1 A + 1 HR
	e.g. 10000 m^2	2 A + 1 HR
other	General	$1/2000$ m^2
	Minimum	1 HR

* To convert to square feet multiply these figures by 10.5.

LR = Light Rigid Truck Bay
HR = Heavy Rigid Truck Bay
A = Articulated Truck Bay

Source: TTM Consulting (1989)

Table 6.4
Typical parking requirements for couriers and taxis

Development	Spaces per 10000m^2 Spaces per 100,000 ft^2 (rounded)
offices	5.0
retail	10.0
industry	2.5
other	4.0

Source: TTM Consulting (1989)

Table 6.5
Number and size of loading spaces by land use, Dallas, Texas

Land use	Gross area per space (after first two)		Percent of space sizes		
	m²	ft²	artic truck	large rigid	small rigid
office	100,000	9,300	-	40	60
retail and personal services	60,000	5,600	-	40	60
retail (if over 60,000 ft² (5,600 m²)	60,000	5,600	25	25	60
commercial and industrial	100,000	9,300	-	40	60
hotel/motel	200,000	18,600	1 space	75	balance
food and beverage	50,000	4,600	-	40	60

Source: Walters (1989a)

- entry ways and loading docks should be laid out so as to permit through movement of trucks, and minimize the amount of manoeuvring needed; for larger installations, there should be separate entry and exit lanes;

- a sawtooth dock arrangement has some advantages over a straight dock face in terms of manoeuvrability;

- attention should be given to the entry and exit arrangements to the loading dock area, in terms of such aspects as sight distance along the street, gradients of ramps serving the loading area (5 percent maximum is suggested although much higher values - 12 percent - may be necessary in some instances), and grade changes where the ramp meets the street level (5 percent maximum);

- potential conflicts with pedestrian traffic should be avoided by site layout; where driveways or access ramps cross sidewalks, sight lines should be splayed so as allow adequate visibility of pedestrians;

- adequate ventilation must be provided;

- the facility should be protected from the weather; and

- attention needs to be given to the details of traffic management and control, e.g. signs, signals, pavement markings, warning devices at bends and on columns, etc.

Table 6.6
Loading bay dimensions

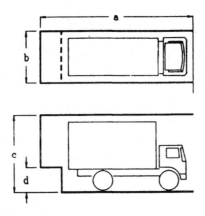

Truck type	Recommended minimum dimensions							
	a		b		c		d	
	m	ft	m	ft	m	ft	m	ft
light rigid	8.0	26.2	3.6	11.8	4.0	13.1	1.0	3.2
heavy rigid	11.0	36.1	3.6	11.8	5.0	16.4	1.3	4.3
articulated	17.0	55.8	3.6	11.8	5.0	16.4	1.3	4.3

Source: TTM Consulting (1989)

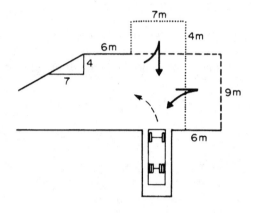

Light Rigid Truck

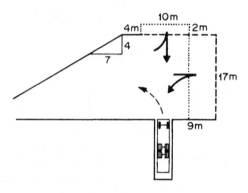

Heavy Rigid Truck

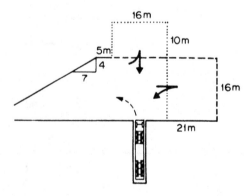

Articulated Truck

Source: TTM Consulting (1989)

Figure 6.15 Truck manoeuvring spaces

Table 6.7
Widths for driveways and access roads

Configuration	one way road		two way road	
	m	ft	m	ft
no parking	4.5	14.8	6.5	21.3
car parking, one side	6.9	22.6	8.9	29.2
car parking, both sides	7.5	24.6	9.5	31.2

Source: TTM Consulting (1989)

Walters (1989a, p 59) has documented some examples of design and operation which have been found to be 'questionable' in Dallas, Texas:

- a two-way, one-lane truck ramp with a 16.5 percent grade crossing a sidewalk with poor sight distance;

- a truck ramp on a sharp curve having a blind merge with a parking garage exit;

- a loading facility some 180 m (600 ft) from the building it serves, leading to long access hauls and extended occupancy times of trucks in the loading area (Walters suggests that each 30 m (100 ft) of haul length over 15 m (50 ft) to the freight elevator should be accompanied by a 5 percent increase in the number of loading spaces provided); and

- a combined parking-loading ramp with an awkward merge on a steep grade.

Pedestrian malls

For good commercial and aesthetic reasons, many urban centres have removed vehicular traffic from retail streets to create pedestrian malls. This can create a need for alternative access to premises (e.g. shops) in the mall area, especially if those premises are not served by rear alleys or laneways (Cooper, 1990).

A typical arrangement is to allow truck access to the mall itself until, say, 10 am, since there are relatively few pedestrians in the mall until that time.

177

After 10 am, goods must by wheeled in by handcart. (One problem is that since there are few shoppers before 10 am, some shops do not open for business until that time, thus forcing truck operators to deliver in hours where trucks cannot enter the mall.)

In Perth, Australia, part of the downtown mall redevelopment included the construction of an underground truck delivery area, with the intention that deliveries to premises in the mall could be made from that facility. In practice, trucking firms prefer to make their deliveries direct to the stores before 10 am, to avoid the delay associated with entering the delivery dock and the longer access haul from there to the consignee's receival point (Ogden, 1990).

Habib (1981, p 67) has suggested that the desirable maximum haul length from the parked truck to the pick up or delivery point in a mall should be about 75 m (250 ft).

Truck parking

Trucks, especially those used within urban areas, spend a considerable proportion of their day at rest. Trucks used for long distance or ex-urban operations may sometimes have to wait for hours or even days to pick up a new load. Truck parking is thus an important issue in urban freight; Hall and Worden (1982, p 5) have noted that 'well-sited and designed facilities for (trucks) and their drivers can have considerable effects on the achievement of policies which aim to maximize efficiency and reduce both the costs incurred in transporting goods and consequential environmental costs.' These difficulties include the following (Hall and Worden, op cit; Cooper, 1990, p 53):

- trucks parking in residential streets causing a loss of amenity to residents living nearby;
- the potential safety hazards caused by truck parking on streets;
- security of vehicles and loads; and
- facilities for drivers, in terms of rest, food, etc.

On-street truck parking is becoming less acceptable, and in many cities there are regulations prohibiting the overnight parking of trucks in residential areas; Figure 6.16 shows the regulatory sign used in one city in California. Even in commercial and industrial areas (e.g. near freight terminals) it is considered that trucks which are parked for an extended period of time interfere with other traffic and do not represent the best use of that roadspace. Thus, there is a definite tendency towards the provision of explicit facilities or areas for truck parking.

Truck parking may be:

- a public truck park, providing either parking only, or parking in conjunction with other facilities such as fuel, food, repair, sleeping accommodation, and maybe even some transhipment facilities; there have been a number of these built in Britain (Hall and Worden, 1982); Figure 6.17 shows a multiple use facility in Britain - car parking by day, truck parking at night, and free shopping car park at weekends;

- a private truck park, or 'truck stop', providing a full range of facilities to road users, including truck parking; generally truck stop operators are unwilling to provide free parking space to operators who do not wish to use other facilities such as fuel, accommodation or truck servicing;

Figure 6.16 Truck parking restriction in residential area, USA

Figure 6.17 Multiple use car and truck park, Britain

Figure 6.18 Private truck parking yard, Australia

- a private truck park, essentially providing nothing more than overnight parking in a fenced enclosure, as a commercial operation; these are likely to become more common as truck parking in residential areas is increasingly restricted (Figure 6.18 shows a facility of this sort in Perth, Australia), or

- a truck operator's depot or yard where the firm's own trucks (and possibly sub-contractors trucks also) are kept when not in use.

Figure 6.19 shows typical dimensions of truck parking bays for light rigid trucks, heavy rigid trucks, and articulated trucks (tractor semi-trailers).

Clearways. As noted previously, clearways (i.e. streets where curbside parking or stopping is prohibited during peak periods; see Figure 6.13) are a double-edged sword so far as trucks are concerned; they facilitate the movement of all vehicles (especially trucks, which commonly use the curb lane, and have more difficulty in manoeuvring around a vehicle parked in that lane), but provide difficulties to those truck operators which need to service premises along the clearway.

This raises three points:

- the need to explicitly consider the benefits to moving trucks in developing clearway warrants;

- the need for enforcement of clearway provisions; and

- the need to consider provision of commercial vehicle access to premises along the road during clearway hours; this may include alternative access provisions (e.g. rear access), or off-street facilities.

Access to industrial estates or to specific sites requiring truck deliveries can be difficult. These problems are especially acute in older inner-city areas with narrow streets, but can also be a problem elsewhere, especially where transport requirements vary; for example, Staley (1989b) has highlighted problems with the delivery of goods in containers to sites not built to accommodate them.

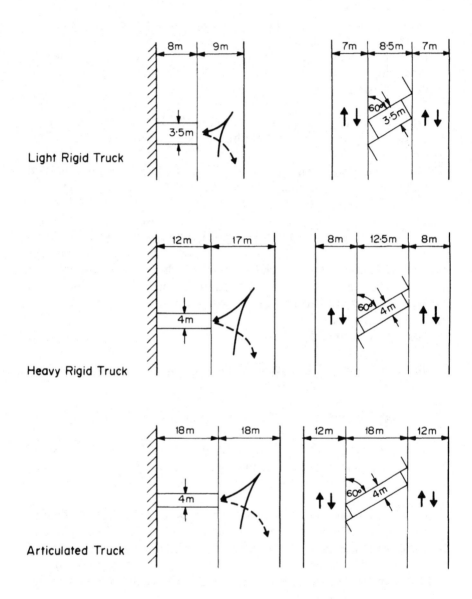

Source: TTM Consulting (1989)

Figure 6.19 Typical truck parking area dimensions

Access and egress to sites

The appropriate location of access to industrial and commercial developments by trucks depends upon the layout of the particular site, and the types of road which abut it. In general however, it is desirable that such access roads should be at least 100 m (330 ft) away from signalized intersections in order to provide adequate lengths for deceleration lanes and tapers (if they are required) and to minimize any interference of turning vehicles with the signal operation (TTM Consulting, 1989). The location of access roads may also be affected by the need to minimize traffic impacts in nearby roads and streets, especially residential streets.

For large developments, it may be desirable to separate car and truck access to the development for operational, aesthetic, or security reasons. In particular, where trucks are subject to security checks, weighing, or need to have documents checked on entry to the site, it is desirable to have separate car and truck access points. Pedestrian access ideally should be separated from both car and truck access. Truck access roads or lanes should be of adequate width; see Table 6.7 above.

Attention to sight lines and access conditions at the property boundary is also needed; see the discussion above on design of off-street facilities.

Removal of physical impediments

This final traffic management measure involves removing physical impediments to the smooth flow and economic operation of trucks. Examples might include:

- poles or signs which are close to the edge of the road provide a hazard to high vehicles (refer Table 6.2 above);

- low overhead clearances, especially on overbridges, should be signed as such (see Figure 6.11 above), and where truck volumes are significant, they should be protected with a hanging beam or similar device installed upstream of the bridge; there is also scope for the development and installation of dynamic height warning devices which sound a warning on the approach of a vehicle exceeding a height corresponding to the bridge clearance;

183

- rehabilitating deformed road surfaces will benefit all road vehicles, but provide particular benefits where trucks are concerned, through reduced vehicle operating costs, reduced damage to goods, and reduced noise and vibration;

- reconstruction of intersections, especially through the provision of curb returns with larger radius, will facilitate truck movement and reduce truck interference with other traffic (refer Figure 6.10 above);

- greater consideration could be given to the needs of trucks in providing access to industrial and commercial estates, especially in such areas as the location of median openings, the geometric design of turn lanes, etc;

- adequate direction signs benefit all road users, and are especially helpful to out-of-town truck drivers who may find great difficulty in redirecting themselves if they take a wrong turn; there should also be adequate advance warning of the need to take alternative routes, e.g. in the case of bridges with low clearances; and

- provision of ramps or 'curb cuts', handcart lanes, etc facilitate access by handcart or fork lift from a truck parked at the curb.

Truck traffic generation rates

In major new developments, or consideration of traffic management at existing sites, it is necessary to make an estimate of the traffic generation likely to be associated with the development in the future. Truck traffic generation may not be a significant contributor to the overall level of traffic generated by a site, but it may be necessary to make a separate estimate of its likely incidence in order to plan and design truck access and goods delivery facilities.

Even less quantitative information is available about truck traffic generation than about car traffic generation, and what is known suggests that there is wide variation from site to site and land use to land use. Consequently, each case should be assessed on the basis of what is known about that site, and the particular types of land use activity (commercial, industrial, retail, etc) which are present.

Quantitative examples of truck trip generation rates for various land uses are reviewed in Chapter 13.

Similarly, traffic generation variations throughout the day can be quite different from site to site. In general however, truck traffic generation tends to be somewhat less peaked that car traffic generation, being more uniform over the working day (say from 8 am to 4 pm). Hourly flows over this period are typically 10 - 12 percent of the daily total (see Figure 2.1).

Traffic engineers' attitudes

The various traffic engineering measures described in this chapter have the potential, when applied in appropriate ways, to assist truck movements and freight deliveries in specific circumstances. However, of perhaps greater significance in the long run is the necessity for a change of attitude on the part of traffic engineers towards these freight activities. The need for this change of perspective is evidenced in a number of ways (Ogden, 1991; Anon, 1989a; Hedges, 1978, 1985; Goettee and Cadotte, 1977; Cadotte, et al, 1977):

- most of the day to day work of traffic engineers is affected primarily by their own driving experience and their level of tolerance regarding traffic congestion and delay, and traffic elements are therefore planned on the basis of their own perceptions which may be quite different from those of a truck driver or freight firm;

- similarly, traffic problems are perceived primarily from the viewpoint of motor cars (and perhaps pedestrians and cyclists) because traffic engineers empathize with these problems; simply to consider the road traffic system from the viewpoint of the driver of a high, wide, and slowly accelerating vehicle, with constraints on rearward visibility, could go a long way towards appreciating the difficulties which drivers of trucks face in negotiating the road system;

- there is evidence that traditional economic evaluations of road proposals underestimate the costs incurred by the road freight industry in avoiding periods of peak congestion, and the benefits which accrue to the economy through more efficient urban freight delivery;

- consideration of trucks and freight movements tend to be limited to specific projects where there are particular concerns, such as a truck route or access ban, rather than on a systematic overall analysis with clear objectives; when the issue ceases to be 'fashionable', the work stops, perhaps leaving the truck operator in a difficult or costly position;

- an attitude amongst some traffic engineers that their role is to regulate and restrict a rapacious private sector, rather than to assist it to provide goods and services to the community; this leads (or results from) polarization of attitudes rather than cooperation between the public and private sectors in finding mutually satisfactory solutions;

- truck operators and freight generating firms (manufacturers, retailers) perceive that municipal government does not appreciate the needs of the freight sector or the contribution of trucks to the viability of local industry, but take much more notice of residents' concerns in local traffic management schemes; and

- to a large extent, traffic engineers consideration of truck movements focuses on the negative - restricting truck operations rather than facilitating truck movement and access.

Thus, the conclusion is not just that the traffic engineer be aware of and use the various measures (outlined above) which can be of assistance when addressing traffic issues associated with trucks. In addition to this, the traffic engineer should make an attempt to understand the needs of the road freight industry and its customers. It is important to recognise that the road freight industry has legitimate and important needs, and that the perspective of the road freight system from this viewpoint (or the viewpoint of a truck driver) is different from that of a driver of a motor car.

Solutions to problems always involve a tradeoff between the needs of competing interests, and traffic planning and design for trucks should consider not only ways of reducing adverse effects of trucks but also ways of enhancing the movement of goods in the interests of efficiency and economic development. In the words of Noortman (1984, p 57), 'much more success is to be expected from a positive approach towards urban goods movement (and) to this end the integration of goods vehicle characteristics in traffic engineering and traffic management can be an important first step.'

Implementation of freight planning and policy is discussed in Chapter 14, including some suggestions as to the means of developing and assessing traffic management proposals.

Notes

1. STAA: Surface Transportation Assistance Act. See Chapter 11.

2. Figure 6.10 is for vehicles driving on the left side of the road. Typical dimensions for these vehicles in Australia would be:

   Light rigid: 2 axle; length 6.6 m (21.6 ft); width 2.1 m (6.9 ft); wheelbase 3.7 m (12.1 ft); swept circle radius 15.4 m (50 ft).

   Heavy rigid: 3 axle; length 11.0 m (36 ft); width 2.5 m (8.2 ft); wheelbase (to mid-point of rear axles) 5.5 m (18 ft); swept circle radius 23.2 m (76 ft).

   Articulated truck: 3 axle tractor; 3-axle trailer; overall length 17.0 m (55.8 ft); width 2.5 m (8.2 ft); tractor wheelbase 3.7 m (12.1 ft); kingpin to mid-point of trailer axles 8.6 m (28.2 ft); swept circle radius 22.0 m (72.2 ft).

3. It is important to note that the urban goods movement system in any urban area is unique, and reflects the particular land uses, economic bases, population characteristics, street networks, planning ordinances, traffic regulations etc applicable to that area. The result is that the experience in any one area may not transfer comfortably to another. Therefore, the quantitative results presented in this part of the chapter should be taken as indicative only for their application to other cities at other times. Nevertheless, they are useful in that they indicate what has been found to work in certain areas, and they may be of interest to those responsible for urban freight planning and policy in other areas. In Chapter 14, we discuss implementation of freight planning and policy, and mention there ways in which experience from one urban area may potentially be related to another.

4. See footnote 2 above for typical vehicle sizes.

7 Location and zoning of land use

Freight activities in an urban area and the truck movements associated with them are generated by the land use patterns within that area. These include industrial, commercial and residential land uses as well as transport terminals. Consequently, by influencing the location of land uses through the land use planning process, the amount, type, location and intensity of freight and trucking activities can be affected. Conversely, as noted in Chapter 5, the magnitude of urban freight costs are such that freight is an important considerations in metropolitan planning. These two aspects are discussed in this chapter.[1]

Freight considerations in metropolitan planning

Transport planning in general, and planning for goods movement in particular, should not take place in isolation from planning for future metropolitan structure and form. Transport policy is, or should be, subservient to metropolitan policy.

Therefore, freight planning and policy should normally take cognisance of any broader considerations related to overall metropolitan development. Obviously, it is impossible to generalize about this, because such broad considerations will vary considerably from area to area. However, examples might include:

- amount, type and location of future employment growth;

- the future size and role of the central city;

- the future of specific economic bases, such as manufacturing;

- the future role and location of key activities such as a port;

- future urban development strategy, including proposals for urban renewal; and

- key environmental issues such as air quality.

This is not the place for a discussion of these issues. However, two general points can be made (both of which were discussed in Chapter 5, so we will keep the discussion here brief).

First, because freight costs (defined broadly to include not only economic and financial costs, but also environmental, social and other costs as detailed in Chapter 5) are so large, metropolitan growth strategies should recognise the importance of freight to wider metropolitan goals. Indeed, one of the criteria by which alternative urban development strategies might be assessed is urban goods movement, i.e. the reduction (even minimization) of total freight costs as just described.

Second, to the extent that freight transport facilities affect urban development patterns, it might be possible to use the location and operation of those facilities as a tool to help shape urban form.

Land use strategies to reduce freight costs

A succinct statement of the issues in relation to urban freight and land use patterns has been presented by Chatterjee (1982, p 226), as follows:

It is well known in urban transportation that traffic is generated by land use and that the locations of activity centres influence travel patterns. Therefore, the amount of travel can be minimized and undesirable travel movements avoided by proper manipulation of the locations of activity centres.

Unfortunately, the land use planning process in most (US) cities pays little attention to these opportunities with respect to urban goods movement and the dispersed locations of industries cause trucks to travel all over the area, creating pollution and wasting energy and time. Similarly, it is found in many cases that improper locations of truck terminals cause not only difficulties for truck travel, but also result in adverse impacts on residential areas and other incompatible land uses.

There are several strategies for reducing urban freight costs through land use planning. These are discussed below.

Zoning

Zoning is the practice, widely if not universally adopted in modern industrial countries, of prescribing the uses to which individual pieces of land may be put. While zoning practices and procedures vary considerably, the effect of such land use planning is to control (or at least influence) region-wide allocation of land for designated purposes, and to prescribe the activities allowed to be undertaken thereon.

Clearly, zoning has a very significant effect upon freight generation and flow. As noted in Chapter 5, in past decades the emphasis has been to separate the various land uses - heavy industry, light industry, freight terminals, warehousing, retailing, etc. However, this has had the effect of building into cities the need for massive and sustained flows of goods. It is clear therefore that the converse opportunity exists, i.e. by locating complementary land uses in close proximity to each other, freight costs (both economic and environmental) can be reduced.

In other words, the opportunity exists in long range land use planning to build in to the future urban area a greater level of efficiency; needless to say this must be considered alongside other goals of long range planning. Specific strategies for doing this might include the following:

- Land use policies could aim to encourage groupings of industry on the basis of complementary trade, e.g. to encourage back hauls. This may first require surveys to establish what such land uses and commodities might be, since such information may not be currently available, but an example might be to locate a container repair and storage facility near to a container depot area; this would not only reduce the distance which an empty container has to move as it goes to or from the depot, but would also enable a truck carrying a full container from the port to the depot to carry an empty container back to the port if that container is to be taken out empty, as quite often occurs if inbound and outbound container flows do not balance (Ogden, 1985). A similar effect may be felt in an industrial park, provided that it is occupied by firms which have the potential to trade with each other (Chatterjee, 1982, p 230) - e.g. a steel merchant and an engineering firm.

191

- As noted above, land use policies have tended to separate the location of various activities, such as heavy industry, light industry, processing, warehouses, etc. There may be potential to reduce freight demands by allowing, even encouraging, integration of complementary activities. In part at least, modern industrial processes, and the increased importance of service industries are tending to achieve this integration. Traditional classifications of industry and land use are breaking down so that there is no longer a clear distinction between (say) retailing, wholesaling, storage, maintenance, administration and even manufacturing, as all may be carried out within a single premises. This is particularly the case with such activities labelled as (say) computers, research, communication, services, etc. This makes close control of land use activities not only more difficult but less relevant, and is therefore likely to lead to, if anything, a diminution of land use controls in these sectors of the economy, as well as a reduction in freight demand from what it would have been if such controls had aimed to keep these activities separate.

- Because freight terminals (and especially trucking terminals) exist to consolidate freight from several shippers, there is merit in allowing those terminals to locate near to their customers. This would include, for example, allowing trucking terminals to locate in an industrial zone, or creating a so-called 'transportation park', which would encourage the clustering of freight terminals, warehouses, and distribution centres (Chatterjee, Staley and Whaley, 1986). As an example of this, Hall (1991) has analysed the location of freight terminals in Los Angeles, and has developed proposals for terminal location which, if implemented, would provide a better service with less truck-induced traffic congestion.

Access and infrastructure

It is axiomatic that if land uses are heavy generators of freight traffic, the costs of moving freight will be reduced if those generators are located with good access to transport infrastructure, ceteris paribus. From the viewpoint of urban planning, which is concerned with determining the location of land use activities, the following considerations apply:

- Decisions about the zoning of land for industrial, commercial and transport purposes should give due consideration to transport infrastructure, to ensure sensible use of existing resources. In particular, those land uses with high freight requirements should be located near good arterial roads or freeways, with easy access to them (Anon, 1978a, p 75).

- It is generally considered to be good practice to encourage terminals for inter-urban trucking on the fringe of an urban area, so that large line haul trucks do not have to penetrate the urban area. This reflects industry practice, particularly in the US, where it is common for such terminals to be located near the intersection of an inter-urban freeway and a circumferential 'beltway'.

- Consideration should be given, where relevant, to servicing industrial sites with rail facilities. This factor is commonly cited in Britain (Hall, 1982, p 30), but is applicable to most urban areas with rail freight services. However, the land use planner in this case must keep abreast of the changing needs of industry and the relative technical and marketing features of rail and other modes of transport. For example, in Perth, Australia, a number of firms located on sites well served by rail, with direct rail access on private sidings, do not use them because with deregulation of transport in the State of Western Australia, rail services are no longer provided to many centres, so that these firms now use road transport services (Ogden, 1990, p 79).

Relocation and urban renewal

Cities change over time. Industries which were historically located in or near the central city may find those sites unsuitable because they are too small, have no room for expansion, or are no longer near their markets. Encouraging or allowing such industries to relocate may assist with urban freight problems also, since to the extent that activities move out, so the freight movements associated with those activities will move. Noortman (1984, p 56) has commented that if other measures are unsuccessful or inadequate in resolving the problems of urban freight, 'a relocation of those activities which generate undesired freight transport seems to be the ultimate answer.'

Of course, one such activity may be transport terminals themselves; they require extensive areas of land, are typically found in low-rent areas which are often prime targets for redevelopment, and may find it expedient to relocate to follow their customers to suburban locations (Anon, 1982a, p 47). Not all such activities can or should move; in particular, terminals associated with ports, which for historical reasons are often found near the centre of cities, need to remain there. However, even in this case, there is some scope for relocation, as in many cities ports have tended to move from their historical locations along a river towards deeper water and larger land areas downstream.

The other side of the relocation coin is urban redevelopment, or urban renewal, in which new uses have to be found for the sites formerly occupied by inner city firms and activities. Spielberg (1982, p 218) has noted that truck access can be important in this, as the need for freight deliveries should be taken into account in the planning and design stages, especially if the redevelopment involves the creation of pedestrian malls (see Chapter 6). Plant Location International (1983, p 6.1) in a study in Sydney, Australia, noted the trend, for the reasons outlined above, for manufacturers and their associated freight services to relocate to suburban areas. As a corollary, there will be trend towards greater non-manufacturing land uses in inner suburban areas, and they suggested that warehousing and distribution can be a suitable activity for inner urban, formerly manufacturing, sites. This location not only facilitates the servicing of central city and inner urban areas, but also means that trucks are tending to travel in a counter-peak direction, outbound in the morning and inbound in the afternoon.

Notes

1. The discussion in this chapter does not include the location of freight terminals; this is discussed in Chapter 11. The broader issue of the inclusion of freight in the urban transport planning process is taken up in Chapter 14.

8 Infrastructure

A key aspect of any public policy on urban freight is the power of government to provide and maintain capital infrastructure. The three prime areas are investment in urban roads, urban freight terminals, and incident management, especially on urban freeways.

Road investment

Road networks

Governments have a virtual monopoly on the provision of roadspace, and for that reason if for no other there is a public policy role in urban freight since, as noted in Chapter 2, virtually all intra-urban freight movements take place on the road network. Road network improvements include:

- rationalizing the spacing and pattern of urban arterial roads and freeways;

- improving access roads which serve freight generating areas;

- constructing new or upgraded roads in congested corridors;

- redesigning intersections to ease the passage of trucks, especially turning movements by longer or wider trucks;

- increasing capacity, increasing travel speeds, or reducing variability in travel times by intersection works, installation of linked signal systems, or other road improvements (see Chapter 6 for a discussion of traffic management measures); and

- ensuring that road maintenance practices keep the road network in a serviceable and safe condition.

While these activities reflect common practice in urban road authorities worldwide, they may be of special cogency in the case of urban truck operations. Specific freight-related benefits which may result from urban road investments include:

- potential for travel time savings, leading to higher productivity from the urban truck fleet;

- potential for regional economic growth, as a result of more efficient links between industrial areas, and between manufacturers and ports, rail and truck terminals, or airports;

- potential for reduction in environmental impacts, especially noise, if trucks can be diverted onto arterial roads (it was noted in Chapter 6 that an important concomitant of local area traffic management, to the extent that it aims to reduce or eliminate extraneous traffic from residential areas, is the upgrading or nearby arterial road links to make travel on the arterial network a viable alternative to travel on the local network);

- similarly, potential for reduction in environmental impact from the construction of bypass routes (Cooper, 1990, p 23);

- potential for safety benefits from the explicit consideration of truck performance characteristics (e.g. braking) in road and traffic design (Hutchinson and Parker, 1989);

- reduction of the costs of congestion, including vehicle operating costs, costs of driver stress, etc (see Chapter 5); and

- improvements in delivery schedule reliability, which is growing in importance with the tendency for manufacturers, retailers, etc to hold minimum stocks on site.

Examples of specific instances where urban road investment has been determined or substantially influenced by freight considerations include:

- Melbourne, Australia: The urban road development program for the 1990s is largely directed towards roads which will benefit the regional economy; this primarily involves circumferential roads linking key industrial areas, and other roads connecting these areas to the port and airport (Road Construction Authority, 1987).

- London, England: During the 1970s and 1980s, much effort was devoted to the construction or upgrading of a limited network of key roads which linked the main industrial, warehousing and trade areas with each other and with the national network. This was aimed both at reducing travel times and increasing their reliability, and at providing environmental benefits (Hasell, Foulkes and Robertson, 1978b).

- Other British Towns: During the 1970s, a key priority in the development of the national road network was the construction of bypass routes to divert traffic, but especially heavy vehicles, from built-up areas. Clearly, the effectiveness of this policy depended upon the size of the town, since as urban size increases, the proportion of local traffic (whether intra-urban or traffic which needs to service the town) also increases. However, the program was successful in improving environmental conditions in smaller and medium sized urban centres; in 1976-77 alone, some 17 towns were provided with by-pass routes (Button and Pearman, 1981, p 158 ff).

- Los Angeles: A major upgrading of infrastructure to serve the port area is to take place during the 1990s. This includes the development of a road and rail 'consolidated transportation corridor' some 28 km (17 miles) in length between the port area and the central city (and especially the rail terminals located nearby), an extensive program of road-rail grade separations nearer to the port, and the extension of on-dock and near-dock rail facilities in the port area itself. This proposal aims to 'facilitate port access while mitigating potentially adverse impacts of port growth, including highway traffic congestion, air pollution, vehicle delays at grade crossings, and impacts of train noise in residential areas' (Joint Powers Authority, 1990, p 2).

Details of some of these are presented in the case studies in Chapter 15. They are mentioned briefly here to emphasize that the explicit consideration of freight needs in urban road (and rail) investment is taken very seriously in some urban areas.

Investment appraisal

From the viewpoint of planning and policy in relation to urban freight, the key question is whether existing project appraisal techniques suitably reflect the benefits and costs of freight-related impacts of candidate projects.

That question is a difficult one to answer because it has not been subjected to study. There is some evidence to suggest, however, that the answer is probably 'no'. For example:

- In economic cost-benefit analyses, the only benefits commonly included are user benefits, i.e. travel time and operating cost savings for all vehicles (including trucks) are taken into account, but other economic impacts are not usually considered (Meyer and Miller, 1984, Chapter 9; Wohl and Hendrickson, 1984, Chapter 5).

- A study in Sydney, Australia by Plant Location International (1983, p 4.8) concluded that traditional economic evaluation of road proposals 'overlook the significant costs that are incurred by the freight transport industry in trying to avoid the use of roads during periods of peak congestion'.

- Several studies, including one in Melbourne, Australia (Road Construction Authority, 1987) and others in England (Hasell, Foulkes and Robertson, 1978b; Quarmby, 1989) have drawn attention to the benefits to the national and state economies resulting from more efficient urban freight operations made possible by road investment. The Melbourne study concluded that 'benefits to the national economy from major urban road improvements should involve increasing the benefits conventionally calculated to the freight sector (for time and cost savings) by about 50 percent' (op cit, p 6).

- Bowyer and Ogden (1988) argue that freight needs are not sufficiently taken into account in road investment decisions. They suggest that savings to operators from urban road investment are mainly revealed in savings in labor cost, and this should be valued at the overtime rate.

These are perhaps little more than 'straws in the wind' but together they would seem to suggest that perhaps freight impacts are not sufficiently taken into account in road investment economic appraisal in general.

To this must be added doubt about the extent to which the non-economic impacts of freight can be accommodated, at least in analytical sense. In Chapter 13 we discuss freight models, and show that these are, at best, very crude and simplistic, and in fact have had very little influence in transport planning decisions. Moreover, models which aim to estimate various environmental impacts, such as noise, emissions or energy consumption are either non-existent, or based upon scant data. As a result, it can only be concluded that the ability (let alone the will) to incorporate explicit consideration of non-economic freight impacts into transport appraisal is limited to the point of being almost non-existent. This is exemplified in the recent proposals to restrict truck usage of streets in the City of Los Angeles at peak periods in the pursuit of ostensible air quality objectives; the ability to predict the consequences of such a policy is extremely limited because of uncertainties about how truck trip patterns and truck usage factors (e.g. truck size) will change, how these may affect traffic conditions, or how land use locational factors may be affected (see Chapter 15).

In conclusion, the state of the art in urban road investment appraisal, whether in terms of economic impacts or environmental impacts, is extremely crude. It is doubtful whether current road planning and appraisal procedures take sufficient account of the wider economic benefits to regional and national economies which flow from improved freight efficiency, whether they adequately value the benefits and costs which are typically included (usually only user benefits and the costs of providing and maintaining public infrastructure), or whether the environmental and other objectives of urban freight outlined in Chapter 5 are capable of being incorporated in a formal project appraisal process.

Terminals

Terminals and modal interchanges are covered in detail in Chapter 11. However, there are some considerations related to public sector infrastructure which are worth a brief mention at this point.

Some freight terminals are provided by government (seaports, airports, rail terminals in many countries), while the location of other terminals, especially road freight terminals, is influenced by government through the planning process.

The size and location of freight terminals has a significant influence on the magnitude and orientation of urban truck movements but it is almost certainly true to say that this factor has little influence in road investment decisions (except perhaps at the micro level - e.g. it may be a requirement that freight terminals are located on arterial roads).

Nevertheless, there is possibly scope for government to influence urban freight through greater control on the size and location of freight terminals and through investment in terminals. However, this should be done with caution, as terminal costs can be a significant part of total freight costs, and if greater government control led to higher terminal costs (or to trucks by-passing terminals altogether), the net effect could be to increase urban freight costs, not to decrease them.

Incident management

An increasingly important aspect of the management of the urban road infrastructure is the establishment of procedures to deal with incidents which cause delay. For example, as noted in Chapter 5, non-recurrent incidents (accidents and incidents) account for about half the delay which occurs on Los Angeles' freeway system, the other half being from traffic congestion (Cambridge Systematics, 1988b, p ii). Trucks are involved in a high proportion of such incidents.

An incident management program involves four elements (Cambridge Systematics, 1988a, Technical Memorandum 2.3; Grenzeback, et al, 1990), as follows.

Improved surveillance and communication. Incident management is most effective when problems are diagnosed and stabilized in their early stages. In truck-involved incidents on freeways in particular, information about the type of truck, its position, traffic on the freeway, and conditions on parallel arterial roads is critical.

The incident management program could use such surveillance techniques as closed circuit television cameras, aircraft or helicopter observers, and in-pavement or overhead traffic flow monitoring devices

200

to alert traffic control personnel to the occurrence and location of an incident, and provide information to incident management teams before they are despatched so that decisions on equipment, personnel, and system-level traffic management can be made early.

Equipment and procedures. Pre-positioning of heavy tow trucks, helicopter delivery of emergency equipment and personnel, video recording of crash scenes to speed up documentation and administrative, legal and insurance reports, etc are techniques which can be used to facilitate work at crash sites and minimize the amount of time that lanes or links are closed.

Systems operations management. The incident management program could make extensive use of real-time traffic monitoring devices to record system-wide traffic flow patterns, test the efficacy of incident management plans, and evaluate the effectiveness of their implementation.

Organisation and coordination. Major incidents often involve a range of personnel, including those responsible for police, fire, ambulance, hazardous materials, road maintenance, traffic management, and vehicle removal functions. The incident management strategy should be a vehicle for strengthening and streamlining the institutional capabilities to coordinate and manage these functions effectively.

A major study of incident management in America (Trucking Research Institute, 1990, p 20) found that incident management programs can be highly cost-effective. For example, a Chicago program was estimated to return $17 for every $1 of investment. Key organisational elements of a successful program were:

- the formation of traffic management teams to organise multiple jurisdictions and multiple agencies;

- traffic operations centres to coordinate incident management activities at a metropolitan level;

- dedicated service patrols to speed detection of and response to incidents, especially small incidents;

- incident command systems, contingency planning, and quick clearance policies to minimize inter-agency conflicts over roles and responsibilities;

- partnership with commercial radio and television to send information to motorists; and

- a strong service orientation to build a constituency and maintain a commitment to the incident management program.

It has been estimated that a comprehensive incident management strategy for the Los Angeles area could reduce the duration of major incidents by 50 percent (from an average of 4 h to 2 h), and of less major incidents by 20 percent (from 60 min to 50 min) (Grenzeback, et al, 1990). While the results may be less dramatic in other urban areas, the message is clear that as congestion increases, the need for comprehensive incident management procedures increases. While not overtly or specifically aimed at trucks, the fact that trucks are involved in a high proportion of such incidents means that this strategy is particularly relevant to urban freight.

9 Licensing and regulations

Types of regulation

Regulations and licences are the instruments by which policies developed in other areas are implemented. Thus, for example, regulations applying to traffic flow, parking, off-street loading bays, etc are the means by which the particular traffic management strategies outlined in Chapter 6 are introduced.

In general, regulations on the freight industry may be of two quite different types, often referred to as *quantity* (or *economic*) regulation and *quality* (or *operational*) regulation. The former involves direct intervention in the road freight industry by control of such aspects as entry and exit to the industry, total numbers, routes, schedules, rates, etc. The latter involves controls on such aspects as vehicle standards, safety measures, emissions, management, etc, which have as their objective the maintenance or improvement of the quality of service provided by the industry. In essence, quantity regulation covers what the industry does, and quality regulation covers the way in which it does it.

There has been a clear trend worldwide, in the transport sector as elsewhere, towards a reduction in quantity licensing ('deregulation'), and often a concomitant increase in quality licensing. This is predicated on the one hand by a realization that industry is better able to respond to market forces if it is less controlled by essentially arbitrary government regulation, while on the other hand, the community is becoming more demanding of industry in such areas as minimising its effects on the environment and society as a whole.

However, of all components of the freight sector, the urban freight area has been least subject to quantity regulations, in western industrialized countries at least. There are usually no controls on entry or exit to the industry, no rate controls, no route licensing, etc, for movements entirely within urban areas. This has been so firstly because there has not been the necessity (e.g. there are no railway interests to protect, and competition has generally seen that prices have not been unreasonable), and secondly because of the administrative complexity which would accompany any attempt to apply economic regulation to urban trucking (Magee, Copacino and Rosenfeld, 1985, p 130).

Quantity regulations certainly affect ex-urban goods movements - i.e. trips to and from an urban area. Discussion of these regulatory controls is beyond the scope of this book. However, it might be noted that deregulation of long distance and inter-urban freight movements could lead on the one hand to a greater number of trucks on urban roads in total, (to the extent that such deregulation leads to less traffic on rail), while on the other hand, the number of trucks near rail terminals (typically close to the city centre) may decrease.

The quality regulations which affect urban freight are of three main types, traffic regulations, vehicle regulations, and building regulations.

Traffic regulations

These give effect to many of the strategies discussed in Chapter 6 on traffic management. In general, traffic regulations provide direct benefits to urban freight activities through control of congestion and the operating environment of trucks, in order to affect delivery times, fuel consumption, loading and unloading arrangements, etc. They also assist in reducing some of the adverse environmental effects of freight delivery, such as noise, emissions, and intrusion (Crowley, et al, 1980, p 15).

In essence, traffic regulations attempt to ration the use of road space by either time or space controls. These may take several forms, as outlined below.

Allocation of curb space

In many urban areas, particularly in older central cities, pick up and delivery operations take place with the truck parked at the curb. Often, the streets in which these operations take place are heavily trafficked, and there are competing demands for the use of the curb space from car parking, customer pickup, bus and taxi stops, pedestrians, and moving traffic (Habib, 1985). It is the objective of curb space allocation regulations to allocate the use of the curb amongst these various demands, by location and by time of day. While freight pickup and delivery is commonly regarded as a legitimate use of curb space, it is nevertheless valid to note that curbside loading zones 'are public subsidies to land owners as contrasted with off-street facilities provided within private property' (Anon, 1974a, p 69).

Key points to be considered in the development of regulations covering curb space allocation include the following (Anon, 1974a, p 69; Anon, 1978c, p 88 and 94; Habib, 1985):

- because the process involves rationing of a scarce resource (public road space at a particular time of day), equity considerations demand that regulations be developed by a public authority (e.g. a city council) and not be subject to private control;

- adequate enforcement is essential if the allocation process is to work, and the development of regulations should be consistent with the level of enforcement available;

- in some cases, more stringent enforcement of existing regulations may be a better alternative to creating more loading spaces;

- consideration must be given to the types of vehicle permitted to use curbside loading spaces (e.g any commercially-registered vehicle, trucks as defined by size or mass, etc);

- similarly, the types of activities in which such vehicles may be engaged must be determined (e.g. pick up and delivery of goods only, delivery of services, or unrestricted use by any vehicle legally permitted to stop at the space);

- determination of appropriate curbside uses should involve a detailed block by block analysis, with the aim of allowing pick up and delivery operations as close as possible to customers' premises, consistent with other demands for the use of roadspace (note that this may also vary by time of day and day of week - see below);

- development of a curbside allocation program should involve extensive consultation with affected parties, including the traders and businesses in the street, shipper and trucking representatives, police and emergency service authorities, and local residents;

- implementation is usually through the use of signs mounted on posts at intervals along the curb; this may be supported by other means of communication to drivers, e.g. a painted curb with a colour coding system is used in some places in the US and Europe, while a distinctive 'clearway' sign is used in Australia to denote roads where the curb lane is allocated to moving traffic in peak hours.

- the curb space allocation should be reviewed periodically to ensure that current needs are being met in an equitable way.

Loading time restrictions

Restricting the amount of time that a vehicle may occupy a loading space is often a concomitant of the above-mentioned allocation of curb space. It aims to:

- encourage greater use of off-street facilities (where these are available) for time-consuming deliveries;

- increase the turnover of vehicles and thus reduce the amount of curbside loading space needed;

- prevent the misuse of loading spaces, e.g. vehicle parking, lunch breaks, extended visits by service vehicles, etc; and

- allocate curb lane space amongst competing uses by time of day.

Time restriction may be of three types:

- a limit on the length of time for which a vehicle may use a curbside loading space;

- designation of the hours of the day for which the space is allocated to loading operations (with the space being used at other hours of the day for other purposes, such as moving traffic, car parking, pedestrian malls, etc); and

-   allocation by day of week (e.g. the regulations may not apply at weekends).

Considerations to be taken into account in the determination of time allocation are quite similar to those listed above for space allocation, especially those related to the need for enforcement, implementation procedures, signing, and consultation with affected parties (Anon, 1974a, p 69; Anon, 1978c, p 90; Walters, 1982, p 252).

Truck route regulations and truck access controls

As noted in Chapter 6, regulations aimed at restricting trucks to particular routes usually involve either the use of 'no entry except for access' controls, or absolute limits on the size or mass of vehicles permitted to use a street. It is therefore necessary to consider truck route regulations and truck access controls together as they are, in effect, two sides of the same coin.

Advisory truck routes, also mentioned in Chapter 6, merely require the determination of an appropriate route network and its signing; they do not involve the preparation and enforcement of regulations because they are advisory in nature.

Truck route regulations may also be required where particular classes of truck are limited to a restricted network of roads. Examples of this situation include:

-   in the US, longer and wider trucks are permitted to use the federal-aid primary arterial network, and federal law requires the states to provide reasonable access to this network; in this case, where trucks permitted on the federal network would not be allowed as-of-right on a state or local road, those state or local roads where access is permitted are designated and signed as such (see Figure 6.2 above);

-   in Australia, so-called 'road trains' (combination vehicles up to 50 m (164 ft) in length and 136 t in mass) operate in remote parts of the country, but usually their operation is by permit only; the permit typically specifies, amongst other things, the routes which the vehicle may use; and

- a variation on this occurs with extractive industries (which may produce large numbers of truck movements) where a condition of the extractive industry licence specifies the route to be used by such trucks; this applies for example with mineral sands activities near Perth, Australia, with the purpose of keeping heavy vehicles away from residential areas and off lightly-constructed roads on the urban fringe (Ogden, 1990, p 94).

However, within urban areas, truck route controls are more likely to be an absolute restriction on truck use of the street, perhaps by time of day (Figure 6.3), or a 'no entry except for access' regulation, so that only vehicles with legitimate business in the area or street are permitted (Figures 6.5 and 6.6 above).

In Chapter 6, the factors to be taken into account in developing and designating a truck route system or entry bans were discussed. Factors to be considered in the development of regulations to implement such controls include the following (Anon, 1974a, p 64; Anon, 1978c, p 97; Hasell, Foulkes and Robertson, 1978c; Button and Pearman, 1981, p 156):

- match vehicle mass and/or dimension limits to roadway facilities having adequate structural strength, geometric design, and environmental sensitivity;

- notwithstanding the previous point, as far as possible there should be consistency within municipalities (and if possible between municipalities) in the mass and/or dimension limits of trucks which are permitted access (this is to enable truck operators to select and use vehicles capable of wide use, and not have to invest in vehicles just to be able to access a limited area);

- in some cases, access control may not be on the basis of vehicle characteristics, but be limited to vehicles which have been issued with a permit or licence of some sort to operate in that area; this raises the possibility of making a charge for the issue of the permit as a means of paying for enforcement;

- trucks should be able to use a reasonably direct route in order to minimize travel distances and thus minimize their contribution to congestion, emissions, energy consumption, etc;

- adequate enforcement is necessary if truck entry restrictions are to be effective, especially for 'no entry except for access' controls which may require an enforcement officer to establish whether a truck has a legitimate need to be in the area;

- development of truck entry bans or route controls should involve extensive consultation with affected parties, including shipper and trucking industry representatives, police and emergency service authorities, and local residents;

- implementation is usually through the use of signs mounted on posts at the entrance to the street or area; ideally, such signs should indicate the allowed route for a truck whose entry is not allowed (in some cases this is obvious - an entry ban into a local area for example implies that the truck must stay on the arterial road (see Figure 6.3 above), but in other cases it may not be obvious);

- similarly, it is helpful if detailed maps indicating the location of entry bans or truck restrictions are produced as part of the implementation program; once again these should aim to show drivers where they are permitted to travel as well as where they are not permitted;

- restrictions, if applied at all, should be applied only to the degree necessary to achieve the desired reduction in truck movement, since all such restrictions impose costs on the road freight industry (and thus on the community as a whole), and require enforcement; and

- further to the previous point, alternatives to regulation as a means of controlling undesired access should be considered; these might include local area traffic management schemes employing roundabouts, street closures, etc, although even in these cases, it should be noted that trucks have legitimate access needs, and means of allowing such access must be preserved.

Building regulations

Building codes are commonly used to prescribe off-street loading requirements, and thus have a direct effect upon urban freight. These codes specify, for given land uses and building sizes, the number of off-street loading, unloading and commercial vehicle parking facilities, their sizes and access conditions. They should also include clauses related to the use (or misuse) of such facilities. In some cases, building regulations also apply to environmental factors, e.g. the provision of noise fences or buffers at freight terminals (Technical Advisory Group, 1990, p 31).

Because the provision of off-street loading spaces is usually viewed as 'dead space' by a building developer, some form of public intervention is usually necessary to ensure that these facilities are provided. To ensure consistency and equity between building developments, this intervention should take the form of publicly promulgated regulations, codes, ordinances, or some similar legal form. Wood (1979, p 25) has correctly interpreted this as a symptom of the failure of the pricing mechanism: 'Under the existing system, building developers and managers pay for improvements and tenants and carriers reap the benefits. The market mechanism is unable to resolve this inequity and therefore the most practical solution is municipal level by-laws which require the costs to be internalized and therefore passed on through the system.'

The usual application of these types of regulation is to require that building plans include the necessary provisions as a condition for granting planning approval and/or issuing a building permit, and to verify that they have been provided as a condition for issuing a certificate of occupancy. They typically apply to office buildings, apartment buildings, manufacturing plants, larger retail stores, distribution and warehousing buildings, and institutional land uses such as schools and hospitals.

The estimation of the number of off-street loading spaces required for a range of land uses in relation to their size is discussed in Chapter 13, while general comments about the value of such facilities are included in Chapter 6. Key aspects to consider in the development of regulations covering off-street loading facilities include the following (Anon, 1974a, p 66, 73; Anon, 1978c, p 85; Crowley et al, 1980, p 14; Walters, 1982, p 244; Anon, 1989a):

- the number of loading spaces to be provided should be determined on the basis of the proposed use of the building and its size (typically measured by gross floor area); there may be a minimum size of building below which the regulations do not apply;

- similarly, the range of sizes of loading spaces should be determined on the basis of the type and size of trucks likely to use the building; in particular, the likelihood of tractor semi-trailers using the building in question should be considered;

- the dimensions and geometry of access driveways (height, width, turning and manoeuvring space) must be specified to ensure that trucks which use the off-street facility can actually gain access to it;

- the buildings to which the ordinance shall apply must be defined; for example, all new buildings exceeding a certain size may be subject to the provisions of the regulations, but redevelopment of existing buildings may be exempt unless they involve a significant increase is size, traffic generation, etc;

- there needs to be flexibility in interpretation to allow innovative solutions, such as shared facilities at adjacent buildings, or even remote loading spaces;

- the regulations must specify not only the number of spaces and their size, etc, but also the use to which they may be put; in particular, their use for car parking, trash dumpsters, etc should be prohibited as this can negate the purpose for which the regulation was introduced (there may be enforcement implications of this provision);

- the regulations should specify, in addition to the above, that adequate linkages in the form of ramps, cartways, elevators, etc are available to connect the loading area with the various pick up and delivery points within the building;

- the regulations should recognise that not all freight and service vehicles using a particular building can or should use the off-street facility; in particular, courier vehicles which may be present for only a few minutes and which involve the pick up and delivery of parcels or documents would normally be permitted to use on-street facilities, and these should be provided even where off-street loading spaces are required;

- development of regulations covering off-street loading provision should involve consultation with the building development industry, building owners and managers, the trucking industry, and other interested parties such as police and emergency service agencies;

- the provisions of the regulations should be reviewed from time to time to ensure that they are still adequate in terms of changing truck technology, freight delivery patterns, and new land and building use; and

- it must be remembered that there are costs in both underprovision of facilities (e.g. congestion on streets) and overprovision of facilities (e.g. construction costs and lost revenue to building owners).

Vehicle regulations

These effect such aspects as truck mass and dimension limits, environmental factors such as emissions and noise, and safety factors such as braking and seat belts. By their very nature, these must apply to the truck fleet as a whole, rather than just to urban trucks, and thus they are not peculiarly urban freight strategies. However, the degree of enforcement of the regulations may vary between urban and non-urban areas, and there may be some specifically urban applications, such as restrictions on truck idling (Technical Advisory Group, 1990, p 11).

It is likely that there will be increased community demands for trucks which are more 'environmentally friendly' (Cooper, 1990). In the main, this relates to noise, but other factors such as emissions, safety and visual intrusion are important also. It is technically possible to build trucks which are more environmentally benign in these ways, but at a cost. Historically, such improvements have come about not so much from market competition as from government regulations affecting truck design and use (Anon, 1982b, p 81 ff).

Application of regulations

As noted in the introduction to this chapter, the recent worldwide trend towards so-called 'deregulation' has in reality seen a reduction in quantity regulation and an increase in quality regulation. The question arises therefore as to how such regulations should be applied in the context of urban freight.

Regulations in general should satisfy certain general criteria if they are to be beneficial and not merely create confusion, frustration and excessive cost. These criteria are that the regulation should be (Sach, 1984):

- shown to be needed;

- acceptable in principle and practical application to the majority of the affected population;

- framed in such a way as to be clear and unambiguous;

- consistent with other regulations;

- made known, and

- enforceable.

Whether these criteria are satisfied in any given city and at any given time is a matter for judgement. However, to the extent that they are not, there will be excess cost of urban freight (defining cost in the broad way outlined in Chapters 4 and 5 to include not only operational costs but the associated economic, social and environmental costs). For example, Noortman (1984, p 47) notes the that effects of restrictions aimed at reducing truck traffic flows will inevitably have repercussions, up to and including the closure of businesses. Crowley, et al (1980, p 14) note that government (especially local government) has been accused of:

- continuing to use regulations that are out of date;

- inadequately enforcing existing regulations;

- implementing regulations which are oriented towards traffic flow rather than towards efficient goods movement; and

- lacking concern for goods movement problems because of failure to recognise the importance of freight to the urban economy.

Staley (1989c, p 50) points to a need to achieve a balance between regulations which have the effect of restricting truck activity in urban areas, and the absence of any such restrictions. He paints a gloomy picture of the scene as it applies in the US in particular, with lack of understanding of the trucking industry's view by government, and vice versa; mutual suspicion and distrust; and public antipathy towards aspects of the urban freight industry, all of which result in the development of regulations which are costly, only partially effective, and potentially counter-productive. He calls for the development of an independent ombudsperson who would come to an area, assess its needs and the efficacy of its regulatory structure, and make recommendations. He asserts that 'a community and its delivery systems represent a delicately balanced mechanism where efficiency, economy and utility must be constantly balanced against intrusion, the environment, and the overall welfare or common good. (Regulations) swinging between restriction and facilitation must be made to come to rest at a proper balance point.'

Whether by the appointment of an ombudsperson or by some other means, Staley's advice is salutary, and of relevance to all concerned with the development and enforcement of regulations related to urban freight.

10 Pricing

Pricing strategies in general aim to affect the nature and extent of urban freight activities through the pricing mechanism. While anything which attempts to internalize externalities might be regarded as a form of pricing, it is more usually held that these approaches reflect alternative strategies, e.g. the provision of off-street facilities, or the requirement that vehicles be fitted with noise or emission control devices.

Pricing therefore in this chapter covers three distinct strategies: road pricing, charges levied on trucks entering a congested area, and commercial rates.

Road pricing

In theory, a system of 'road pricing' is the key to solving traffic congestion problems in any city (Hills, 1990; Thompson, 1990; Small, Winston and Evans, 1989). The essence of road pricing is that all vehicles are charged for the use of road space according to the marginal costs that they impose on others, including congestion costs and perhaps other external costs as well. It is important to note that road pricing is just that - a scheme to allocate a scarce resource (road space) and not a scheme explicitly aimed at reducing congestion or reducing the number of trucks (or any other class of road user) on the road, or even raising revenue. To the extent that it had those effects, that would be a consequence, not a purpose, of the pricing policy.

In practice, technological, political and equity considerations mean that its applicability has been limited. Only Singapore could be said to have implemented a comprehensive urban road pricing scheme, with its central area cordon scheme. However, as these technological, political and equity

215

issues are resolved, it is possible, even likely, that more cities will adopt some form of real time road pricing, i.e. vehicles will be charged for the use of roadspace depending upon the amount of congestion which they produce. This would likely have the dual effect of raising revenue, and discouraging the marginal traveller from using congested roads.

If a form of direct road pricing was introduced, it is likely that trucks would be required to pay a higher price than, say, private cars because their larger size means that their effect on congestion and other externalities is greater. It is interesting to speculate therefore upon what might happen to the demand for truck activity in urban areas in the presence of a road pricing regime.

Assuming that the demand for the use of road space is not totally inelastic with respect to price, the imposition of a road pricing charge would lead to some reduction in the demand for the use of the road. However, the effect of this would not be uniform across all road users; it may be that an individual, or certain classes of road user, find that their costs have actually decreased, i.e. the benefits of operating in less congested conditions actually outweigh the charges imposed by the road pricing scheme. This outcome is likely if the particular road user has a high value of travel time. It is generally considered that most trucks would, in fact, fall into this category. For example, Hicks (1977, p 112) commenting on this feature, noted that 'as commercial goods vehicles are likely to have a high time valuation, it is therefore possible that their generalized costs of travel may diminish with road pricing and their road use consequently increase... with labor costs usually making up well over half of vehicle operating costs, a congestion charge will be far outweighed by any driver overtime rates which need to be paid if a vehicle is scheduled outside normal hours of operation. Off-peak delivery is not likely to be encouraged if, to avoid the congestion charge, overtime wages are incurred.'

House (1979, p 81) also speculated that this outcome might occur, while Button and Pearman (1981, p 167; see also Button, 1978) also reached similar conclusions: 'reduced congestion will almost certainly have favourable consequences for urban goods movement, i.e. it will speed up journeys, which permits greater utilization of vehicles and crew and possibly results in indirect benefits from a smaller fleet requirement, and it also reduces the wear and tear on vehicles which accompanies frequent braking and acceleration. There is likely therefore to be some reduction in the generalized costs of haulage to offset at least part of the road price.' Button and Pearman quantified this by quoting the results of a study undertaken in the 1970s in Coventry, England. Although trucks were to be charged at twice the rate for cars, all categories of truck (and also business cars) showed a significant reduction in trip costs, while private cars showed an increase.

Button and Pearman (op cit, p 169) therefore concluded that the effects on urban freight of the introduction of a system of road pricing would be:

- in the short term, to have little effect on freight or truck flow;

- in the longer term, to encourage the use of both smaller and larger trucks at the expense of medium trucks (this is happening anyway);

- to encourage some re-routing of trucks away from central city areas, on the assumption that prices would be higher there; and

- to encourage shifts in land use patterns and their associated freight demands; these could be quite complex, depending for example upon the relative extent to which residential, commercial and retail establishments relocated towards the centre for greater access or towards the suburbs for lesser congestion, and also upon the extent to which a road pricing regime encouraged the use of public transport.

Hicks (1977, p 112) notes that the somewhat counter-intuitive outcome of no reduction (or even an increase) in truck flows might invite the response that trucks were not being charged enough and that their toll should be increased until a sufficient number had been removed. However, he correctly notes that such a response 'loses sight of the economic efficiency basis of road pricing (and) to take this approach is to make an arbitrary decision as to the amount of truck traffic to be allowed on the route. Taxation, not road pricing, is being used.'

Road pricing has been criticised on several grounds in so far it might be applied to urban goods movement. It has been argued that it might increase prices of retail goods,and thus contribute to inflation. It has also been suggested that it is regressive in that the demand for necessities is highly inelastic and thus road pricing will impact most severely on low income groups. However, as Button and Pearman (1981, p 170) correctly point out, these fears are unfounded, since it is likely that a road pricing regime would have little effect on road freight costs and may actually reduce them.

A more valid criticism is that road pricing may produce a particular split between passenger and freight vehicles, which may be unacceptable on equity grounds: 'the poorer man is being priced off the road whilst the richer man and his commodities are not' (Hicks, 1977, p 113).

A form of real time road pricing is not on the political or technical agenda for most cities at the moment, but as mentioned above, it is possible that it will be more seriously considered in the years ahead. Therefore in the context of this book, it is relevant to note that should such a proposal be made, serious consideration would need to be given to the freight transport implications of road pricing.

Charges on truck access

In some cities, especially in Europe, trucks require a permit or licence to access the central city. The question then arises as to whether a charge can be levied for such a permit, as a crude means of charging trucks for the congestion which they cause.

Button and Pearman (1981, p 166) have examined the likely range of consequences of such a system on the demand for freight movement, and concluded that the outcome would depend upon the 'strength of a number of interacting forces, notably the final demand elasticity for the good being carried, the importance of transport costs in total production and distribution costs, and the market structure under which the hauliers and retailers operate.' In particular, to the extent that trucking firms were able to pass on costs, such a scheme would push up prices of those commodities for which transport costs were a high proportion of total costs. Whether this applied solely to the area covered by the charging scheme, or whether it was averaged out across the metropolitan area (assuming that the charging scheme applied only to a congested central area) would depend upon the pricing policy of the trucking firm, and its willingness or ability to price its services selectively.

A variation on this arrangement would be to levy a charge on trucks at peak periods only. In this case, the same result would apply, but limited to those goods which had to be moved during peak periods. Hasell and Christie (1978, p 29) examined the effects of a scheme of this nature in London, England, and concluded that there would be some rescheduling of trips to other hours of the day, and greater use of smaller vehicles which were not subject to the charge. However, much freight demand was not elastic, and even with a quite substantial charge, 45 percent of operators of large vehicles (>24 t GVM) were not likely to change their pattern of activities. On the other hand, 12 percent indicated that they would relocate their activities to areas not subject to the charge, or even go out of business.

Finally, it is sometimes suggested that charges be levied on the firms which generate freight demand, not on the road freight industry. This may be done, for example, by installing metered loading zones, with the payment of the metered fee by the firm being served; the amount of the fee would vary by time of day, so that the firm wishing to avoid the charge would schedule its freight loading and receipt to off-peak hours (Hicks, 1977, p 113). Whether this is practical is doubtful, although it might be noted that meters are in use at curbside loading spaces in Dallas, Texas, but this is to encourage turnover, not to levy a charge (Walters, 1989a, p 62; Habib, 1985). However, in a study related to air quality impacts of large trucks in California, the Technical Advisory Group (1990, p 29) suggested that road pricing (as discussed above) 'could lead to unintended results, such as consolidation of the trucking industry', and a better approach might involve 'assessing peak period pick up and delivery fees on shippers and receivers in an attempt to reduce truck travel during commute hours.'

Commercial rates

Competition between carriers is on the basis of both service and rates. Trucking firms may be reluctant to refine their rates to more accurately reflect costs attributable to a particular customer, since they would run the risk of losing the business. If they were willing to do so, they could possibly encourage greater efficiency by such measures as:

- extra charge for non-acceptance;

- demurrage if a truck is unduly delayed;

- higher prices for peak-period delivery or pick up;

- minimum charges per delivery to discourage multiple small shipments;

- pricing to reflect higher costs in certain areas, e.g. central city deliveries, deliveries to shops on malls, etc;

219

- FOB[1] pricing for delivered goods, so that the price is paid by the receiver, not the shipper; this would mean that the costs and impacts of poor receival facilities (especially those in downtown offices, apartment buildings, or sites with difficult access) were recognised by consignees;

- pre-paid shipments or electronic documentation to minimize the need for face to face contact between truck driver and shipper and/or receiver.

These are all essentially commercial decisions, with little if any public sector role, and their introduction depends upon the pricing policy of the trucking firm, the competitive position which would determine the acceptance of price discrimination on the basis of costs, the extent of geographical price discrimination (e.g. a trucking firm may quote a common price to deliver to any location in a given metropolitan area) and the relative market power of shippers, receivers, and carriers. They are included here for completeness however.

Note

1. FOB means 'free on board', and refers to a pricing regime where the shipper's responsibility ends when the goods are on the transport vehicle. The system whereby the shipper arranges and pays for transport is known as CIF ('cost, insurance, freight'), or delivered pricing (Magee, Copacino and Rosenfeld, 1985, p 372).

11 Terminals and modal interchange facilities

Intermodal freight transport

Modal interchange facilities are a key component of what is commonly referred to as intermodal freight transport, wherein goods are consigned from an origin to a destination via a variety of modes and/or carriers, in order to minimize costs or maximize service to the customer.

In one sense, intermodal freight transport is as old as freight transport itself, but in another sense the concept has a freshness to it as transport companies and logistics managers increasingly realise that each mode of transport has particular advantages in particular environments, and that the best service is often provided by using a variety of modes. This concept has been given impetus in recent times through technological developments which have seen the introduction and increasingly widespread use of containers (which may be carried on several modes of transport), the development of equipment to handle containers and other forms of unitized freight, and information systems which are able to keep track of individual consignments as well as facilitate the documentation associated with freight delivery.

The whole subject of intermodal freight transport is a vast one covering aspects of transport equipment design, government regulation, documentation and process control, terminal design and operation, marketing and management, industrial relations, politics, etc. (See for example Mahoney, 1985; Transportation Research Board, 1986a; Muller, 1989 for reviews of various aspects.)

For the purposes of this book, the interests are more specific, and relate to those aspects of intermodal freight transport that are within the province of the traffic engineer or urban planner, and in particular how such a person may contribute towards achieving the objectives outlined in

Chapter 5. In general, these contributions are in two areas - location and size of modal interchange facilities, and some aspects of their design.

Before discussing these however, it is necessary to briefly describe the functions and operations undertaken in modal interchange facilities, and review some of the broader issues related to them, so that the more specific aspects can be seen in context.

Functions and operations

The function of a modal interchange facility has been succinctly described by Marino (1974) as:

- to receive and/or deliver customer shipments;

- to consolidate individual shipments into larger units to take advantage of line-haul economies of scale;

- to transfer shipments between carriers and modes;

- to provide short term storage; and

- to provide short term domicile for transport equipment.

It is important to note that the essential function of such a facility is to enable economies of scale to be achieved; they are not required when large shipments such as full truck loads, unit trains, or barge loads can move freight directly from origin to destination. In the case of overseas transport (sea and air) an intermodal transfer at a seaport or airport respectively is almost always necessary. This operation has been depicted in Figure 3.1.

Terminals may be single-mode (e.g. a rail switching yard) or multi-mode (e.g. a seaport). They may be online facilities (moving freight between vehicles of the same company) or interline (passing the freight on to another operator). They may involve individual components (e.g. parcels, manufactured equipment, pallets, cartons, etc), containerized freight (in which the terminal is only concerned with handling the container, and not the individual consignments therein), or bulk products such as petroleum, minerals or grain.

Truck terminals mostly allow the interchange of freight between urban pickup and delivery vehicles (which are often rigid trucks, ranging in size from small courier vehicles to 3-axle rigid or van type trucks) and line-haul vehicles, which are usually articulated trucks with one, two or three trailers, depending upon the regulations governing vehicle mass and dimensions. Truck terminals may also occasionally involve 'hub' type operations which transfer freight between large line-haul trucks, but these are not so common (Anon, 1989a, p 16).

Shipping terminals may be served by a variety of land-side modes, including trucks, rail, pipeline, barge, etc. Sea terminals may cater for conventional break-bulk ships, container ships, bulk carriers (bulk liquid or bulk solid - usually these would be at facilities purpose-built for the particular trade, e.g. coal, petroleum, grain), or combinations thereof.

Container berths are adjacent to large areas of land where containers are stored temporarily before being loaded onto a ship, or after being off-loaded. Most container terminals are served by road, and some are served by rail. However, the latter is comparatively rare in the United States, because of the 'cost, time and effort involved in spotting railcars in sequence so that they will be within reach of ship-loading cranes' (Mahoney, 1985, p 90).[1] Rail-served container ports more typically have the rail facility some distance from the port, with connection between the port and the rail facility by truck. The Intermodal Container Transfer Facility (ICTF) operated by Southern Pacific Railroad serving the Port of Los Angeles and the Port of Long Beach is a case in point. (Roberts and Felts, 1983; Muller, 1989, p 73; Goodwin, 1986; Radzikowski, 1983).

Air freight terminals are usually served on the land side by trucking services only. In some cases there may be a short road-based connection between the airport itself and an off-airport air freight terminal, especially at larger and busier airports where airline practices and terminal inadequacies force the intermodal transfer functions to a remote site (Mahoney, 1985, p 90).

Issues and problems

There are a number of issues and problems specifically related to intermodal terminals. Those of relevance to urban freight planning and policy are reviewed below.

Location. Many terminals are poorly sited, resulting in (Staley, 1989a, p 10):

- little if any opportunity for facility expansion or modification;

223

- conflicts with other nearby land uses;

- terminals subject to environmental constraints such as noise, hazardous materials storage, flood lighting; and

- access for emergency and support services may be limited or difficult.

Traffic congestion. Partly as a result of the locational aspect, access to many terminals, especially in the older areas of cities (typically near seaports or rail yards) can be quite congested. Staley (1989a, p 10) has listed various sources of congestion:

- traffic volumes on the streets near the terminal;

- inadequate access to major highways;

- overcrowding of the facility;

- queuing on adjacent streets;

- poor access for emergency and support services; or

- spillover parking on nearby streets.

Problems can be particularly severe near ports. This is due partly to the irregular and peaked demand generated by ship arrival times, but is exacerbated by institutional factors which result in a low priority being given to delays to trucks which are sent to pick up containers. In some ports at certain times, delays of 2 or 3 days have occurred, although these instances are becoming less common with improved information and control systems.

Infrastructure. Intermodal operations can affect public infrastructure in a number of ways (Staley, 1989a, p 10):

- damage to roads and bridges with overloaded trucks (see below on container mass and dimension limits);

- damage to roadway signs, signals, poles wires, etc; and

- problems at railway at-grade crossings; in many instances both rail and sea terminals are served by rail facilities which feature numerous at-grade crossings. Because of the shunting and wagon spotting activities which take place on many of these lines, delays can be excessive. For example, in the case of Los Angeles, there are a total of over 300 at-grade rail crossings on rail lines serving the port area and linking it to the downtown rail yards (Roberts and Felts, 1983).

Institutional problems. There are many 'actors' involved in terminal activities (see Chapter 3). Hence, it is hardly surprising that there are problems of an institutional nature, with institutional factors causing some of the other problems listed above. These include (Staley, 1989a, p 11; Ogden, 1985; Rimmer and Tsiporous, 1977):

- availability and adequacy of financing for road infrastructure, handling and transfer equipment, etc;

- maintenance of standardized mass and dimension limits for containers and equipment (see below);

- inadequate data bases for planning and research;

- lack of inter-jurisdictional coordination, caused in part by facility inadequacies and (in the case of ports) by inter-port competition;

- the influence of traditional labor and work practices, which can be extremely difficult to modernize;

- mis-match of hours of work, with different segments of industry working different hours, with non-coincident lunch breaks, etc (e.g. at the port of Long Beach, California, union agreements allow the gates to the terminals to be open between the hours of 8 am - 12 noon and 1 pm - 5 pm only); and

- slow progress on reforming and integrating documentation; in principle with modern information systems, all documentation should be swift, efficient and accurate, but this is not always the case, especially at sea ports.

In the case of shipping terminals, the terminal operator, i.e. the stevedoring company, plays a pivotal role. These companies see their priority as serving the shipping company, either because they are owned by the shipping company, or because their principal concern is to provide a good service to ships so that shipping companies will continue to use their terminal. By contrast, there is little incentive to provide a good level of service on the land side, because once the shipping company has decided to use that terminal, all other land-side actors are 'captive'. In fact, some ship terminal operators see a line of trucks waiting outside their terminal as desirable, since it ensures that the terminal operator's staff and equipment can be fully occupied! The costs associated with truck delay are not borne by the terminal operator, so there is little incentive for the terminal operator to relieve the situation.

Many ports have attempted to resolve these institutional issues. One recent example is the Port of Melbourne, Australia, which established a Project Team comprising representatives of all interested parties to attempt to develop an action plan to reduce truck delays (Smith, 1990). Four avenues for overcoming the causes of truck queuing were identified: improved cargo handling operations; more compatible work practices between stevedores, truckers and warehouses; improved documentation processing; and better communication for queue management. Twelve specific strategies were identified. These, together with the party responsible for implementation were:

- pay customs duty prior to ship arrival (customs);

- standardize import delivery order (shipping companies);

- port-wide truck booking system (truck industry);

- export cartnote (shipping companies);

- queue monitoring and communications (trucking companies, Port Authority and terminal operators);

- continuous service of trucks (terminal operators);

- more truck back-loading (trucking companies and terminal operators);

- stevedoring equipment availability (terminal operators);

- early start time at terminals (terminal operators);

- more bulk runs (i.e. containers moved en-block) (trucking companies and terminal operators);

- anti-queuing regulations (Port Authority); and

- extended hours at warehouses (shipping companies and terminal operators).

Environmental impact. Intermodal terminals can have a number of environmental impacts. These include:

- Noise at the terminal, associated with vehicle loading and unloading, truck movements within and to/from the terminal, vehicle servicing and maintenance, etc. This is particularly relevant since many terminal activities take place at evening or early morning hours.

- Noise generated by vehicles moving to and from the terminal, including trucks and trains. As noted, many of these movements take place at night, because of the need to provide overnight service, or a preference to move at uncongested times of the day. Roberts and Felts (1983) note the requirement that trains in the US sound their whistle before each at-grade crossing, and since, as noted above, these are numerous in many cities, the noise problem can be severe from this source alone.

- Air quality, associated with both vehicle emissions and dust from the load (e.g. coal and grain trains).

- Given that much terminal activity takes place at night, lighting at terminals can be a nuisance to nearby land uses.

- Hazardous materials which pass through terminals can be a major problem is there is a spill, a fire or some other incident which may render the material unsafe or injurious to health.

- Stormwater runoff from the site can be a problem if not properly dealt with; spillage and dripping of oil and grease, and water from truck washing facilities all contribute to runoff pollution.

In part, these problems can be tackled through terminal location decisions, as discussed below.

Container mass and dimension limits. Given that containers must be capable of being handled and carried by a wide range of operators in different countries and across all modes, it is axiomatic that some form of standardization of mass, dimensions and design (e.g. lock down devices) is necessary. The International Standards Organization (ISO) in 1964 established an initial set of standard sizes, basically a 6.1 x 2.4 x 2.4 m (20 x 8 x 8 ft) or a 12.2 x 2.4 x 2.4 m (40 x 8 x 8 ft) box. The maximum permitted mass of these were 24.4 t and 30.5 t respectively.

However, there are now numerous variations on these standards (Staley, 1989b, p 78; Nix, 1990). These include ISO 2.6 m (8.5 ft) high or 3.2 m (10.5 ft) high containers, European 2.5 m (8.2 ft) wide containers, US trucking 13.7 m (45 ft), 14.6 m (48 ft) and 16.2 m (53 ft) containers, 6.1 m (20 ft) containers with a maximum rated mass of 30 t, etc.

There are three main problems with lack of standardization, so far as urban freight is concerned. (There are obviously additional concerns for carriers and terminal operators, but they are beyond the scope of our interest). These are (Hutchinson, 1988; Nix, 1990; Kiesling Euritt and Walton, 1991):

- Increasing the maximum permitted mass on a container may mean that the truck carrying the container is overweight. Since it is usually the truck driver or owner who is responsible for ensuring that the truck complies with mass and dimension limits, this can put such people in a difficult position.

- Similarly, extra-long or extra-high containers may exceed the dimension limits of some jurisdictions, and trucks carrying these containers must travel with special permits, often at higher cost.

- Many containers are (illegally) overweight; this is particularly so for containers imported from some third world countries where containers are not routinely weighed before being loaded onto a ship. (It is interesting to note that at some shipping terminals, the terminal

228

operator weighs incoming trucks - those with containers for export - but does not weigh trucks carrying newly imported containers out of the terminal.) Again, the responsibility is shifted to the truck driver or owner - who is usually unable to do anything about it!

- Containers may not be uniformly loaded, with the result that although their aggregate mass is not excessive, they cause overloading on one set of axles of the truck carrying them. Again, this is a problem for the truck driver or owner.

These problems are relevant to the traffic engineer or transport planner, since they affect the road infrastructure. Local jurisdictions may allow overweight trucks to use specific roads, e.g. those connecting the port with an intermodal container transfer facility. However, in general, the solution to these problems lies in the field of international conventions, or enforcement standards by particular transport or terminal operators not to accept overloaded containers.

Location and size of terminals

As noted in Chapter 5, one of the principal ways in which the public sector in general, and traffic engineers and planners in particular, may influence freight terminal activities (and hence the location and intensity of freight movements generated by them) is through controls or incentives on terminal location.

At the macro-level, location of freight facilities is influenced by a number of factors. Young, Ritchie and Ogden (1980) in a study of factors affecting the location of freight facilities found that the four main influences were proximity to arterial roads, freeways, and services; proximity to customers and other facilities operated by the same firm; site availability; and labor availability. Of these, the first had the greatest impact. The study concluded that 'this result is of value in a transportation planning context, because it means that, by varying the transportation system and by influencing the perceptions of this attribute, the planner is able to have some influence on the location of freight facilities in urban areas.'

Sites with good access are thus both attractive to the industry, and desirable locations from a public viewpoint, because they minimize the amount of travel on local streets. For example, in US urban areas, many of which feature a circumferential freeway, or 'beltway', freight terminals are commonly located on or near this facility, often near the interchange with an inter-city freeway. In Australia, the guidelines for locating new development proposals in New South Wales (Traffic Authority, 1982) state that 'transport terminals should as far as possible be located in an industrial area and should be sited so as to be adequately served by an arterial and sub-arterial road network, thereby ensuring that intrusion into residential streets does not occur.'

Moreover, judicious siting of terminals can affect the amount of travel generated by urban trucks. For example, Southworth, et al (1983) and Southworth (1982b) in a Chicago study found that particular combinations of future terminal location patterns allied with future road networks reduced the modelled estimates of future truck travel in the region.

A study of freight terminal facilities in London, England (Greater London Council, 1977, p 7) revealed several problems, including: the lack of criteria by which government could formulate policies concerning freight facility location; the scarcity of suitable sites acceptable in both operational and planning (environmental) terms; the inequitable distribution of freight activities across the urban area, with some locations being much better served than others; many sites which would be suitable for freight facilities currently being used for other, less desirable, uses; and the poor reputation of freight terminals from an aesthetic and environmental viewpoint, which hindered their acceptability.

The report (op cit, p 16 ff) went on to develop recommendations for freight location policy in London which included the following elements:

- freight terminals servicing essentially local needs should be accommodated in London;

- in the interests of employment, preference should be given to those freight activities which had employment densities comparable to modern industry;

- terminals essentially serving a single large manufacturer should be encouraged to locate as close as possible to that client;

- larger terminals which generated high truck flows should be given preference for the use of sites near a major arterial road; and

- sites with water (canal) or rail use should be encouraged to remain as freight terminals.

While these concerns and strategies are particularly applicable to London, and formed a major focus of that city's freight planning activities in the late 1970s (Hasell, Foulkes and Robertson, 1978b, d), many of the same sorts of problems will be found in other urban areas, particularly denser cities with a more mature land use pattern and industrial base.

Specific site location is influenced by a number of factors (Staley, 1978; Chatterjee, Staley and Whaley, 1986; Anon, 1989a; Staley, 1983; Mahoney, 1985, p 88; Muller, 1989, p 104). The attributes ideally possessed by sites which are suitable for use as modal interchange terminals (especially for truck terminals) include the following:

- adequate site area (see below), of suitable shape and terrain;

- adequate local street and road capacity;

- no restrictions on truck operations in the area, such as:
  - truck bans at particular hours,
  - school zones which restrict traffic operations,
  - roads or bridges with inadequate load capacity,
  - bridges with sub-standard height clearance, or
  - railroad crossings which may impede access;

- permitted access by largest vehicles allowed on the line haul routes;[2]

- no adverse noise or zoning restrictions which might inhibit 24 hour terminal operations, such as restrictions based on noise or lighting;

- adequate power and water supply, and drainage;

- safety and security considerations; and

- favourable local tax climate.

These considerations usually imply a fairly large site in a suburban location, near freeways or arterial roads, and not abutting residential or other sensitive land uses. Taken to the limit, it may be that a number of trucking terminals could congregate together in a so-called 'transportation park' (Chatterjee, Staley and Whaley, 1986).

While these factors may seem logical and straightforward, ideally they should be determined in some explicit policy context which recognises the significance of freight activities to the local economy, the specific access and other needs of industry, and the particular environmental and other problems associated with terminals. The findings of a probe group in the 1973 Conference on Goods Transportation in Urban Areas (Anon, 1974c, p 91) are worth quoting here:

> At a minimum, policy statements should define the extent to which government planning should influence and control the location of freight terminals; the extent to which government should be involved in the design, construction, and operation of freight terminals; the extent to which location of freight terminals should be influenced by desired urban form; the priorities when freight terminal operation and complementary goods movement conflict with person movement; the extent to which freight terminals are allowed to impact on the environment and surrounding community; and the allocation of costs and benefits resulting from freight terminal location and operation.

Terminal size is essentially a private-sector decision, based upon operational factors at the terminal, terminal throughput, market area, etc. However, for illustrative purposes, it might be noted that Staley (1978) found that in the Los Angeles area, the average trucking terminal had about 100 doors and occupied about 6 Ha (15 acres). The largest terminal had 300 doors and several small satellite terminals had as few as 12 doors. In London, on the other hand, freight terminals are generally much smaller, being more typically 1-2 Ha (2.5 - 5 acres) (Hasell, Foulkes and Robertson, 1978b).

Design

Detailed discussion of the design of modal interchange facilities is beyond the scope of this book, and in any case would depend upon the specific needs and operational practices of the freight firm or terminal facility (see for example Goodwin, 1986). However, Staley (1978) has given some indicative information which may help envision what is involved in a trucking terminal:

232

- the terminal is typically a long, narrow building with doors along each side;

- arriving trucks unload on one side of the building, and departing trucks are loaded on the other;

- there may be a variety of materials handling equipment inside the building, ranging from conveyor systems to manual handling; the most common system probably involves the use of fork-lift trucks with pallets;

- the floor of the building is flat, and is above road level by about 1.2 m (4 ft) - i.e. the height of the tray of a truck, so that goods can be loaded and unloaded directly from the truck; there is still a need for an adjustable ramp to allow smooth access to the truck by fork-lift trucks, carts, etc;

- each gate position usually has its own door, for security and weather protection; the door should be at least 2.4 m (8 ft) wide and 2.7 m (9 ft) high;

- there may be an overhanging weather roof over the trucks, which needs to be at least 4.3 m (14 ft) high to accommodate maximum height trucks;

- the truck loading docks should be concreted, to ensure a safe and flat surface;

- the remainder of the exterior space used by the trucks should ideally be paved, to avoid dust, mud, etc;

- the terminal building would include office space, etc, and depending on the activities carried out there may also need to be facilities for computers, radio despatching, drivers' lounge, truck maintenance, truck washing, storage and spare parts, etc; and

- the whole yard would be surrounded by a security fence, and the yard may be flood lit at night for safety and security purposes.

These design guidelines for terminals should be related to the general design, layout and access requirements for off-street loading areas discussed in Chapter 6.

Notes

1. There are some on-dock rail facilities in the US, including terminals at Long Beach California, Tacoma Washington, and Port Elizabeth, New Jersey.

2. For example, in America the Federal Government has legislated for the use of longer combination vehicles (including twins and 14.6 m (48 ft) tractor semi-trailers) on designated federal-aid primary arterials. States are prohibited from denying 'reasonable access' by such vehicles from the Interstate system and designated primaries to terminals; facilities for food, fuel, repairs and rest; and points of loading and unloading for household goods carriers (Transportation Research Board, 1986b, p 50).

12 Operational strategies

Cost cutting measures through modification of operational procedures are essentially the responsibility of the private sector - shippers, receivers, and carriers - and the public sector has little direct role to play (see Chapter 4). However, although detailed discussion of urban freight operations is outside the scope of this book, it is useful to review operational strategies which are potentially available to pursue some of the objectives outlined in Chapter 5. In part this is for completeness, to indicate that the private sector can introduce strategies which go some way towards achieving these objectives, and in part it is to indicate that there are opportunities for the public sector to intervene in the operations of the urban freight sector in pursuit of such objectives.

Discussion of operational strategies is therefore directed at six topics, as follows:

- the urban freight task;
- improved urban pick up and delivery practices;
- urban freight consolidation;
- off-hours shipping and receiving;
- truck technology; and
- road system technology.

The urban freight task

Possibly the biggest area of change is new demands from customers. Increasingly, customers are demanding 'just in time' deliveries (see Chapter 3), which, as the Organisation for Economic Cooperation and Development (1985, p 126) has noted, 'imply new demands for service quality in which regularity counts for more than speed, a demand for ancillary services, and a greater variety of requirements; in terms of actual transport, the main change is that freight is characterized less in terms of its physical properties or value and more in terms of density and logistical requirements.' Similarly, Nicolin (1989, p 14) has noted that 'high quality goods transport is a *sine qua non* for efficient production systems in industry and thus for economic growth and expansion.' He went on to list five key service factors:

- high punctuality and reliability;
- high frequency;
- high speed point to point;
- capacity and flexibility; and
- low risk of goods damage.

This has a number of consequences. First, it is leading to more sophisticated management and control techniques and a wider range of services, especially real-time monitoring of freight flows. This in turn requires (and is made possible by) greatly increased use of information systems, both in the internal organisation of carriers and in their dealings with shippers and receivers (US Department of Transportation, 1990, p 9.20).

Second, there will likely be a continuation of the trend towards reorganisation of the structure of the urban trucking industry. This has several aspects, including the emergence of transport firms which have taken over the whole of the logistics chain (warehousing, stock control, transport, etc) on behalf of, say, a manufacturer. It will also likely lead to the emergence of larger, better capitalized and more sophisticated firms, as the smaller firms with lower level management and technological skills will be less able to manage an increasingly complex task involving ordering, consolidation, and distribution using computer-based inventory and despatch systems.

Third, as mentioned in Chapter 4, it will mean that the goals of the transport-logistics task will change from one which essentially minimizes transport costs alone to one which minimizes costs for the logistics system as a whole. From a transport policy viewpoint, this is an important change, as firms will not necessarily seek the lowest cost of transport, but will place other demands on the transport system, especially those related to reliability and quality of service.

A paper produced for the Central Area Transport Study in Melbourne, Australia (Road Traffic Authority, 1988, p 29) suggested that changes in the urban freight task over the next decade may be associated with:

-   increased consolidation of loads to achieve economies of scale;

-   even greater use of containers;

-   smaller and lighter consumer products, of higher value per unit mass;

-   development of specialized commercial and industrial precincts;

-   more exacting demands on reliability of delivery and pick-up;

-   growth in highly specialized freight for export;

-   growth in very small manufacturing activities at home or in small high-technology 'cottage' industries;

-   more small-scale delivery services (cooked meals, etc); and

-   extended hours of operation, particularly for freight receipt and despatch.

Improved urban pick-up and delivery practices

There are a number of ways in which the efficiency and level of service of urban freight operations might be increased by changes in operator practices. As well as the increased use of consolidation of deliveries and off-hours operations which are discussed in the following sections and which potentially involve some form of public sector participation, those which are essentially within the province of the operator include the following.

Radio or in-vehicle telephone despatching. Radio despatching (and increasingly, the use of in-vehicle telephones), enable the despatcher to control the pick up and delivery patterns of truck drivers on a real-time basis. This practice is already common but not universal, because some delivery patterns are sufficiently fixed that it is not necessary. Better truck routing, which may be assisted by computer programs to alter truck route patterns in real time (Franz and Woodmansee, 1990) can both reduce the cost of urban freight by increasing the productivity of trucks, and also provide a higher level of service to customers.

Block booking, or time slotting. With this arrangement, a truck is required to arrive to pick up or deliver a load in a given time slot, say of 15 minutes duration. In reality, it is applicable only when the shipper or receiver has considerable market power over the carrier, as for example at maritime container terminals, supermarket distribution centres, or large manufacturers (e.g. as a component of a 'just in time' operation).

Materials handling techniques. The greater use of materials handling techniques such as shrink wrapping, palletization and containerization have the potential to improve pick up and delivery operations because goods are consolidated into larger shipping units. Improved packaging can also reduce spillage and breakage losses. The introduction of insurance and pricing structures which encourage the use of better packaging may be the best way of stimulating the introduction of these improvements. There may also be implications for the road freight sector, in terms of perhaps the use of larger vehicles, or specialized vehicles with on-board handling equipment.

Larger order quantities. A variation on the previous point is that freight costs are lower, ceteris paribus, if goods are shipped in larger lots, e.g. a pallet instead of several individual items, or a container instead of a pallet, etc. This is not always possible of course, but in the urban freight context, the development of a pricing regime which aims to have rates more accurately transport costs would assist in encouraging shippers to despatch in larger lots where possible (Kearney, 1975, p VI-5).

Standardization. At present, there are impediments to the smooth flow of goods between shipper and receiver, and especially between modes or between different carriers when goods are inter-lined. Some of these impediments could be reduced by rationalization and standardization of certain aspects of the freight system, such as standard sizes and masses for pallets and containers, standard bills of lading, and standard commodity classifications. Problems associated with the lack of standardization of container mass and dimension limits have been discussed in Chapter 11.

Documentation. The increasing availability of cheap computer hardware and suitable software will doubtless lead to a much wider use of electronic documentation, with attendant efficiency gains. This is a necessary concomitant of 'just in time' deliveries, while computerized documentation is beginning to appear in imports and exports, with consequent potential to significantly reduce costs and delays on the waterfront and at international airports. One of the major benefits to the road freight sector of road system technology involving electronic vehicle identification (see below) is that it can greatly simplify the documentation associated with inter-state or international travel.

Coordination of working hours. There is room for greater coordination of working hours of those involved in urban freight. Pick up and delivery operations usually require the active participation of shipper or receiver personnel, to physically hand over or accept the goods and associated documentation. Thus freight activities are frustrated by lunch and other breaks which do not coincide between the freight industry and shippers and receivers. This is particularly a problem on the waterfront in many countries, where for traditional reasons, the hours of working are different from industry as a whole. Moreover, many businesses limit the hours during which they will accept goods (and sometimes also to despatch them), such as no afternoon deliveries, no deliveries on Friday, etc. Greater coordination and cooperation between shippers, receivers and carriers, or possibly a pricing structure which includes the provision of a surcharge for unsuccessful attempts to deliver goods, could eliminate or reduce these delays.

Urban freight consolidation

All else being equal, fewer vehicles will be required to accomplish a given freight task if the amount of goods picked up or delivered at any stop is increased, and if the mass and/or volumetric capacity of the vehicle is more fully utilized. There is evidence that certain aspects of urban freight, especially central city pick up and delivery operations, exhibit quite low levels of vehicle capacity utilization (Schuster, 1978, p 561; Plowden, 1983). Reduction in the number of trucks, especially on central city streets, would in turn lead to reduced costs of freight transport, reduced traffic congestion from both moving and parked trucks, reduced fuel consumption, lower levels of emissions and noise, and less interference with pedestrian traffic (Crowley et al, 1980, p 17).

In order to pursue this objective, goods can be despatched in larger lot sizes, points of delivery can be concentrated so that fewer sites need be visited, or shipments from multiple sources can be accumulated into a single delivery (Kearney, 1975, p VI-4). To the extent that they are able, urban freight firms attempt to do these things. Market forces are leading to this development, particularly through company amalgamations or takeovers which tend to place deliveries in the hands of fewer carriers, and also through the economies of scale made possible through the establishment of large distribution centres (which are becoming more common for grocery items, frozen food, liquor, paper products, and many other goods).

However, there are potentially a number of consolidation strategies which, if more widely used, could encourage greater urban freight efficiency. In general, these strategies are of three types:

- terminal consolidation;
- route consolidation; and
- consolidated despatch and receival facilities.

Terminal consolidation

In most cities at present, deliveries to the central city may be made by a large number of individual freight firms, which may lead to substantial duplication of effort. Under a terminal consolidation regime, each freight company would deliver specified types of freight (typically small shipments of less than, say, 450 kg (1,000 lb)) for delivery to a specific area (usually the central city) to a single consolidation terminal. At the terminal, shipments destined for delivery would be sorted into routes, and despatched with a single truck serving all premises along one route (much like mail delivery). The trucks would also pick up outbound shipments and return them to the terminal, where they would be sorted for collection by the freight company (Crowley, et al, 1980, p 18; Robeson, 1978, p ii).

This terminal is variously known by such terms as consolidation terminal (the term we use here), consolidation centre, transportation facilitation centre, transhipment centre, or goods distribution centre. The concept has been more highly developed in Europe than elsewhere (Eckstein, 1985; Plowden, 1983; Button and Pearman, 1981, p 171; Hasell, Foulkes and Robertson, 1978b). It excited a great deal of interest in the US in the 1970s

(Anon, 1974b; Parsons, 1974; Robeson, 1978; Schuster, 1978; US Department of Transportation, 1978), but for various reasons has not taken off in the highly coordinated, centralized fashion that its early protagonists envisaged. We will return to discuss the reasons for this shortly, but first we will examine the nature of the concept, and its advantages and disadvantages.

Institutional factors. Various institutional forms for a consolidation terminal are possible, depending at least in part upon the regulatory regime in the country or city in question, and in particular upon anti-monopoly legal constraints on trading practices which may limit the extent of cooperation or joint ownership. However, in general, three forms of ownership are possible:

- ownership by a single private corporation, perhaps owned in turn by one or more freight companies (Robeson, 1978, p iii);

- a cooperative venture in which each freight company using the facility contributes to its operating expenses and/or receives income from it; this appears to be the common form in Germany (Eckstein, 1985); or

- a public corporation, usually owned and operated by the municipality of the area concerned.

If a consolidation terminal was to be established, consideration would need to be given to the question of whether participation by firms serving the central city would be voluntary or mandatory. If the latter, some form of licensing of trucks allowed to serve the central city would need to accompany the introduction of the scheme. This would be a bureaucratic nightmare, as there would obviously have to be the facility for exemptions from the compulsory use of the terminal (see below). The question of how to cater for private (i.e. own account or ancillary) trucking and service vehicles would be very difficult to resolve in a way that did not create inequities or massive inefficiencies. On the whole, a voluntary system, whereby the advantages of the system (assuming that they exist) were sufficient to make it worthwhile for freight firms and shippers to use it, would seem to be superior to a regulated system with its inherent inefficiencies and inequities.

Markets. As noted, a consolidation terminal would not be suited to all freight movements to and from a central city. Noortman (1984, p 52) has suggested that those shipments to which a consolidation terminal concept is suited are concentrated in space (which would be the case if the system was focussed on the central city), small (i.e. limited to shipments of less than, say, 450 kg (1,000 lb) (Robeson, 1978)), and where the distance between origin and destination is not too short. Hasell, Foulkes and Robertson (1978b) concluded that in London, England 'it would be more attractive commercially to use smaller vehicles over even quite long distances rather than have arbitrarily to transship into (larger vehicles)'; they quoted a British study which indicated that it was more economical to ship goods in a 3 t vehicle up to nearly 200 km (120 miles) than to tranship into a 32 t truck from a 3 t truck at the urban boundary.

Robeson (1978, p 42) concluded that the use of a consolidation terminal would only be economic if there was a single item to be picked up or delivered at any site, since freight firms operating in the usual manner would be able to provide pickup and delivery service to shippers with pick up *and* delivery, or multiple shipments, at less cost than would be the case if a terminal was used. Clearly, this provides a significant limitation to the efficacy of a consolidation terminal for central city deliveries.

Kearney (1975, p VI-12) also points out that some commodities are not suited to transport via a consolidation terminal. Fresh food, bakery products, frozen food, fragile or perishable products, hazardous materials, construction materials, urgent deliveries such as courier services, newspapers, etc would be in this category.

Economic viability. The economic viability of a consolidation terminal has been succinctly outlined by Kearney (1975, p VI-14): 'the cost savings from the consolidated pickup must at least offset the additional handling costs associated with the sorting of shipments for individual carriers.'

Several studies of the economic viability of the concept have been made. Parsons (1974), based upon a study in Chicago, USA, concluded that a consolidation terminal for the urban pick up and delivery of inter-city shipments less than about 450 kg (1,000 lb) would produce savings of 3.5 percent. Schuster (1978, p 578) built upon this and other work to conclude that the concept was especially 'cost effective' in areas where there were concentrations of pick up and delivery operations including (but not only) central cities. Anon (1974b, p 138), based on a study in Los .Angeles estimated a cost saving of 5.6 percent for shipments of less than about 230 kg (500 lb), compared with conventional operation.

Environmental effects. Although the environmental effects of the consolidation terminal concept may well be positive, they are likely to be quite small. A probe group at an Engineering Foundation Conference on Goods Transportation in Urban Areas (Anon, 1974b, p 144) examined this issue and concluded that because the number of trucks engaged in central city delivery is only a small percentage of total motor traffic in an urban area, the effect of consolidation on the total urban environment is insignificant. However, the concept has recently been considered in Los Angeles as one possible means of managing trucks for air quality (Nelson, et al, 1991; Technical Advisory Group, 1990, p 15).

Difficulties with consolidation terminals. If there are benefits, albeit perhaps small, to be gained from a system of consolidation terminals to facilitate freight movements to and from a central city, and perhaps other areas, the question that follows is why the concept has not been further developed, except for certain instances in Europe.

To answer that question, we need to note that there are many objections and difficulties with the concept, of both an economic and an institutional nature. These include the following (Crowley, et al, 1980, p 18; Anon, 1974b, p 146; Urban Consortium for Technology Initiatives, 1980, p 8; Robeson, 1978, p iii-iv; Mohr, 1974; Kearney, 1975, p IV-12 ff; Bloch, 1978):

- road freight firms may lose their competitive edge through the loss of identity to their customers;

- large carriers would lose the economic and marketing advantage of their own consolidation operations which they have achieved by virtue of their size;

- conversely, small carriers which aggressively compete with large carriers on the basis of service would lose the ability to compete;

- freight firms sell more than just transport; they sell a service which includes not only delivery of the goods per se, but also reliable pickup and delivery schedules, special handling of freight, efficient billing and tracing, claims processing, etc, some of which would be lost or compromised if a third party was introduced;

- as a corollary to the previous points, a consolidation terminal could not serve all areas of the market; it may suit those where costs are important but urgency is less important, but transhipment through a terminal would likely lead to a lower level of service for urgent deliveries;

- a freight firm's truck acts as a mobile billboard, and the driver acts as a salesperson as well as the prime point of contact between carrier and customer; neither feature is likely to be given up lightly;

- if a scheme was introduced, a non-participating firm could gain a market advantage by advertising that it was *not* a participant, and that the customer was dealing only with that firm without the involvement of a third party;

- service quality and reliability could be lowered in a number of ways: door to door delivery times may take longer; there is increased risk of loss and damage (due to extra handling) and theft (due to more parties being involved); there would possibly be a lower frequency of pick up and delivery, and longer times to respond to a request for a pick up service;

- maintaining accountability, and accepting responsibility when things go wrong, would be more difficult as the freight passes from the control of the terminal operator to the freight company, and vice versa;

- freight firms would be reluctant to surrender direct control of shipments for which they are legally responsible;

- shippers may lose leverage in dealing with freight firms; the option of taking business away from an unsatisfactory operator and giving it to a competitor (or being able to threaten to do so) would be partly lost if there was a centralized pick up and delivery operation;

- there is no certainty that the consolidation terminal would operate efficiently, and indeed there may not be economies of scale in large terminals;

- management problems are likely to be greater at a single centralized terminal, and the potential for labor disputes to disrupt freight deliveries would be much greater;

- there would be extra documentation associated with the additional freight handling inherent in a consolidation process; and

- a likely consequence of the system would be that there would be a change in the pattern of deliveries to the terminal of an inter-city operator; at present urban pick up and delivery trucks arrive at the terminal over an extended period of time, whereas if deliveries were coming from a consolidation terminal there would be more peakedness in arrivals, leading to potential inefficiencies in operation.

With such a formidable list of objections, perhaps it is not surprising that the concept, so strongly embraced during the 1970s, has not really taken off, at least in the highly centralized, coordinated fashion envisaged at that time. (As noted before, many private trucking firms consolidate their own traffic using individual terminals or distribution centres, so aspects of the concept are being introduced through normal market pressures.) Robeson (1978, p vi) concluded that while there was widespread recognition that there were potential economic benefits to be gained through the use of consolidation terminals for central city deliveries, the major problem was that 'no one has a clear understanding of how these benefits will be shared among the users.' Wood (1979, p 19) after case study examinations of the concept in Vancouver and Saskatoon, Canada, concluded that 'the value of consolidated terminals was found to be inconclusive ... and therefore to suggest that a significant outlay of public funds to build and operate a terminal was not recommended'. deNeufville, Wilson and Fuertes (1974) after a study of consolidation concepts in New York City, concluded that consolidation terminals were cost-effective only under limited conditions where the savings could be obtained at low cost; they mentioned garbage collection as one example, an example which is of course common in many cities throughout the world. Their overall conclusion however was that consolidation terminals, as the concept has been described above, were too costly.

Route consolidation

Route consolidation is an arrangement whereby a single truck serves pick-up and delivery functions in a particular area, rather than having several trucks on similar journeys. It is an essential component of a terminal consolidation concept as described above, but we mean it here as a stand-alone concept, without the use of terminals.

Route consolidation already exists *within* a company of course, and its use is common with particular categories of freight such as mail, newspapers, milk, garbage, etc.

Extending it to deliveries involving multiple firms may take several forms (deNeufville, Wilson and Fuertes, 1974). One form is for each individual freight firm to sort its deliveries as at present, but instead of loading those goods into its own vehicle, a common vehicle among several companies is used; this however raises many of the objections listed above in relation to terminal consolidation, particularly those affecting the market strategy of a freight firm and its relationships with customers.

Another variation is for delivery rounds of a particular product to be pooled amongst carriers. An example of this flowers in Portland, Oregon (US), where florists meet in a suburban parking lot at an agreed time each day, and swap their deliveries, so that each individual delivery vehicle covers only a portion of the total metropolitan area (Treichler, 1990). The Urban Consortium for Technology Initiatives (1980, p 9) has reported a similar arrangement with some florists in Richmond, Virginia (US).

There is another form of what is in effect route consolidation which is widely practiced in many cities, and that is to use taxis for freight delivery, especially for urgent movements. To the extent that both passengers and freight are being carried simultaneously, this could be said to be route consolidation.

In their analysis of freight consolidation strategies in New York City, deNeufville, Wilson and Fuertes (1974) concluded that route consolidation was the most effective of the various consolidation concepts, and could result in quite substantial savings. However, the constraint on the widespread introduction of the concept was the institutional one, i.e. the identity and responsibility of an individual delivery firm and its relationships with its customers.

Consolidated despatch and receival facilities

This form of consolidation involves the establishment of a central despatch and receival facility to serve a range of individual shippers and receivers in a localized area. As generally envisaged, it would serve, say, all (or most) tenants in an office building, or all residents in an apartment building. Goods coming in or going out of the building would be received at the central facility, and pick up and distribution within the building would be the responsibility of the facility staff, not that of the truck driver.

The concept is based on the assumption that truck and driver dwell times are a major contributor to costs, including the time spent parking and unloading vehicles, waiting to use elevators, waiting for the consignee to sign for the goods, and possibly having to return a second or third time to affect the delivery because no-one is available to accept the goods (especially at residential addresses, such as apartment buildings) (Crowley, et al, 1980, p 85; Tee Consulting, 1979b).

Benefits from the establishment of a central facility therefore potentially arise from greater productivity of trucks and drivers, reductions in on-street congestion, and reductions in emissions, noise and energy consumption. Costs include the wages and overheads of facility staff (including perhaps extra security services), loss of rental space within the building, and reductions in level of service to clients. In addition, many of the institutional problems described above for terminal consolidation apply here also: introduction of a third party into the transaction, complication of relationships between delivery firms and clients, and the pricing difficulty that those receiving a benefit are not those paying the price.

A major experiment involving the trial establishment of a central despatch and receival facility at a downtown office building in Ottawa, Canada, was funded by Transport Canada in the 1970s (Tee Consulting, 1979b; Wood, 1979, p 21 and 197; Habib, 1983, p 77). Among the observations made about the effectiveness and use of the system were:

- the system was suited only to relatively low value products such as paper and office supplies; higher value products such as cash, securities, jewellery, etc would not pass through the facility;

- there was some reduction in truck dwell times, but many drivers chose to use the time savings in other ways (e.g. coffee break);

247

- there was some rearrangement of pick up and delivery patterns, in particular an increase in late afternoon pick ups;

- many stops involved multiple pick ups and deliveries to several office buildings, and for this reason a service concentrated on a single building would be effective only for a very large building; and

- there is no simple mechanism to transfer the cost of the system from the building owner (who pays) to the delivery firm (which receives the direct benefit) and/or the community (which receives indirect benefits).

The essential conclusion was that the concept was justified only in a heavily congested area, and then only if most major buildings in the area used such a service (Wood, 1979, p 224).

Habib (1983, p 82) was more specific, suggesting that the concept was only applicable in the following circumstances:

- minimimum building size of 46,500 m² (500,000 ft²);
- poor elevator service;
- problems with freight security under existing arrangements;
- over-utilized loading docks;
- location in a street environment with little or no available curb space; and
- costs borne by the building owner, and staffed by building personnel.

Even under these circumstances, Habib concluded that 'the final effectiveness of such a system could not be guaranteed'.

Off-hours shipping and receiving

Off hours shipping and receiving may be broadly defined as any urban freight pick up and delivery operation that takes place outside normal working hours. The term particularly applies to evening operations (say between 6 pm and 6 am) although it could also be applied to weekend operations.

Where there are benefits to shippers or receivers, this process is in use at present. It is common for example in the case of petroleum deliveries (which is a 24 hour operation in many urban areas); deliveries to supermarkets, particularly those which have extended hours and therefore have personnel present to receive incoming goods; delivery of perishable goods to stores for morning sales, such as newspapers, milk, fruit and vegetables, etc; and positioning of goods between terminals, e.g. mail and parcels.

However, there may well be societal benefits resulting from the expanded use of off-hours shipping an receiving, and discussion of this strategy as a component of urban freight policy focuses on encouraging off-hours operation in order to achieve these objectives. Supposed benefits include (Crowley, et al, 1980; Organization for Economic Growth, 1979; Grenzeback, et al, 1990; Cambridge Systematics, 1988 a,b; Cooper, 1990):

-   reduced daytime (and especially peak period) traffic congestion;
-   improved car, pedestrian and public transport access and circulation in central city areas;
-   reduction in truck-generated emissions; and
-   reductions in fuel consumption, etc.

Some argue that as the system became more widely used, there would be efficiency advantages as a result of greater truck productivity from round the clock utilization.

Techniques. Among the techniques to implement such a system are (Organization for Economic Growth, 1979, p 104; Hicks, 1977, p 111):

-   pick up and delivery in the evening hours, with a receiver being present to accept delivery; this may involve:
    -   the use of existing staff or the engagement of additional staff for premises which are open at night;
    -   staggering the working shifts of staff so that someone is available at night, whether or not the premises are normally open; or
    -   creating a special staff or shift for despatching or receiving goods in those premises which are not normally open at night;

-   use of a two key storage room, in which the truck driver delivers the shipment, unloads it, and locks the door of the storage room as the truck leaves; this may have implications for other driver duties such as the need for documentation and cash collection, and certainly has security implications in terms of both driver exposure to violence and theft of goods;

- use of a locked container or trailer, which is dropped off during the night, either at the curb or in a locked yard; this has similar implications to the above in terms of both driver duties and security implications;

- use of freight bins or slots, analogous to mail boxes; or

- consolidation of receiving facilities of a group of premises, whereby goods are received at night and distributed amongst the customers the following day.

Target groups. For reasons such as these, the California urban gridlock study (Cambridge Systematics, 1988a, Technical Memorandum 2.4, p 2; Grenzeback, et al, 1990) argued that there were two prime targets for expanded night operations; large establishments, for which the additional cost would be relatively small and could be spread over many receivals and despatches, and establishments that normally operate for extended hours, up to 24 hours, such as oil refineries, large warehouses, some supermarkets, and continuous manufacturing operations. Firms which could not shift to night time shipping and receival were smaller businesses, or those which by their very nature must perform their business operations during normal working hours (e.g. small manufacturers, retail stores, banks, most offices, etc).

There would be some industries which could potentially shift their overall hours of operation, but at a certain cost, e.g. for lighting; examples mentioned here included the building construction industry, plumbing and heating services, etc. Chambers Group (1990) for example have examined the air quality benefits of early start times (6 am) in the construction industry in Los Angeles, and concluded that there would be a small reduction in overall emissions, no change in traffic congestion (as cars would use the spare peak period road capacity made available by reduced truck activity), and significant increases in noise nuisance due to both construction activity and truck movements in the early morning hours.

Problems. Problems associated with off-hours operations are mainly felt amongst receivers; those despatching goods are more easily able to accommodate to a change in hours, while the urban freight industry could, if required, work around the clock (and does so already where customers demand it). There are also some environmental impacts, particularly noise.

More specifically, the difficulties with off-hours operations include the following (Hasell, Foulkes and Robertson, 1978b; Hicks, 1977, p 111; Churchill, 1970; Bloch, 1977; Crowley, et al, 1980, p 19; Organisation for Economic Growth, 1979, p 101 ff; Cambridge Systematics, 1988a, Technical Memorandum 2.4; Grenzeback, et al, 1990):

- noise: this has been probably the major impediment to wider use of evening operations among those firms and industries which could, or would like to, use it; many local governments have noise ordinances which prohibit night-time truck operations and these would need to be relaxed or revised if more widespread night-time truck operations were to be encouraged;

- costs of staff and associated overheads, especially where they would be additional to other requirements;

- costs of heating and lighting;

- concerns about security of personnel and goods, leading to direct costs (security services, additional insurance costs) and concerns about personal safety;

- costs to government of enforcement, if there was an element of compulsion to the scheme;

- problems with labor contracts, which may make off-hours operation difficult or expensive;

- management difficulties associated, for example, with supervision of off-hours operations, or changes resulting from elimination of direct contact between drivers and shippers' or receivers' personnel;

- potential for inefficiencies in pick up and delivery operations if delivery firms have to make two rounds per 24 hours (one at night and one during the day) instead of one at present;

- equity issues related to the relative incidence of costs and benefits (e.g. if freight rates as a whole increased because of the need to undertake more expensive night time operations, should those firms which only ship during the day be required to pay extra?);

251

- reduced level of service for some shipments, e.g. a consignment now picked up in the late afternoon can be delivered to another city the next morning (by either inter-city trucking, express rail, or air freight, depending upon distances and services available); if the pickup were required to be delayed for several hours, this may mean that it became a second-day, not next day, delivery;

- the whole question of service trucks is often overlooked in discussion of off-hours operations; many trucks in central cities are occupied on service, not freight, activities, and focussing on pick up and delivery operations would not affect these (or, conversely, if there was some form of program directed at trucks as a way of encouraging off-hours operations, this may have serious consequences for the supply of services in central cities); and

- there is likely to be resistance to change from potential participants, either because of the common human preference to keep the status quo, or because people or firms are not convinced of the benefits (if indeed there are any!).

Assessing costs and benefits. A number of case studies or experiments with off-hours operation have been conducted, and some of these have examined the relative advantages and disadvantages of the practice.

In 1968, an experiment in evening retail deliveries was conducted in London, England (Churchill, 1970). This was discontinued after less than 6 months. Although the nature of the experiment and the way it was monitored precluded any comprehensive assessment of benefits and costs, it is relevant to note that the study concluded that for the concept to produce net benefits, there must be economies of scale (i.e. it is not worth putting trucks on the road at night unless they can be productively employed), and that firms need to perceive a real benefit to themselves or they will seek to withdraw.

The US Federal Highway Administration funded a review of the feasibility of off-hours operations (Organisation for Economic Growth, 1979). It took the form of interviews with shippers, receivers, carriers and government officials, and concluded that where off-hours operation was commercially attractive, it would occur provided that there were no regulations to prevent it (e.g. noise regulations). Societal advantages associated with off-hours activities were perceived as being remote. The study recommended the development of a simplified procedure which could be used by a business to assess the cost advantages of its moving to off-hours operations, and the mounting of a small scale demonstration project to assess the broader environmental and social impacts.

Cambridge Systematics (1988 a,b), in its urban freeway gridlock study for the California Department of Transportation, considered evening deliveries as one of the strategies for managing urban freeway congestion. It included an assessment of the economic benefits and costs; these are summarized by Grenzeback, et al, (1990) and Cambridge Systematics (1988a, Technical Memorandum 3.6) as follows:

-   there would be modest effects on traffic congestion; total truck travel would increase slightly, there would be some reduction in peak period truck travel, but most of the truck movements would be shifted from the less congested daytime off-peak period;

-   there would be positive effects on air quality, due to trucks operating in less congested night-time traffic;

-   there would be additional costs to shippers and receivers totalling $1.45 billion per year in Los Angeles and $0.71 billion in San Francisco; and

-   there would be an increase in the costs of doing business in Los Angeles and San Francisco, resulting in a decrease in statewide employment of 31,500 jobs (0.2 percent) by 1995, and a decline in output (without offsetting savings) of $3.4 billion (0.3 percent) by 1995.

The City of Los Angeles is currently developing a program aimed at reducing the number of heavy trucks (3 or more axles) by 50 percent in peak hours. This program is described in Chapter 15.

In summary, the greater use of off-hours operations will occur without the need for government stimulation where there is a financial benefit to the shippers and receivers concerned, and where regulations (especially noise regulations and labor agreements) do not prevent it. The urban freight industry will readily, even willingly, participate in evening and weekend operations because it increases the productivity of capital equipment.

A program which aimed to coerce shipper or receiver participation could be very costly unless it was directed only at firms or industries which could find offsetting savings. Thus, the active involvement of shippers and receivers, as well as carriers, in the design and implementation of any such program would appear to be essential. The likely effects of such a program would vary from location to location, but in general would have only a modest beneficial effect on traffic congestion and air quality (Cambridge Systematics, 1988b, p viii).

Truck technology

Trucks and equipment

The technology associated with the truck itself and its equipment is in a state of continuous evolution. Commercial forces will continue to encourage the development of trucks and their equipment more suited to the cost structure associated with urban operations. Moreover, government regulation has been, and will continue to be, used to achieve improvements in safety, emissions and truck noise.

Among the major recent changes in truck technology are (Stadden, 1989; Erickson, 1989; US Department of Transportation, 1990, p 9.20):

- engines: improved power:weight ratios through the use of engines with larger capacity, greater use of turbo-charging, more efficient engine design (e.g. inter-cooling, electronic fuel injection and intake-air management); these developments improve both economy and safety, and contribute to air quality;

- braking: the wider use of anti-lock brakes, the introduction of electronic braking, and the development disk-drum brake combinations;

- improved tyres, wheels and suspensions: the introduction of smaller wheels (as operators seek to increase the cubic capacity of their vehicles), the greater use of wide single tyres on trailers, the use of polymer composite springs which are less subject to breakage, and the introduction of air suspensions;

- cabs and instruments: better seats (to improve comfort and reduce costs of back-related injuries to drivers), improved visibility, more ergonomic cab and instrument layout, air conditioning, more silent cabins, and the development of seat belt systems which are suited to a truck cab;

- goods handling techniques: these will both do general tasks more efficiently (e.g. elevator tailboards, on-board hydraulic cranes, canvas-sided pantechnicons and vans, side-loading vehicles for operation in congested streets, etc), and accommodate the particular needs of special cargo (e.g. frozen, liquid, etc);

- design of vehicles to reduce aerodynamic drag, and thus improve fuel economy;

- more productive vehicle combinations: this includes twin trailered trucks, which (while having mainly a line-haul emphasis) have advantages over long tractor semi-trailers in urban streets because of their better manoeuvrability and safety performance; and

- communication: the increasingly common use of two-way radios and/or mobile telephones (as means of enabling real time re-routing and re-assignment of urban trucks), real-time truck location and navigation systems, electronic data interchange (linking the computer data bases of trucking companies with those of their clients), and on-board engine diagnostic systems.

Alternative energy sources

The immediate future is likely to see further advances in all of these areas. In addition, there are clear pressures from both energy conservation and environmental sources for the development and wider use of alternative energy sources for trucks. In general, these are of three types (Institute of Transportation Engineers, 1981; Southern California Association of Governments, 1989b, p 198, Ryder, 1990; Constantinou and Janus, 1990):

Liquid fuel based sources. These involve minimum changes to existing engines, fuel storage and refuelling systems, and for this reason they are attractive to both engine manufacturers and fleet operators. The options here include:

- Gasoline: This has the big advantage that major improvements in the air quality aspects of gasoline-engined vehicles (both the fuel itself and on-board emission control devices) have been and will continue to be developed for automobiles. The adaptation of these for truck use is therefore fairly straightforward. It has the disadvantage that gasoline engines are less suited to heavy truck applications because they are less efficient, and produce less torque.

- Clean diesel: It is technically possible to produce a diesel fuel which has acceptable levels of particulate *and* nitrous oxide emissions (see Chapter 5), but at a significantly greater cost.

- Methanol and ethanol: These are alcohol-based fuels. Engines require some modifications to achieve efficient performance, but it is possible, with suitable measures, to achieve acceptable levels of emission. However, these fuels have a much lower energy:mass ratio than petroleum-based fuels, and are expensive to produce. Storage is also expensive, since they are corrosive liquids.

Gas based fuels. These sources have the advantage that they involve little change to engines, and they have good emission characteristics. However, they involve considerable costs in fuel storage and refuelling arrangements, since they involve high-pressure tanks. The options here are:

- Liquid petroleum gas (LPG, or propane): This has long been used as a transport energy source, so there is some experience with it, and a certain infrastructure exists. It can be used in spark-ignition (i.e. gasoline) engines with little modification, and it has better emission properties than gasoline or diesel. Being a petroleum-based fuel, it has the same energy supply disadvantages as gasoline or diesel.

- Compressed natural gas (CNG): From an emissions and fuel supply viewpoint, CNG has major advantages, since it is both clean burning and abundant. Its main disadvantage is the expense of storage (both in bulk and on the vehicle), and refuelling, since it is stored at around 21,000 kPa (3000 psi). Also, it has a low ratio of energy:mass, meaning that a greater mass of it has to be carried and used for a given freight task, so there are productivity (payload) losses.

- Liquified natural gas (LNG): This is the same product as CNG, but is stored in a liquified form, which means very low temperatures (minus 150°C (minus 240° F)). This means very expensive storage facilities on the vehicle and in bulk, and expensive refuelling. However, the liquefied form means that the energy:mass ratio is much higher. Although there is industrial experience with the storage and handling of both CNG and LNG, there is virtually no public infrastructure in place, which must provide a very serious limitation on their early introduction on a widespread basis. Any usage is therefore likely to be limited to local fleets initially.

Electric vehicles. Electric vehicles involve a new technology, in the sense that the engines and energy sources are fundamentally different from existing truck engines. They involve the engine (which is not a major technological challenge since electric powered applications are widespread), the storage medium (i.e. battery), and refuelling. These latter two aspects constitute the main limitations on electric vehicles, since existing battery technology involves substantial weight, limited capacity (i.e. vehicle range), and very time consuming refuelling (i.e. hours, rather than minutes for liquid fuels). However, research is being conducted to attempt to develop practical electric powered vehicles for urban use. In the freight field, their main applications, at least in the short term, would appear to be with central city pick up and delivery operations, or in applications involving frequent stop-start operations, such as mail delivery.

The incentive for the introduction of these energy sources may be economic, in those countries where the tax structure makes such sources more economical than gasoline and diesel, or regulatory requirements in those countries (especially the US) where regulation rather than the market is the preferred mechanism for introducing technological change.

In the longer run, there may be potential for more exotic technologies, especially those involving a greater degree of automation. These might include the use of intelligent vehicle-highway systems (see below), or alternative modes such as pneumatic or vacuum commodity pipelines, freight conveyors, or automatically routed, unstaffed vehicles in their own right of way (e.g. tunnel).

Road system technology

There are a range of emerging developments in the technology of the road system itself. Primarily, these revolve around communication systems and electronic navigation and route guidance systems, but the technology is readily extendible to such applications as electronic log books, real time road pricing (see Chapter 10) and vehicle management. While the hardware and its proposed applications vary, several major research projects under way in the United States, Europe and Japan aim to have such systems operational within a few years (French, 1990).

The generic term for these systems is 'Intelligent Vehicle/Highway Systems' (IVHS). This has been described by Euler (1990) in the following terms:

The essence of IVHS is to make significant improvements in mobility, highway safety and productivity by building transportation systems that draw upon advanced electronic technologies and control software. The term applies to transportation systems that involve integrated applications of advanced surveillance, communications, computer display, and control processes, both in the vehicle and on the highway.

Euler (op cit) went on to describe four categories of IVHS:

Advanced traffic management systems, which activate traffic control and management strategies (such as traffic information, demand management, freeway ramp metering, arterial road traffic signals, and incident response procedures) in real time, based upon area-wide surveillance and detection systems.

Advanced traveller information systems, which provide drivers with real-time information on congestion and alternative routes, navigation and location, and roadway conditions.

Advanced vehicle control systems, which aim to dramatically improve safety and highway capacity by ultimately providing complete control of the driving function and even allowing for external (in-road) energy sources.

Commercial vehicle operations, which aim to improve the productivity, safety and regulation of all commercial vehicle operations, including large trucks, local delivery vehicles, buses, taxis, and emergency vehicles.

The first two of these stand to benefit all classes of vehicle on the road, although since commercial vehicle travel time and reliability of arrival time is probably greater for trucks than most other vehicle categories, these technologies offer special promise to urban goods and service vehicles. The third of the above categories is some time in the future, although extensive research is being conducted to attempt to develop practical automatic vehicle control technologies. Hence, our discussion here will focus on the fourth of the above categories.

Despatching and routing. As noted above, real-time routing and re-direction of trucks in urban areas is common now, especially for those on pick up and delivery rounds. However, this is generally done without detailed knowledge of either current traffic conditions or the exact location of a truck at any point in time. Real time traffic information, perhaps supplemented by a route guidance system, would thus enable faster despatching, more efficient routing, and more timely pick ups and deliveries (US Department of Transportation, 1990, p 9.4). It would doubtless lead to the development of improved despatching techniques, based perhaps on some form of expert system software (Goetschalckz and Taylor, 1987). A study of road freight transport operators in Australia indicated that this real time vehicle identification and location in urban areas was the industry's highest priority need from advance technology (Pearson, 1988, p 22).

Regulation and administration. Amongst the earliest applications of advanced technology are those directed at enhancing regulatory control and reducing industry's costs in complying with regulations. These essentially involve fitting the truck with a transponder which enables automatic vehicle identification (AVI) from roadside or in-pavement detectors. Specific applications include the following:

-   In those jurisdictions where trucks pass through various check points (e.g. state boundaries, international borders), the documentation can be facilitated by electronic surveillance and monitoring. Such documentation might include driver licence validation, safety inspection certification, fuel tax and registration payments, load permit checks, customs and quarantine laws, etc. Full automation of the process could eventually lead to 'transparent borders' (US Department of Transportation, 1990, p 9.6). The well-known HELP (heavy vehicle electronic licence plate) program in the US, with its associated Crescent demonstration project, (involving all western US states between Texas and Washington, as well as British Columbia,

Canada) is directed primarily towards this end (Hill and Davies, 1990).

- Similarly, the monitoring and control of hazardous material movements is enhanced with real time detection. This not only facilitates the movement function per se, but also enables more rapid detection of incidents, and speedier response by emergency service personnel.

- Weigh-in-motion (WIM) technology aims, as its name suggests, to weigh vehicles speedily, and to identify the truck type. WIM facilitates weigh station control (thus assisting industry by speeding up the checking process). It is also being used to provide valuable data on truck axle and gross loads, which is useful for road design and load enforcement purposes. Overloaded vehicles not only cause undue wear and tear on the road, but provide unfair competition to legally loaded vehicles. It is thus in the interests of both the public and private sectors to attempt to control or eliminate overloading.

Positioning and communication. This technology is being rapidly adopted by the road freight industry, especially in the US. It incorporates three aspects: location (the current location of a vehicle is relayed to a central site), navigation (the location of the vehicle is known to the driver) and communications (data and voice transmissions to and from the vehicle) (Garrison and Scapinakis, 1990). Systems in use are formatted to use satellites for vehicle position finding, and mobile cellular telephones for communication. Their main benefits are to long distance trucking operators, and arise from reduced long distance telephone charges, and better truck productivity. There can be improved customer levels of service, especially if these systems are linked to customers' data base systems (electronic data interchange - EDI). There is also potential to link on-board electronic monitoring systems to base computers for such purposes as maintenance scheduling (engine monitoring systems), load control (e.g. refrigerated container temperature monitoring), and driver schedules (US Department of Transportation, 1990, p 9.20).

In-vehicle technologies. Increasingly, archaic monitoring technologies such as tachographs and hubodometers are being replaced by more advanced computer-based systems which monitor not only basic information such as time and speed, but also have the potential to monitor a range of truck parameters (e.g. fuel consumption, engine performance). Potentially, they could be enhanced to monitor driver functions as well, such as fatigue. Given the inadequacy of existing driver log book regulations, some form of 'electronic log book' offers potential to enhance truck driver safety.

Electronic road systems technologies offer a range of potential benefits, including (Pearson, 1988; Garrison and Scapinakis, 1990; Euler, 1990; Grenzeback, Stowers and Boghani, 1988; US Department of Transportation, 1990):

fleet management
- estimating time of arrival
- two way communication with drivers
- enhanced driver and load security
- hazardous vehicle routing
- location of closest vehicle
- historical route and time information
- interface with on-board computer systems

driver management
- monitor driver performance (speeds, fuel consumption, etc)
- check breakdown and unauthorized stops or detours
- controlling overloads

operations
- automatic distance recording
- efficient routing
- credit facilities
- information on potential delays
- engine, drive train and load diagnostics
- electronic data interchange (EDI) between operators and customers

community and government
- assist transport planners with travel information
- crime detection
- reduced cost of regulation
- enhanced and better-targeted enforcement
- lower cost of freight movement

13 Urban freight modelling

Engineers and planners have long used mathematical models to assist in the tasks of estimating demand for travel and the impacts of proposed land use or transport system changes. It is appropriate therefore to consider whether models depicting aspects of the urban freight system are useful, and if so, what form they may take.

It is essential to realise at the outset that models are not a end in themselves. Models will usually be part of the process of estimating future travel demand and impacts, and this may in turn be an important part of a planning process. That process in turn may (or may not) assist in public policy and decision-making. As Meyer and Miller (1984, p 226) correctly point out:

> Analysis is only one component of the planning process, and, in fact, demand estimation is only one component of analysis. Analysis provides input into the planning and decision-making process. As such, it is only of use to the extent that it aids in that process.

In this chapter, we first discuss a possible framework for urban freight modelling, and then examine the form which such models have taken. A review of currently available models is then presented, and the chapter concludes with a discussion of the role and usefulness of these models.

Modelling framework

The modelling framework must reflect the scale and nature of the planning issues concerned and provide relevant input to the decision-making process. As such, it is not possible to be prescriptive about an overall modelling

263

framework. However, it is probably true to say that models of urban freight are likely to be relevant and helpful at a range of levels, including:

- a metropolitan-wide transport systems planning level, the output of which may be used for metropolitan scale planning; perhaps the most common example would be to provide estimates of truck traffic flow as an input to urban transport planning, although recently there has been an interest in planning at this level from the viewpoint of regional economic analysis;

- a sub-regional or corridor level, where again the most common case would be to provide truck traffic flow estimates; and

- a local or site level, concerned essentially with traffic impact analysis; the application here is with design aspects both on-site (e.g. number of loading docks) and on the nearby road system (e.g. intersection design and capacity).

Of these three, the state of the art modelling framework at the local or site level is very simple, involving usually no more that an estimation of truck movements as a function of land use variables. We will return to this later, but for the moment will concentrate on a modelling framework appropriate to metropolitan or corridor analyses of freight and truck movements.

In one of the few discussions of the role of models in such a context, Hedges (1971) suggested that a freight modelling framework should have the following characteristics:

- it should be *behavioral*, in the sense that it would describe the relationships between the specific transport service demanded and the key determinants of demand;

- it should be *multi-modal*, or at least capable of handling more than the truck mode;

- it should include *passenger* as well as goods movements, and show how the two are related (especially where conflicts occur);

- it should show *feedback* effects of changes in policy variables;

264

- it should be *dynamic*, in the sense that it would show the movement from one equilibrium position to another in response to changes in policy variables; and

- it should have *general applicability*, so that it could be applied to urban areas with similar topological, demographic, economic and transport system characteristics.

This is an ambitious prescription, and it would be true to say that no urban freight modelling framework even comes close to meeting it. We will discuss the reasons why this might be so in the conclusion of this chapter.

Many models which have been used in urban freight, as we will see in later, have followed an analogy to passenger demand models. There are however some quite fundamental differences between the movement of people and the movement of goods which may make such analogies unrealistic. These differences include:

The decision-maker: With person movement, the decision-making process is mostly with the person making the trip. With freight transport, it is more likely to be a complex process in which a number of actors are involved, influencing each others decision-making. Chiang, Roberts and Ben-Akiva (1980, p 12) state that 'it is clear that the firm is the basic decision-making unit in freight transportation. However, the role of the firm in selecting freight transport service has not been explored satisfactorily'. Noortman (1984, p 35) illustrates the complex interaction between shipper, receiver and carrier: 'a familiar pattern shows the shipper as the main decision-maker on distribution and mode choice, whereas the receiver's interests find their reflection in the frequency and size of shipments.' Moreover, policy changes by government, which may be quite unrelated to the freight transport system, can have a significant effect upon the amount and composition of urban freight. Such factors as the general level of activity in the national or regional economy, tariffs and currency fluctuations which affect imports and exports, and policies aimed at boosting or suppressing particular industries (e.g. agriculture or building construction) have an indirect effect upon urban freight.

The unit of transport: In passenger transport, the unit concerned (i.e. the individual) does not change throughout the whole decision-making process, i.e. the individual moves from origin to destination at a given time by a given mode and route. In freight transport by contrast, as Noortman (1984, p 32) notes, 'this non-changing unit does not exist. At the starting point of the decision-making process it is the commodity flow on a yearly basis which forms the subject of decision-making, followed by the forming of shipments as the next relevant units and resulting in vehicle trips within a specific transport system.'

Delivery patterns: Many urban pickup and delivery operations involve very circuitous routing and a multitude of origins and destinations. Southworth (1982, p 190) notes that 'the major problem facing the analyst is to find a way to estimate zone-to-zone commodity flows, or their equivalent in truck trips, while taking account of the highly circuitous multi-destination nature of most urban pickup and delivery services.' Sonntag (1985) and Pitfield (1978) have made similar points.

Animate vs inanimate objects: People are animate objects, and can therefore be relied upon to make certain decisions for themselves, which the modeller may not need to consider. For example, a passenger trip may end (for modelling purposes) at a car park, a transit stop, or a 'zone'. By contrast, a piece of freight must be handled by mechanical or manual means every time it moves from the very point of origin to the final destination. Thus, for example, the availability of a crane, fork lift or container receival facilities at a site may have a major influence on the freight transport decision-making process.

Demand factors: While all travel is a derived demand, it is especially so that in goods transport the amount of freight generated and the types of commodities which are moved vary with the needs, desires and fashions of an urban community, and are a complex function of social, economic and technological forces (see Chapter 3). Moreover, urban freight may be affected by conditions in areas quite remote from the urban area under consideration; e.g. import and export flows may be dependent upon social or economic conditions in markets or supply centres for those goods.

Relationship of demand to independent variables: Commonly, models of person movement relate trip generation to a range of independent variables representing land use factors at the origin or destination. This is less likely to be valid in the case of goods movement. Technological change over time may result in such changes as higher labor productivity (so that the amount of freight generated per worker in an industry increases), and larger trucks (so that a given freight task can potentially be handled by fewer truck trips). Structural economic changes have seen a clear move towards service industries, and towards consumption of higher value but lower mass products. Both of these trends cause smaller amounts of freight per employee, so that a model based upon (say) number of workers would likely not be very robust.

The model builder's task when faced with these complexities is a formidable one. None of these items are readily incorporated into a model (at least not one structured like a model of person movement), nor are they capable of being independently predicted with any degree of precision.

Moreover, some of the independent land use variables do not respond quickly to changes in these more fundamental variables. Land area, floor area and population may change in response to factors such as lifestyle and economic conditions, but only over a fairly long period of time. On the other hand, tariffs, the state of the economy, and government support for particular sectors may change abruptly. A model based upon variables such as floor area could not predict changes in commodity flow or truck trip generation which resulted from changes in these more fundamental factors.

Thus a model which expressed, say, the amount of goods movement as a function of land use variables has only a limited applicability, especially in a forecasting sense. It has some use however in analysing the contributions which various components of the economy make to freight generation at a given point in time, and for this reason is a tool for which the transport analyst may have a use. Models of this general type have been developed in several places, and are reviewed below. They typically relate truck trip generation on an areal, industry-wide or site basis to measurable variables describing the area, industry or site respectively.

In summary, while there are good reasons why a framework for modelling urban freight activities should be different from that for modelling person movements, in practice most urban freight modelling is based upon analogies with urban passenger modelling.

Categories of urban freight model

In general, existing urban freight models of relevance to the engineer or planner may be categorized into two main groups, as follows:

- *Commodity-based models.* These are based upon the notion that since the freight system is basically concerned with the movement of commodities, the movement of these should be modelled directly. The state of the art for *urban* freight models of this type is based upon a sequential modelling approach (generation, distribution, modal split, assignment). However, an alternative is to use a direct estimation approach which truncates the stages of generation, distribution and modal split into a single step. In either case, truck trips are then derived from commodity movements via a vehicle loading model, or equivalent, and the output of the model is the assignment of truck trips to the road network.

- *Truck trip-based models.* These estimate truck trip activity directly. Three sub-categories may be identified: a sequential modelling approach and a direct estimation approach, similar to those described above for commodity-based models, and a 'truck traffic generation' approach which merely estimates the number of truck trips generated by a site or area. This third approach would suffice for the local or site application mentioned above.

Within each group, there are a range of specific models or stages, as outlined diagrammatically in Figures 13.1 and 13.2. It should be noted that these figures are deliberately kept simple, and represent only those models concerned directly and explicitly with truck trips and/or commodity flows. Obviously, these models need to be considered and applied within a wider modelling framework that would, for example, provide inputs of such parameters as travel times, and would integrate the outputs with the outputs of other stages of the modelling process (e.g. add assigned truck trip volumes to car trip volumes to get total link volumes). Examples of how truck-related models may be incorporated in a wider modelling framework are given in Meyburg and Stopher (1974), Zavattero (1976), and Southworth, et al (1983).

Both categories of model have their place. Commodity-based models recognise that fundamentally the demand for the freight is for the movement of commodities, not the movement of vehicles. Producers and consumers of goods in a region create a demand for commodity movement, and the movement of vehicles merely represents the supply-side response to that demand (see Chapter 3). On the other hand, truck trips are of direct interest in themselves because many of the costs and problems of urban freight result from the presence of trucks on the road system. Thus, the different modelling approaches result from differing policy and planning issues, and to an extent from differing conceptual frameworks. (However, it should be noted that recent work by Bowyer (1991), based upon the conceptual framework of Harker (1987) and the modelling process of Roberts and Kullman (1979) has postulated an approach which attempts to integrate these two streams.)

The following sections consider both of these groups, firstly defining what is meant by each of the terms used in Figure 13.1 and 13.2 respectively, and then going on to review models which have been actually been developed in each of the various categories.

Commodity-based models

Commodity generation

Commodity-based models, as discussed above, are predicated on the fact that the freight system is essentially concerned with the movement of goods, not vehicles, and therefore an attempt to understand and model freight must commence with a study of commodities - their generation (by site or firm, etc), markets (by land use, location, etc), and logistics management (warehousing, transport, mode use, etc). It is probably true to say that no urban[1] transport modelling packages have developed this notion with any degree of sophistication, but there have been some attempts to model the generation and distribution of urban commodities, as distinct from urban truck trips.

Two examples of urban commodity generation models are presented below:

Watson (1975) examined commodity generation in terms of *shipments*. Using data collected at 12 manufacturing plants in Chicago, USA, models were developed at three levels of sophistication, a simple uni-variate model, models based upon the sub-components of employment and floorspace, and log-linear relationships (op cit, p 65). The best results were obtained from a simple floorspace model:

Total shipments per plant per week =
13.97 + 0.044 (total floorspace per plant in square feet)

$(R^2 = 0.88)$

269

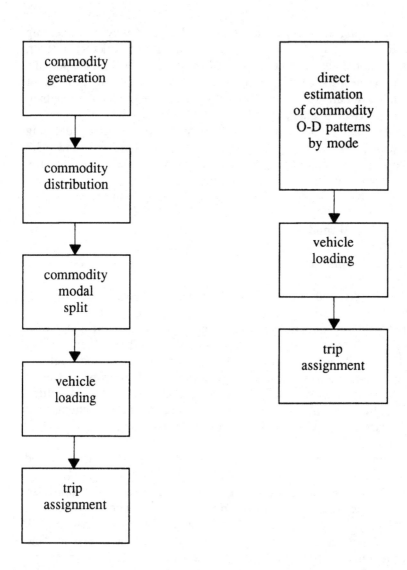

Figure 13.1 Commodity based models

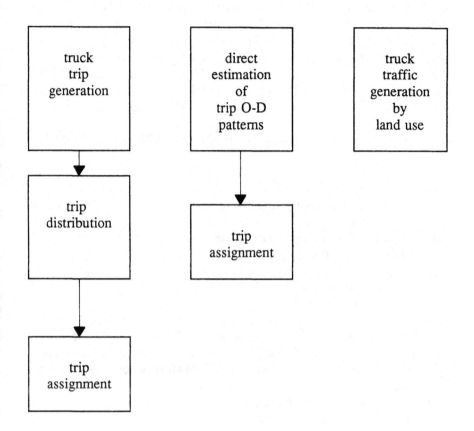

Figure 13.2 Truck trip based models

Ogden (1977a) using data on commodity generation (in tonnes) for Melbourne, Australia, developed a series of models for the *mass of commodity groups attracted to or produced by a zone*, in terms of zonal land use variables. His models were as follows (R^2 values shown in parentheses):

271

food and agriculture	$Y = -391 + 0.0894\ X_2 + 0.0158\ X_9$	(0.65)
building materials	$Y = 333 + 0.0957\ X_4 + 0.138\ X_8$	(0.44)
manufactured products	$Y = -731 + 0.0798\ X_2 + 0.146\ X_4$	(0.67)
petroleum products	$Y = 30.5 + 0.0163\ X_2 + 0.00202\ X_8$	(0.46)
waste	$Y = -191 + 0.0450\ X_2 + 0.0214\ X_9$	(0.58)
other commodities	$Y = -173 + 0.0704\ X_2$	(0.84)
all commodities	$Y = -1417 + 0.467\ X_2 + 0.0317\ X_8$	(0.68)
	or	
	$Y = -749 - 0.224\ X_1 + 0.726\ X_2$	(0.84)

where

Y = tonnes of commodity attracted to zone (in the case of waste, mass produced by zone)
X_1 = white collar employment in zone
X_2 = blue collar employment in zone
X_4 = manufacturing employment in zone
X_8 = population in zone
X_9 = number of households in zone

Noortman (1984, p 35) in a review of modelling approaches to urban goods movement concluded that goods production and attraction models 'can best be expressed in tons, with a breakdown by categories of goods that are relevant from the point of view of the transport activities.' He suggested that for retail activities, floorspace and number of employees were appropriate independent variables, while for industrial activities, the number of employees may be preferred. However, he cautioned that in this case, for long term planning purposes, it is necessary to introduce assumptions concerning development of labor productivity. For activities high in the chain of production, he suggested that 'the least complicated way to estimate the production volume ... will probably be by using the potential output capacity the plant has been designed for, plus an assumption of the degree of utilization.'

Noortman did not develop models as such, but suggested that a linear regression model relating the mass of a commodity attracted to and produced by a zone as a function of zonal variables (c.f. Ogden's model described above) would suffice, with perhaps the need to introduce zonal accessibility measures (undefined) 'in case these (accessibility) differences have an influence on the level of the inputs and outputs'.

It must be recognised however that any zonal model will likely not reflect a wide variation in commodity generation of individual sites within the zone. For example, Hutchinson (1974) has quoted data for the Province of Ontario, Canada, which shows the number of input tons per employee varying by several orders of magnitude across different manufacturing industries. Similarly, Chatterjee, et al (1979) have shown that there are considerable differences between urban areas in truck trip generation rates as a function of land use.

Commodity distribution

A commodity distribution model would take the commodity attraction and production estimates produced in the commodity generation phase, and link origins to destinations. In fact, very few models of this sort have actually been developed at the urban level, probably because of lack of commodity flow data to calibrate the models.

Ogden (1978), using data on inter-zonal commodity flows in Melbourne, Australia, developed gravity models for the distribution of commodities between zones. His model was a singly-constrained gravity model, constrained at the destination zone, not the origin zone. Ogden's reasoning here was that since the movement of goods is determined by the demand for commodities, it is more meaningful to consider a customer or receiver of goods examining alternative supply points, or origins. By contrast, with passenger movements, it is reasonable to consider a traveller at an origin considering alternative destination points, and thus the usual gravity model approach of an origin-constrained model is appropriate. Winston (1981) also supports the view that the receiver is usually the controlling influence, and this should be reflected in the modelling framework.

Ogden's model used airline distance between origin and destination as a measure of separation, on the grounds that for many commodity movements, neither travel time nor road distance was valid, because of the circuitous truck trip routing adopted by urban pick up and delivery trucks. His model was therefore:

$$Q_{ijk} = \frac{O_{ik}D_{jk}d_{ij}^{-b}}{\Sigma_i(O_{ik}di j^{-b})}$$

where

Q_{ijk} = tonnes of commodity k moved from origin zone i to destination zone j

O_{ik} = total production of commodity k in zone i (tonnes)

D_{jk} = total attraction of commodity k to zone j (tonnes)

d_{ij} = airline distance between zone i and zone j

b = calibration constant.

The calibration constant, b, for various commodity groups was as follows:

all commodities	1.1
petroleum	0.6
building materials	1.1
manufactured products	0.7
food and agricultural products	0.9
other products	1.4
waste	2.1

Zavattero (1976) presented a commodity distribution model structure based upon a gravity-type formulation for Chicago, USA, but apparently this model was not developed, as subsequent work emanating from the Chicago Area Transportation Study (see below) is based upon truck trip distribution models.

Gravity models of commodity distribution have also been used for inter-regional analyses. For example, Chisholm and O'Sullivan (1973) used such a formulation to model the distribution of commodities carried by road in Britain, while Black (1972) performed a similar analysis of inter-regional commodity flows in the US.

Noortman (1984, p 38) was not enthusiastic about the use of gravity models to determine commodity distribution. He argued that 'if there are several origins and destinations in an urban area belonging to the same links of the same chains of production (a situation rather familiar to the wholesale and retail trades) it seems questionable whether the interdependencies of the various locations can be determined using the distance of the generalized transport costs as a resistance factor.' He argued that other factors, such as level of service, need to be considered, and that for some commodities, where transport costs are averaged by the shipper, transport cost may be irrelevant.

While these arguments are valid at the level of an individual firm, they may be less valid at an aggregate level, where it is clear, especially for goods where transport costs are a significant proportion of the value of the product, that distance (or cost) is an impedance function.

Both Ogden (1978) and Noortman (1984) make the point that where there is a large commodity flow from a fixed origin to a fixed destination this can be analysed directly, without recourse to a model. Examples might be the flow of coal into a steel mill, or an export commodity from a processing plant to a port facility.

Commodity modal split

While in principle the distribution of commodity flows within an urban area may be allocated amongst various modes of transport, in practice this stage is rarely if ever modelled. The reason is a simple one: the commodities in which the transport planner or traffic engineer is interested all move by road in most cities. While it is certainly true that many urban commodities move by other modes (e.g. water, waste water, petroleum products by pipeline; specific commodities by barge in some cities), these movements are so explicit and so specific that, for practical purposes, it is not necessary or helpful to model them. Of course, in a research environment, or an attempt to develop a deeper understanding of the relative merits of alternative modes, a model of intra-urban commodity modal split could be quite valid. However, for most cities, it is not necessary or relevant to the planning and policy needs of engineers and planners.

It is interesting that the strongest arguments against this approach have come from Europeans. For example, Button and Pearman (1981, p 103) argue that a modal split model should be included for two reasons - first, that a modal split model could consider different truck types as effectively different modes, and second that 'a considerable number of trips to and from other urban areas, but commencing or ending in the city, are by other modes.' Noortman (1984, p 40) makes similar points. However, it is valid to argue that in a European context, the distinction between intra-urban goods movement (which is the subject of this book) and inter-urban goods movement is less clear, or even irrelevant. Because of the smaller size of the nations, the closer spacing of the cities, and the ability to serve one city from a nearby city, the notion of 'urban' goods movement, which is quite meaningful in, say, America, Canada, or Australia, is not relevant in Europe. In this sense then, Button and Pearman, and Noortman are quite

275

right, but in the context adopted here, their call for modal split to be modelled explicitly should be directed towards inter-urban commodity flows. As for Button and Pearman's point about the need to differentiate between different truck types, it could be argued that this is better (or at least satisfactorily) picked up by a vehicle loading model (see below).

Although beyond the scope of this book, it may be pointed out that there are a number of models of inter-urban commodity mode split, for example Chiang, Roberts and Ben-Akiva (1980), Young, et al (1982), Gray (1982), Friesz and Tobin (eds) (1983), Harker (1985; 1987), and Jeffs and Hills (1990).

Vehicle loading

Notionally, once commodity flows between origins and destinations have been determined (by mode if need be), the conversion to truck trip origin-destination patterns requires a vehicle loading model of some sort. As Noortman (1984, p 42) has put it, 'with the help of this sub-model the goods volumes transported between certain origins and destinations, in number of tons, per mode of transport and per transport system, are converted into number of movements by type of transportation with a given loading capacity.'

For some industries and commodities, the vehicle loading model will correspond essentially to the load capacity of the vehicles serving that industry. This is especially so in the case of bulk products such as sand and rock, bulk cement, petroleum, etc. However, for many urban products, especially urban pick up and delivery operations, vehicle loading is quite complex, and may bear little relationship to the vehicle capacity.

There has been very little empirical work on vehicle loading models, despite their importance in a commodity-based modelling framework (Meyburg and Stopher, 1974; Zavattero, 1976; Noortman, 1984, for example, all describe the purpose of such a model, but do not develop one nor outline it's possible form.) The only known vehicle loading model for application in an urban context was that developed by Watson (1975), and his work was more experimental (i.e. exploring relationships) than an attempt to develop a working model. Moreover, it was based upon observations at only two firms, both in Chicago. He concluded that 'the results on the shipment truck models are not altogether satisfactory, in the sense that no clear-cut relationships between shipment and truck characteristics emerges from the analysis. Nevertheless, there are indications that weight and volume adequately characterize a shipment, and that this combination is correlated with the truck type and capacity variables .... these preliminary results lead us to believe that there is some basis for believing (sic) that a sufficiently stable relationship exists between shipment and truck characteristics to justify attempts to build a 'loading' model to assign shipments to trucks' (op cit, p 82).

Noortman (1984, p 42), commenting on this result, noted that 'because of the importance ... of factors like the physical distribution system, the transport system, and the degree of spatial concentration of origins and destinations, it will be understood that attempts to make a direct link between the size of the shipment ... and the type and loading capacity of the goods vehicles used were not encouraging.'

Button and Pearman (1981, p 107) suggested that a vehicle loading model should not be based upon existing usage rates and consignment mixes, but ideally should allow for:

- the availability, by capacity, of vehicles;

- the nature of the consignments;

- the proportion of vehicle capacity required by each consignment and the aggregate volume of consignments by each shipper in a specified time period;

- the ability to hold up shipments until a full load is achieved; and

- the characteristics of the desired pick up and delivery patterns of vehicles.

It is probably the inadequacy of the vehicle loading model, and the difficulty of relating commodity origin-destination information to truck trip information (especially for multiple-stop pick up and delivery trips) that has prevented the more widespread adoption of commodity-based models. This issue is taken up in the conclusion to this chapter.

Trip assignment

Assuming that the item of interest is an estimate of the number of vehicles using a road network, the assignment of truck trips (based upon origin-destination truck trip matrices determined either from commodity origin-destination patterns, or estimated directly as truck trips) is relatively straightforward. There are widely used trip assignment models which are capable of doing this. However, most of these involve feedback between assigned volumes on a link and the travel 'cost' (e.g. travel time) on that link. This can only be done after *all* vehicle trips using that link have been estimated, and it follows therefore that truck trip assignment needs to be done in conjunction with the assignment of passenger car trips, etc. Thus, as explained previously, the set of models described in Figures 13.1 and 13.2 must be sub-sets of a wider package encompassing other aspects of the urban transport system.

Trip assignment models are described in any text on urban transport system modelling (e.g. Meyer and Miller, 1984, p 254 ff). It is relevant to note that the networks available for cars and trucks may not be identical, due to restrictions on truck usage of some links because of either physical restraints (e.g. low overhead clearances), or regulatory considerations such as truck bans. The modelling procedures should reflect these restrictions. Reilly and Hochmuth (1990) report a case where this was done in Chicago, USA. In this case, there were significant differences in the modelled performance of an unrestricted network (i.e. identical networks for trucks and cars), and a network which incorporated restrictions on truck movements on specific links (reflecting both physical impediments and regulatory controls). Modelled travel times on the restricted network were 10 percent higher, and modelled vehicle kilometres (miles) of travel were 1.4 percent higher.

Direct estimation of commodity origin-destination patterns by mode

Direct estimation methods attempt to include in a single model the stages of generation, modal split and assignment which are usually considered sequentially. Models of this type have been developed for inter-regional freight flow, but not for urban freight flow. For example, Roberts and Kullman (1979, p 563) developed the following multi-nominal logit function:

$$p^k(i,mq/ALTS) = \frac{e^{U(T,C,M,R)}}{\Sigma\, e^{U(T,C,M,R)}}$$

where

p　　= probability of choosing a particular combination (i, mq)
U(T,C,M,R) =　the utility function of the receiver
k　　= commodity index
i　　= supply (origin) point
mq　　= mode/shipment size combination
ALTS = alternatives available to the receiver
U　　= utility function
T　　= transport attributes
C　　= commodity attributes
M　　= market attributes
R　　= receiver attributes

They suggested the following as relevant variables forming the vectors of attributes:

Transport attributes:

W = waiting time (days)
T = transit time (days)
R = reliability (days)
L = loss and damage (unitless, $0 \leq L \leq 1$)
S = freight rate ($/lb) ($/kg)
C = special charges ($/lb) ($/kg)

Market attributes:

P = relative price (unitless)
O = ownership (binary 0-1)

Commodity attributes:

V = value ($/lb) ($/kg)
D = density (lb/ft^3) (kg/m^3)
S = shelf life (days)

Receiver attributes:

A = annual use rate (lb/y) (kg/y)
M = mixed order (unitless, $0 \leq M \leq 1$)
S = seasonal purchase (unitless, $0 \leq S \leq 1$)
Q = shipment rate (lb) (kg)

Harker (1985) presents a good review of inter-urban freight modelling. Because these models have not been applied to intra-urban freight[2], they will not be considered further here.

It is worth mentioning also at this point a conceptual approach to freight analysis based upon direct estimation, namely an adaptation of the input-output formulation. This is in effect a sensitivity model, wherein the effect of a change in one sector of the economy upon other sectors can be estimated. Early researchers in urban goods movement (e.g. Hutchinson, 1974; Goss, et al, 1967) held some hope that this approach would be useful for urban goods movement analyses, but little has come of it. Probably the main reason for this is that the data base which would enable the interactions to be linked and modelled exists in only a very few urban areas. For example, Ogden (1977b, p 235) used an input-output formulation in which the entries in the input-output table were tonnes moved between land uses in Melbourne, Australia (not dollar flows between economic sectors as in the classic input-output formulation). Conventional input-output analysis develops a set of 'technical coefficients', as the amount of input ($) required from each economic sector to produce an extra $1 worth of output in a given sector (Miernyk, 1967). Using the same matrix algebra, Ogden was able to calculate the direct and indirect effects of a unit change in the final demand for the products of each land use. His results were as follows (e.g. a one tonne increase in the demand for products of timber and furniture manufacturing land uses would generate a total additional freight flow in the urban transport network of 1.60 tonnes):

timber and furniture manufacture	1.60
brick, pottery, glass and cement manufacture	1.22
metal and metal fabrication	1.99
machinery and motor vehicle manufacture	1.76
food, drink and tobacco processing	2.03
textiles, clothing and footwear manufacture	2.33
paper and paper product processing	1.67
chemical processing	1.80

petroleum and coal processing	1.08
other manufacturers	1.62
food stores	2.61
retail stores not otherwise specified	2.19
service stations and repair shops	2.24
wholesalers - durable	1.63
wholesalers - non-durable	1.72
storage and junk facilities	1.37

Truck trip-based models

Truck trip generation

Truck trip generation models considered here are those which use independent variables aggregated to a zonal level, and which give as output the number of truck trips attracted or produced for that zone. (Truck trips attracted on a site basis are considered below, under truck traffic generation by land use). It is important to note at the outset that models formulated in this way are unlikely to capture the variance in trip generation characteristics of individual sites, firms, or industries *within* a zone (Slavin, 1976; Button and Pearman, 1981, p 87). They are in fact useful only for the purpose for which they have been developed, namely providing zonal estimates. They should not be used to estimate truck traffic generation characteristics of specific sites.

That having been said, it is also noteworthy that probably more attention has been given to the development of models of this form than of any other. All are based upon least squares estimation using zonal variables, as indeed are most models of urban person trip generation (see for example Meyer and Miller, 1984, p 246 ff). Some of the important and typical models are reviewed below:

Chicago. In the Chicago Area Transportation Study, a battery of truck trip generation models were developed (Zavattero and Weseman, 1981). These showed *zonal truck trips by truck type and land use, as a function of zonal land use variables.* A total of 35 models were developed.

Although the Chicago Area Transportation Study developed these models, and had the data base to do so, it did not actually use these models in its travel forecasting process (Habib, 1983, p 4). Instead, it used a simple relationship showing *zonal truck trips by truck type and land use, as a function of zonal person trips.* This is an interesting approach, entirely empirical (since there is no theoretical relationship between truck trips and person trips), but easily incorporated into the modelling process. The results, in commercial vehicle trips per 1,000 person trips, were as shown in Table 13.1.

Table 13.1
Relationship between truck trips and person trips, Chicago

Destination land use	Commercial vehicle trips per thousand added person trips		
	Light trucks	Medium trucks	Heavy trucks
residential	20.8	26.7	0.2
manufacturing	35.8	65.0	28.9
retail	27.0	34.8	4.8
public buildings	9.9	10.8	1.2
public open space	4.3	5.5	0.6
transport, communications, utilities and warehouses	94.1	170.1	93.2
service	36.1	31.6	6.7
other	369.9	346.6	97.6

Source: Habib (1983), p 4

Vancouver. Swan Wooster (1979, p 5-23), in a major study for Transport Canada and the City of Vancouver, Canada, developed an urban truck modelling package for that city. In the course of the study, several truck trip generation models were developed, the most comprehensive of which expressed *zonal truck trips by truck type as a function of zonal employment*. Their models were as follows (with R^2 values in parentheses):

a. Gross vehicle mass $\leq$ 8,000 lb (3.6 t)

(i) Production:

$$T_1 = -17.94 + 1.29X_1 + 1.24X_2 + 1.15X_3 + .90X_4 + 2.00X_6 \quad (0.93)$$

(ii) Attraction:

$$T_j = 6.59 + 1.54X_1 + 1.05X_2 + .87X_3 + .990X_4 + 1.01X_6 \quad (0.99)$$

b. Gross vehicle mass 8,001 to 32,000 lb (3.6 to 14.5 t)

(i) Production:

$$T_i = 12.19 + .94X_1 + 1.98X_2 + 1.30X_3 + .05X_5 + 1.71X_6 \quad (0.96)$$

(ii) Attraction:

$$T_j = 49.85 + 1.01X_1 + .15X_4 + 6.28X_5 + 1.95X_6 \quad (0.85)$$

c. Gross vehicle mass > 32,000 lb (14.5 t)

(i) Production:

$$T_i = 10.47 + 1.35X_1 + 5.63X_2 + .81X_3 + .29X_6 \quad (0.84)$$

(ii) Attraction:

$$T_j = 9.40 + 1.20X_1 + .71X_2 + .85X_3 + 3.94X_4 + 1.08X_6 \quad (0.88)$$

where

X_1 = manufacturing/warehousing/major repairs
X_2 = utilities/transport/communication
X_3 = automotive/wholesale/outdoor retail
X_4 = motels/hotels/miscellaneous commercial
X_5 = retail/personal service/indoor commercial
X_6 = transport terminals

Melbourne. Ogden (1977a), using data for Melbourne, Australia, developed a series of models of *zonal truck trips by trip purpose as a function of zonal land use variables.* The models were as follows (R^2 values shown in parentheses):

home base	$Y = 119 + 0.143X_2 + 0.0199X_8$	(0.87)
pick-up	$Y = 1.49 + 0.106X_2 + 0.0280X_9$	(0.91)
retail delivery	$Y = -72.3 + 0.00945X_3 +$ $0.0832X_5 + 0.0339X_8$	(0.66)
wholesale delivery	$Y = 783 + 0.102X_2 + 0.160X_6$	(0.83)
maintenance repair and employer's business	$Y = 84.4 + 0.00387X_1 +$ $0.0810X_2 + 0.0759X_{10}$	(0.92)
personal trips	$Y = 222 + 0.0320X_4 + 0.0138X_8$	(0.73)
industrial delivery, construction and trans-shipment	$Y = 95.9 + 0.0730X_2 + 0.0824X_4$	(0.86)
all trips	$Y = 576 + 0.635X_2 + 0.104X_9$	(0.95)

where Y = number of trips in category shown produced in a particular zone.

home base	$Y = 397 + 0.0857X_2 + 0.113X_{11}$	(0.84)
pick-up	$Y = -51.4 + 0.125X_2 +$ $0.0179X_9$	(0.87)
retail delivery	$Y = -69.4 + 0.020X_1 +$ $0.0363X_8$	(0.65)
wholesale delivery	$Y = 643 + 0.0761X_2 + 0.477X_5$	(0.87)
maintenance repair and employer's business	$Y = 84.7 + 0.0162X_1 + 0.0688X_2$ $+ 0.0782X_{10}$	(0.94)
personal trips	$Y = 165 + 0.0556X_4 + 0.0116X_8$	(0.76)
industrial delivery, construction and trans- shipment	$Y = -423 + 0.114X_2 + 0.0502X_4$ $+ 0.00695X_8$	(0.71)
all trips	$Y = 589 + 0.635X_2 + 0.104X_8$	(0.95)

where

Y = number of trips in category shown attracted to a particular zone
X_1 = white-collar employment in zone
X_2 = blue-collar employment in zone
X_3 = total employment in zone
X_4 = manufacturing employment in zone
X_5 = retail sale employment in zone

X_6 = wholesale employment in zone
X_7 = retail sales (\$) in zone
X_8 = population in zone
X_9 = number of households in zone
X_{10} = white-collar resident labour force in zone
X_{11} = blue-collar resident labour force in zone
X_{12} = total resident labour force in zone

Boston. Slavin (1976) in what is still a very cogent review of the state of the art in urban truck trip modelling, discussed the difficulties and theoretical problems associated with the use of aggregate zonal models. He pointed out that they typically:

- have little theoretical justification for either the explanatory variables or the functional form of the relationship;

- as a result, many lack important variables such as transport cost or measures of freight activity;

- fail to satisfy the assumptions which underlie least squares regression; and

- often do not take sufficient account of the fact that urban truck trips are organised in routes which composed of multiple numbers of trips.

Slavin then went on to develop a model, using data from Boston, USA, which he claimed was 'vastly superior to previous versions in terms of theoretical consistency, the degree of explanation obtained, and conformance to ordinary least squares assumptions.' Since the total number of trips attracted to a zone equals the total number produced, he used trip ends (attractions plus productions) as the dependent variable, and his model estimated *truck trip end density per zone as a function of zonal employment and population, together with a measure of accessibility*. His model was:

$$T/A = 1.41 + 0.45E_1/A + 0.91E_2/A + 0.29E_3/A + 6.63E_4/A + 0.07E_5/A + 0.20P/A - 4.7R + 90.8(1/C)$$

where

T = trip ends
E_1 = employment in manufacturing
E_2 = employment in wholesale trade
E_3 = employment in retail trade
E_4 = employment in motor freight transport and warehousing
E_5 = employment in all sectors other than those above
P = population
R = ratio of heavy vehicle trip ends to total trip ends
A = area
C = travel time to the centre of the region in minutes

These examples serve to illustrate the work on urban truck trip generation which has been undertaken to date. Each model is to a large extent unique to the urban area for which it has been calibrated, so that the results are not transferable. However, it is probably true to say that urban truck trip generation has been found to be related to such aggregate variables as employment and land area in relevant categories, and that there appears to be merit in stratifying truck trips by vehicle type. Further discussion of other models of urban truck trip generation is included in Meyburg (1976) who reviews some earlier models, Brogan (1980) who discusses the development of truck trip generation models for a number of small cities in America, Black (1978) who reviews some early truck trip models used in Australian cities, Schwerdtfeger (1978, 1982) who describes models developed in Germany, and Hutchinson (1974) who describes an early model developed in Toronto, Canada.

Truck trip distribution

In urban person trip distribution modelling, the use of the gravity model is now virtually universal (see for example Meyer and Miller, 1984, p 250 ff). This model indicates that the number of trips between two zones, i and j, is directly proportional to the total trip production in i, the total trip attraction in j, and inversely proportional to some measure of the separation, or 'travel cost' between i and j.

In those urban areas which have incorporated truck trips explicitly into their forecasting framework, the approach has generally been to use a gravity model. Vancouver is typical (Swan Wooster, 1979, p 5-50), where three gravity models were calibrated, one for each truck type (defined by gross vehicle mass - see discussion on trip generation above).

A number of researchers have examined the use of various gravity model and intervening opportunities models for their applicability to urban truck trip distribution. These studies will not be reviewed in detail here, but see Southworth (1982) for a study which attempted to incorporate truck route circuity into a gravity model formulation for Chicago, USA; Ogden (1978) for a gravity model analysis of truck trip distribution for various trip purposes in Melbourne, Australia, Meyburg (1976) for a review of some early gravity model experiments, and Button and Pearman (1981, p 96) for a description of British work in the 1970s. The use of an intervening opportunities model for estimating urban truck trip distribution has been investigated by Ogden (1977b) and Swan Wooster (1979).

Direct estimation of truck trip origin-destination patterns

Direct demand models link the modelling stages of generation and distribution on the assumption that the two decisions are made simultaneously, so that truck trip generation is related not only to features at the trip end, but also to some measure of the 'cost' of transporting it to the destination.

Slavin (1976) developed a model of this sort for urban truck trips made by light trucks serving food manufacturers in Boston, USA. His model was:

$$\ln(T_{ij}/A_iA_j) = -10.7 + 0.41 \ln [(R_i/A_i)(R_j/A_j)] + 0.31 \ln [(P_i/A_i)(P_j/A_j)]$$
$$- 1.2 \ln (t_{ij})$$

where

T_{ij} = trips between zones i and j
A_i = area of zone i
R_i = retail food employment (shops and restaurants) in zone i
P_i = residential population of zone i; and
t_{ij} = travel time in minutes between zones i and j

Slavin commented that this model 'illustrates that the supply of transport as represented by a function of travel times between zones substantially affects the generation and distribution of urban truck trips. This is consistent with the hypothesis that the distribution of goods vehicle trips is strongly determined by route choice behaviour.'

Although Slavin's study was extremely limited, it is worthy of mention as it represents a theoretically sound and intellectually appealing approach to urban truck trip generation and distribution modelling. If therefore models are to play a useful role in urban goods movement planning at a regional or metropolitan scale, a model of this sort may be well worth pursuing. The question of the role and value of such modelling is taken up in the conclusion to this chapter.

Dumble (1979) developed a set of direct demand models for truck trips, for 11 trip purposes, using data for Melbourne, Australia. He too found that the use of zonal density measures (e.g. employment density) gave superior results to models based on aggregate zonal variables.

Truck trip generation by land use or industry

This final category of truck trip model is concerned with estimating the number of truck trips associated with a specific site or area. In practice, this is a very common application in such instances as planning site access, determining the number of loading docks or bays, and generally providing facilities for trucks at new industrial, commercial or retail sites. The level of sophistication of the models used is generally quite low, often based upon an assumption about the number of truck trips generated per unit site or floor area.

Models here are of two main types, either simple measures of truck traffic generation, as just mentioned, or models relating truck traffic generation to some measure or measures of site activity, such as employment. (In the latter case, the models may look quite similar to those developed for truck trip generation at a zonal level, and indeed if all relevant sites in an area were considered as a single 'zone', the models could be identical.)

Some examples of both approaches are given below.

Chicago. Zavattero and Weseman (1981) have presented information on truck trips in Chicago, USA, which show, at an aggregate level, the average number of commercial trip ends per unit site area of land in various categories. Their results are shown in Table 13.2.

Site area is not however a particularly useful measure, as it takes no account of intensity of use (e.g. multi-storey buildings; vacant land, etc), and most other studies have attempted to reflect this.

Table 13.2
Commercial vehicle trip ends by land use, Chicago

Land use	Commercial vehicle trips	
	per Ha	per acre
residential	0.3	0.012
manufacturing	8.9	3.61
commercial	35.2	14.25
public building	1.0	0.40
public open space	0.1	0.03
transport, communication, utilities	2.9	1.16
other	0.4	0.15
all developed land	3.2	1.30

Source: Zavaterro and Weseman, 1981

Washington, DC. Spielberg and Smith (1981), in a study of office and service buildings in Washington, DC, recommended the following planning guidelines for US federal office facilities:

- 0.013 truck trips per day per employee;
- 25 percent of trucks in the peak hour (mid morning); and
- 30 minute mean duration.

Australia. TTM Consulting (1989) have presented guidelines, based upon Australian experience, for typical truck traffic generation rates by land use, differentiating between different classes of vehicle. Their results are shown in Table 13.3.

Traffic generation results presented in this way are of course quite common in the case of planning guidelines for urban car traffic generation. However, it is interesting that the standard reference in this area in the US, produced by the Institute of Transportation Engineers (1987) hardly mentions truck traffic at all. In fact, the only mention found in the 4th edition's 1372 pages was on page 79, where for truck terminals it was noted that observations at one terminal found that 70.4 percent of traffic was truck traffic, while at another, it was 34.3 percent.

Table 13.3
Trip generation rates by land use, Australia

Development type	In-bound vehicles per hectare (floor area) per day*				
	Cars	Courier vans	Light rigid trucks	Heavy rigid trucks	Articulated trucks
Offices	500	100	20	0	10
Retailing					
regional centre	2000	20	50	30	5
major supermarket	5000	10	20	20	10
local supermarket	4000	5	50	25	10
department store	2500	10	25	50	5
other	2000	40	50	20	0
Manufacturing	500	5	5	5	10
Warehouse	200	5	1	10	10
Light industry & high technology	500	100	30	25	5
Truck depots	200	50	50	75	200

* to convert to trips per acre, divide these values by 2.47

Source: TTM Consulting, 1989

Britain. Bartlett and Newton (1982) have reported the results of study conducted in Britain, in which a number of analyses of truck traffic generation were performed. One set of results is presented in Table 13.4; this is the mean number of truck trips per site (WT), expressed as a rate per unit employment (TE), per unit site area (SA), and per unit gross floor area (GFA) respectively (areas measured in hectares).

Table 13.4
Truck trip generation by industry, Britain

Category of firm	Mean WT/TE	Mean WT/SA	Mean WT/GFA
manufacturing	2.80	603	779
service	4.14	838	1270
construction	9.62	1740	4047
wholesale/retail/dealer	13.10	2602	3407
haulage/distribution	54.56	2940	59866

Source: Bartlett and Newton, 1982

Starkie (1967) in an early study in Britain, found that the relationship between truck traffic generation at a site and various measures of manufacturing site activity (area, employment) was not linear. He fitted log-linear relationships of which the following are typical; these are for commercial vehicle trips per day (Y) generated by manufacturing and engineering establishments respectively:

$$\log Y = 0.256 + 0.559 \log X$$

$$\log Y = 0.401 + .500 \log X$$

where X = total employment per site

Watson (1975) in his study based upon industrial plants in Chicago, USA, also found that a log-linear relationship between truck trips and employment or site area gave a better fit.

These results of Starkie and Watson may be significant given the tendency in more recent work to adopt a simple linear relationship, although the practice, in results such as those presented above by TTM Consulting, of disaggregating by land use type and vehicle type may achieve similar results.

Dallas. Christiansen (1978) has reported that a value of truck trip generation for use in planning central city office buildings in Dallas, USA, was 22.73 truck stops per day per 10,000 m^2 (2.11 per 10,000 ft^2). This was based on examination of the results at other US and Canadian cities in the 1960s and 1970s, which produced values in the range 16.1 to 25.8 truck stops per day per 10,000 m^2 (1.5 to 2.4 per 10,000 ft^2).

Role of models

Two features stand out from the above discussion. The first is that the state of the art in urban freight modelling is quite undeveloped, having a poor theoretical base, a primitive analytical framework, and very little good data to permit the development and calibration of models. The second is that there has been very little model development since the 1970s, and in fact the whole area of urban goods analysis for planning and policy purposes has hardly seen any advance for over a decade.

One might ask, why is this so? If the topic (urban freight) is important, and if models are inadequate, then surely someone would have been working on developing better models! However, that logic implies that models are helpful to policy and planning issues in urban freight, and it is here that we probably find an answer to the question. It is suggested that the sorts of issues which policy advisers and decision-makers are concerned with in urban freight at this time are not those which better models can assist with - or at least those funding the planning hold that view!

In the introduction to this chapter we mentioned some principles outlined by Meyer and Miller (1984), concerning the role of models, and indicated that models are not an end in themselves, and are only of value in a planning or policy context if they assist the decision-maker to reach better decisions. Meyer and Miller (op cit, p 226) go on to say that for this to be so, analysis must be:

- timely;
- cost-effective;
- responsive to the policy variables of interest;
- sensitive to the scale of the impacts involved; and
- presented in such a way that it is understandable and useful to the decision-makers.

It is suggested that most models of the sort discussed in this chapter fail on some or all of these grounds. In the context of metropolitan-wide transport planning, the interest quickly boils down to one of estimating truck trip flows, and since at peak hours these are a small proportion of the total traffic, there seems to be little need to try and estimate such flows with precision. Even the Chicago Area Transportation Study, which has devoted more effort to urban freight modelling and has a more comprehensive data base on urban goods movement than probably any other urban area, has not used its urban freight models for metropolitan transport systems planning, but has used a simple relationship between truck trips and person trips. At this level then, models are not perceived as being necessary.

Conversely, the sorts of issues which policy-makers are concerned with in the urban freight scene are those which either model developers have ignored, or in which models are not perceived as being helpful. These issues might be elicited from the proceedings of the various Engineering Foundation Conferences on Goods Transportation in Urban Areas. For example, in the proceedings of the most recent conference (Santa Barbara, California, 1988) the preface listed the following 'events and trends' (Fisher, 1989):

- deregulation, and its effect on urban operations;

- role of freight in maintaining the vitality, viability, and functioning of urban areas;

- reduced interest of the US federal government (implying an absence of policy issues from a national perspective?);

- emerging environmental concerns;

- local government rules and decisions made in ignorance of the needs and effects upon the urban trucking industry; and

- academic researchers producing 'their economic studies and mathematical models without a full awareness of the real world of those who transport goods.'

Many of these issues have been taken up in earlier chapters of this book. The point to be made here however, is that the sorts of models described in this chapter bear little relation to these issues.

This is not to say that researchers have been uninterested in those issues; indeed as the discussion in Chapters 4 and 5 would indicate, there has been at least a modest research effort directed at items of current policy interest, such as energy, environmental concerns, effect on regional economies, road safety, urban structure, etc. But in only a few cases (e.g. Southworth (1983), Southworth, et al (1981) and Bowyer, Akcelik and Biggs (1985) with energy) has the researcher made even modest recourse to a modelling framework.

These concerns are summarised in the reported conclusion of a 'Round Table' on goods distribution systems in urban areas organised by the European Conference of Ministers of Transport (1984), as follows:

The Round Table was sceptical about the value of macro-economic models for solving urban freight transport problems and pointed out that:

- There is no theoretical model detailed enough to integrate the different significant variables of city structure, transport quality, the motivations and number of decision-makers.

- In urban freight transport it is difficult to choose a workable elementary unit of measurement. A tonne does not correspond to a trip.

- Models rely on the stability of the variables excluded. At a time of sweeping economic change, that assumption is a steep requirement.

Owing to these shortcomings, the forecasts that can be established are often inaccurate and policy-makers tend to find them unreliable. It takes time, moreover, to construct a model and see whether it works, whereas policy issues usually need to be resolved immediately or in the short term, which means that demands made on models cannot be met.

On the other hand, the following considerations were put forward in favour of models:

- They are preceded by a data collection phase of undeniable value.

- They prepare analyses from the standpoint of causal relationships and the interpretation of processes.

- They promote action by drawing attention to difficulties.

- They provide an ideal basis for simulation. For example, in urban planning, a model may well be used to determine the saturation point for an infrastructure.

As a review of the pros and cons of models, and as an explanation for the relative lack of interest in urban goods models at the metropolitan level over the last decade or so, this summary would be hard to fault.

Hutchinson (1981) has made similar comments about transportation models in general: 'it seems clear that the analysis methods developed during the last 20 years have fairly modest capabilities as aids to policy analysis. (They are) essentially descriptive in nature despite the often extravagant claims made by their proponents ... They are ineffective policy analysis aids when substantial changes are occurring in the environment of transport.' If these comments are true of models applying to person movement, they are even more true of models applying to goods movement.

In conclusion, it is important to note that the use of models at the local or site level continues to be important, and these models enjoy widespread use. However, by their very nature they are very simple in form and intent (often, indeed usually, being merely expressed in terms of truck traffic generation rates). However, their importance at a local planning scale, and in the design of traffic facilities, should not be underestimated. If there is a priority for the development of models of urban freight, it is probably at this level, because it is here that models are of value to decision-makers, and can have a real effect upon outcomes. Given the poor state of knowledge in this area, and the primitive state of development of truck traffic generation models at a site level, research and model development of this sort (e.g. Bowyer, 1991) in this area could be highly beneficial.

Notes

1. More sophisticated models have been developed for inter-regional freight, where the line haul function is simpler, mode is more explicitly defined (e.g. road, rail), and urban pick up and delivery complexities can be ignored (e.g. Harker, 1985; Roberts and Kullman, 1979;

Winston, 1981). Recently, Bowyer (1991) has proposed a framework for development of models of this degree of complexity at the urban level, together with their data and information needs.

2. See Note 1 above.

PART C

IMPLEMENTATION:
FROM IDEAS TO ACTION

14 Implementation of urban freight planning and policy

Introduction

This final part of the book is concerned with the implementation of urban freight planning and policy. Aspects of implementation have been included where relevant in the discussion of specific strategies in Part B (e.g. traffic management, enforcement, land use planning, etc). However, in this chapter more specific comments are made about some of the key points which an urban planning or policy agency should consider if it is to take freight needs and issues seriously, and intends to translate such concerns into action. In Chapter 15, some case studies are presented describing actual implementation of freight policy or planning in several cities.

The discussion in this chapter is directed at a range of key topics which would likely have to be considered in any activity which sought to incorporate freight needs more explicitly into an urban planning or policy context. Such activities might include transport planning, traffic management, land use planning, regional economic development, environmental protection, etc. The specific ways in which these topics may be incorporated would, of course, vary with the context[1], but the topics are likely to be fairly universal. They are:

- the need to be specific about the objectives, problems or issues to be considered;

- institutional responsibilities, and the need for public-private sector cooperation or consultation;

- data and information requirements, and analysis procedures;

- ways in which alternative proposals may be evaluated, and the criteria to be used; and

- research needs, opportunities and priorities.

Identification of objectives, problems or issues

As the previous chapters of this book has made clear, urban freight is a multi-faceted topic, with a wide range of urban impacts. Since it is unlikely that a single agency would have responsibilities or interests which encompassed all aspects of the urban freight system, a necessary starting point for any planning or policy initiative directed at urban freight is to determine what aspects of the total system are to be considered.

While recognising the virtual inevitability that a planning or policy initiative will be directed at a component of the freight system, and not the total system, it must be recognised that this is likely to lead to suboptimization (i.e. one 'problem' might be solved, at the risk of creating a multitude of 'problems' elsewhere in the system) or even that an action may be counter-productive because the effects of a proposed action may be to cause system-wide changes which amplify, not reduce, the problem being addressed.[2]

In Chapter 5, we argued that the objective of freight planning and policy was to reduce total urban freight costs (where costs were broadly defined to include economic factors, environmental factors, social factors, etc). It is implicit in this argument that there will inevitably be a need for tradeoffs between the extent to which the various objectives can be achieved. Therefore, while acknowledging that in reality planning and policy efforts are likely to have a limited focus, the broader consequences of this decision should be kept in mind.

We also suggested in Chapter 5 that 'objectives', 'problems' and 'costs' were three ways of looking at essentially the same thing. So in determining the focus of a planning or policy study, the starting point must be for the agency responsible to determine just what 'problems' it is supposed to be attempting to solve, what 'costs' it is attempting to reduce, or what 'objectives' it is supposed to be pursuing. The distinction is essentially cognitive (and therefore non-trivial), but irrespective of which perspective is taken, a clear statement of the scope of interest of the planning or policy effort needs to be established and agreed.

Generally, planning and policy concerns are reactive, in the sense that they respond to pressures and concerns made known through a political or professional process - truck intrusion into a residential street, regional air quality, downtown congestion, loss of jobs due to poor freight access, etc. Therefore, the initial focus or catalyst of the planning or policy concern is usually obvious.

The challenge is to establish sensible boundaries. As noted above, if the boundaries are too narrow, there may be unforseen and unacceptable consequences elsewhere. Examples might include:

- restriction on truck access may lead to industry closure and job losses;

- peak period restrictions in one part of an urban area may lead to more truck travel in adjacent areas thus defeating (say) a regional air quality goal; or

- restrictions on truck size may lead to a proliferation of smaller trucks, the total effect of which may be to negate any congestion benefits of eliminating the larger trucks.

However, the extent to which freight objectives can be addressed must be considered alongside other responsibilities of the planning or policy agency, as resources are inevitably limited. If an attempt is made to extend the boundaries of the study too far, this may lead to an inability to draw sensible conclusions, or to budgetary needs which cannot be met. For example, it may be that the fairly grandiose plans developed in the 1970s for incorporating freight within urban transport planning processes came to nothing because on the one hand they were too costly, and on the other hand, they had such a broad scope that their proponents were unable to make a convincing case that the outputs would be useful.

301

Institutional responsibilities and public-private sector roles

There are a multitude of participants in the urban freight process (see Chapter 3). Resolution of any given issue or problem is therefore likely to impact upon several interest groups. Given the relative roles of various public sector agencies and a range of private firms and industry groups, it is axiomatic that resolution of freight issues must involve both public and private sector input.

This notion has been well-summarised in the report of one of the probe groups at the most recent of the series of Conferences on Goods Transportation in Urban Areas (Anon, 1989c, p 2):

> Essentially, the idea is to establish a mechanism to facilitate dialogue and promote an understanding of varying points of view in urban goods movement issues. At the very least, such a mechanism could serve as a means of temporarily defusing crisis situations and avoiding the imposition of knee-jerk solutions which have not been thoroughly worked out. At its most effective level, it could provide an entity sufficiently respected by both government and private interests which would be charged with the responsibility of working out satisfactory solutions away from an emotional and often politically charged spotlight. However, the larger objective is to achieve improvements in urban goods movement which are possible when the interested parties act in concert, but are not generally available to any party acting alone.

There are likely to be difficulties and frustrations in forming such a group (National Association of Regional Councils, 1984, p 17). These include the different 'cultures' characteristic of the public and private sectors, as reflected in such aspects as time frames, objectives and decision-making processes. There is rarely a single industry view, and if there is, it is supposed to be expressed by individuals who are in day to day competition with each other; consensus is not easy amongst endemic competitors. Moreover, it is rare that there is a single 'private sector' view, since representatives of different modes, operators in different segments of the road freight sector, small and large carriers, etc, are likely to have a divergence of view, or at least of priorities. (It goes without saying that there is hardly likely to be a single public sector view amongst representatives of different government departments, or from those at different levels of government!) Participation by the private sector is usually expected to be on an unpaid basis, and this contribution of time and effort can be difficult to justify.

Nevertheless, there is increasing recognition that there are mutual benefits to be gained from a cooperative approach to problem identification and resolution. At the very least, everybody stands to gain by consultation and the resultant improvement in understanding of the other party's concerns and viewpoint. As the National Association of Regional Councils (1984, p 17) points out, managers are increasingly 'realising that government's ability to initiate legislation, make infrastructure improvements, and cut red tape can be put to work to help business (while) at the same time local governments, looking for ways to increase tax revenues and create jobs within the community see a need for a coordinated approach to business development and transportation programming.'

However, it must be said that formal, high-level liaison and consultation arrangements in the urban freight sector are the exception rather than the rule in most western countries, although they do exist. For example, Millendorf (1989) has documented the establishment and role of the Freight Services Improvement Conference (FSIC), an entity sponsored by the Port Authority of New York and New Jersey, the New York and New Jersey State Departments of Transportation, and the New York City Department of Transportation. It was established in recognition 'that the bi-state regions's heavy dependency on a viable regional freight transportation industry warranted significantly higher levels of public attention and financial support than the industry had previously received'. The Conference's Advisory Board is an influential group of very high level executives from the carrier, shipping, financial and academic communities.

Another example is the Road Freight Transport Industry Council in the State of New South Wales, Australia. This Council, which comprises representatives of the road freight industry, unions, and government officials, was established in 1981 to advise the State Minister for Transport on a range of matters, including freight services, industrial relations, safety, training and education, environmental concerns, user charges, and regulatory reform. It has undertaken a number of valuable research studies with funds provided by the State government, and its recommendations have been adopted by the government in a number of important areas.

Joint public-private sector coordinating and consultation mechanisms can operate at a number of levels. They may be at Chief Executive level, which is essentially political, ensuring that the industry is acknowledged in broad government decision-making (e.g. the New York - New Jersey example).

303

It may be at a level involving senior industry representatives and public officials, focussing on specific aspects of public policy formulation (e.g. the New South Wales example). Or it may be at a working level, being essentially a consultation mechanism to ensure the practicality of specific design or traffic management measures such as truck route determination, truck access restrictions, or the definition of advisory truck routes.

Private sector representation in a consultation process would depend upon local practice and custom (e.g. in some parts of the world, there is a long tradition of consultation between public and private sectors, while in other areas, there is no such tradition), the issues involved, and (as mentioned above), the level of representation. However, in general, the representation should attempt to cover groups whose interests are relevant to the issue, and/or those who may be affected by potential actions. Without wishing to be exhaustive, such representation may include:

- road freight operators;
- representatives of non-road modes;
- freight shipper representatives;
- terminal operators;
- professional societies, academics, and similar sources of expertise;
- civic organisations, such as chambers of commerce; and
- union representatives.

The benefits to planning and policy bodies arising from public sector representation in such consultation and facilitation forums include:

- to attempt to ensure consistency of action amongst the various government agencies involved in urban freight, and to coordinate the implementation of policy decisions;

- to ensure that government stays aware of issues and concerns in the private sector,

- to assist government officials to gain some appreciation of the role of the freight sector, the practical difficulties which it faces, and actual practices used by the industry;

- to keep public agencies informed of relevant trends, emerging technologies, etc which affect the urban freight task (e.g. industrial location, incidence of 'just in time' demands, etc); and

- to provide early advice to the private sector about potential policy initiatives, with the aim of getting feedback as to effects and industry responses.

The need for consultation and communication, and the difficulties which can frustrate effective facilitation of freight planning and policy, have been well summed up by Millendorf (1989, p 29), commenting upon the aforementioned New York Freight Service Improvement Conference:

Effective solutions to most freight movement problems ... require substantial cooperation between the private sector, where goods are moved, and the public sector, which provides and maintains the vital roadway system infrastructure. That's easy enough to say, but in reality such cooperation requires a degree of credibility and trust which takes time and effort to build.

Data and analysis

Almost any form of planning or policy-making needs at least a modicum of information about the freight system and the likely consequences of planning or policy action. As with the previous points discussed in this chapter, it is not possible to make definitive comments here about data needs or analysis techniques. Clearly, these will vary with the issue concerned, the planning and policy framework within which the issue arises, usual practice in the agency concerning such things as data collection and modelling, and the availability of previous data. However, a few general points can be made about data analysis and collection, and some suggestions offered about the sorts of urban freight data which are potentially useful in a planning or policy context.

Transport system data and analysis

In general, transport system data may be either site-specific or regional.
Site-specific data would relate to applications concerned with site design or use, such as inventories of loading facilities, parking and traffic management provisions, site-based truck trip generation, dwell times, loading facility usage, etc. It may be cross-classified by such variables as

305

time of day, truck type, etc (Anon, 1982d, p 38; JHK and Associates, 1983, p 14).

Site specific data may be analysed to produce site-specific forecasts. These are usually limited in scope and time frame, and directed at estimating future levels of activity at the site in question so that adequate access and loading or unloading provisions can be made. Simple models, for example those relating truck trip generation to some measure of floor space in the building or buildings served, may be beneficial here (see Chapter 13).

Regional transport data may be useful in metropolitan-wide or corridor transport infrastructure planning. Data here may refer to such aspects as truck traffic counts and truck trip generation and travel patterns, perhaps classified by time of day, type of vehicle, owner classification, etc. Other regional transport data, perhaps useful for planning purposes, might include link travel times, truck accident data, hazardous vehicle routing, truck noise data, and perhaps even data on commodity flow (which is not synonymous with truck trip data - see Chapter 2) (Anon, 1982d; Rawling and Reilly, 1987; Rawling, 1989; Strauss-Wieder, Kang and Yokel, 1989).

Analysis at the regional level may be more complex, because of the need to take into account the effect of more variables. (This of course does not necessarily guarantee more accurate forecasts!) Analysis may involve the use of models to predict truck movement on networks, in order to estimate such measures as traffic flow (e.g. for infrastructure design), truck flows (e.g. for emission estimates) or routing (e.g. for the determination of advisory or statutory truck routes). Models are likely to be necessary to enable these estimates to be undertaken, although as noted in Chapter 13 this is rare (i.e. most urban areas do not bother to isolate trucks as a separate vehicle type in their modelling process).

Existing transport data sources should be tapped where they can provide relevant information. In general, such sources as vehicle registration records are usually not very helpful because they do not enable vehicles to be identified by area of usage. Most existing transport data sources refer to long distance (ex-urban) freight, or to very aggregate urban freight indicators such as truck traffic counts on selected arterials or freeways. To the extent that such data are relevant to the question at hand, they should be used, but many urban issues require information at a more specific or disaggregate level than this.

Regional economic data and analysis

In addition to transport system data, it may be relevant to assemble or monitor information about regional economic performance, since urban freight demand is a result of the need to move goods, which in turn is a reflection of a region's economic development. Data here might relate to employment, economic production, income, etc.

Regional economic analyses and forecasts may take several forms. These include (National Association of Regional Councils, 1984, p 13):

- regional profiles, showing such information as income, population, business activity, value added, etc;

- economic base analysis, to identify key trade-exposed industries, and to assess their effects on the regional economy;

- shift-share analyses to show how industries within a region are growing with respect to each other and to the national performance; and

- input-output analyses to determine inter-industry linkages and the direct and indirect responses of the economy to changes in external demand.

Data collection

Data collection methods vary with the type of data sought, their extent and degree of detail, and their availability from existing sources. Data collection is not a trivial task in either financial or methodological terms, and a great deal of care should be given to the design of any data collection and management exercise (Ampt, Richardson and Meyburg, 1991). However, potential data collection methods for use for urban freight include field surveys, industry-based and truck-based surveys (using either interview or mail back methods), and panels. (Robicheaux and Chatterjee, 1978, p 408; National Association of Regional Councils, 1984, p 11-15; Rawling and Reilly, 1987, p 19).

It is very important to note that data should not be collected for its own sake. Data collection programs must be preceded by a very clear statement of needs, to ensure on the one hand that useful data is collected, and on the other hand that time and effort are not expended collecting data which is never used. As Fisher and Meyburg (1983) note, the demand for more data can be 'an excuse for not knowing how to specify and solve (urban goods movement) problems, with the hope that the answers will be revealed in the data.'

Outline study design for urban freight data collection

As emphasised at the introduction to this section, it is not possible to be definitive about data collection and analysis needs except in a specific context. That is, data collection and analysis must proceed from an explicit statement of needs, be directed at clearly defined ends, and have a definite relationship to planning and policy objectives.

However, in a book such as this, it would be remiss not to present some indicative guidelines concerning urban freight data collection, since any person or organisation contemplating such an exercise may expect to find such advice here. Therefore, we present below an outline study design. This study design refers to data needs in the context of metropolitan-wide or corridor transport planning and policy, and outlines the sorts of information and associated data sources which may be helpful in such a context. Whether any given item or source was in fact relevant in any specific instance would need to be assessed on a case by case basis. In other words, this outline should not be used as a definitive prescription; it is only a checklist of the sorts of items which may be helpful to regional transport planning and policy.

In this context, it is considered that information needs fall into five areas as follows:

- truck fleet;
- truck flows;
- commodity flows;
- major freight generators; and
- major freight corridors.

Truck fleet. Information about the truck fleet is important for a basic understanding of the urban freight task. Components might include:

- *number of vehicles*: to establish the dimensions of the task;

308

- *size of vehicles*: to distinguish between 'light', 'medium' and 'heavy' vehicles (to be defined), each of which is associated with a different set of problems or planning issues;

- *type of vehicle*: similar to size, but also to enable results of roadside classification counts to be cross-referenced to the fleet as a whole and to provide information about specialized freight operations; categorized by configuration (rigid, tractor semi-trailer, etc) and body type (e.g. van, refrigerated, tanker, tipper, etc);

- *ownership*, in particular distinguishing between commercial for hire (also known as hire and reward) operations, owner-drivers, private (also known as ancillary or own account) operations, and non-freight (e.g. service) vehicles; this is important since it leads to an understanding of the structure of the industry and enables truck activities to be related to changing customer needs; and

- *sector of operations*, in particular to distinguish between intra-urban, intra-state and interstate (or equivalent) operations, and to isolate the different operational and ownership parameters of these various sectors.

Much of this information can be obtained from an analysis of registration records. However, a major problem is that the locality of ownership does not equate to locality of use, e.g. a firm may operate vehicles which never come to the urban area concerned if all its vehicles are registered at the firm's head office in another city.

Truck flows. Truck flow information is important for road infrastructure and management, and also what it reveals about the location of freight activities (see below), the importance of intra-urban versus ex-urban trucking, and such characteristics as variations in time of day, direction of flow, and type of vehicle used to service different areas and travel markets.

The prime data source for this information would be the periodic traffic counts undertaken by the local or state highway authority. This may need to be supplemented by field surveys, as such surveys are typically sparse, and maybe cover only a portion of the road network (typically those roads for which the authority has administrative responsibility).

It may be possible to use truck counts on arterial roads to synthesize an origin-destination truck trip table, using SATURN or a similar traffic analysis package (van Vliet, 1982). However, if it was desired to establish *commodity* origin-destination tables, this would have to be done using a form of interview survey (see below), and truck origin-destination information could be collected in that survey also.

Specific truck flow data which would be useful in an interview survey would include (for each trip):

- origin location and land use (or industry);
- destination location and land use (or industry);
- time of day; and
- tonnes picked up and/or delivered at each stop, by commodity.

Commodity flows. Commodity flow is not synonymous with truck flow, and since it is commodities which produce the demand for goods movement, information on this is fundamental to an understanding or analysis of the urban freight system. However, as noted above, commodity flow cannot be observed from the roadside, and some form of interview (or mailback) survey is the only practical method of obtaining this information. To ensure that the information obtained in the survey sample can be reliably expanded to give estimates of total flow, a known sample must be used from an explicitly defined population. It is suggested that the best sample frame is the truck population, i.e. to obtain this information, a truck-based sample could be used. This sample frame has the advantage that it would also facilitate the collection of all other data listed here. It has the disadvantage that it is quite expensive to collect.

Data to be sought would include for each consignment (i.e. freight of the same commodity moving from one origin to one destination):

- origin location and land use (or industry);
- destination location and land use (or industry);
- commodity classification;
- commodity type (e.g. frozen, liquid, etc);
- consignment size (mass, volume);
- full truck load or less than truck load consignment;
- type of packaging (pallet, loose, container, etc);
- type of handling (manual, crane, fork lift, etc);
- ownership of goods;
- responsibility for transport (shipper, forwarder, carrier, etc); and
- method of despatch (depot, radio, phone, mobile phone, etc).

Major freight generators. Information about freight generators (i.e. origins and destinations of freight movements) is fundamental to a full understanding of freight movements, and a key to analysing the role of freight in the economy.

There are two possibilities for this analysis, differing in scale and level of detail. The first is a metropolitan-wide analysis, probably on a local government area basis. This would include both freight-related data and economic data, to enable any relationships between them to be established. It might include the following:

- *freight data*
    - mass of freight generated;
    - type of freight generated; and
    - truck trips generated;

- *economic data*
    - employment (by category);
    - population;
    - number of households;
    - number of jobs in relevant categories; and
    - site area (or similar) in these categories.

The freight data could be obtained from the aforementioned truck-based survey, while the economic data should be available from existing sources.

The second possibility would be to focus upon specific freight generators, such as a port, key industrial area, terminal area, etc. Potentially useful information about such localities includes origins and destination of truck movements, and details concerning access to these areas (e.g. delays, routes, time of day, etc). Specific data might include:

- tonneage by commodity by origin/destination;
- type of freight (general, containerized, bulk, etc); and
- mode of transport to/from the area.

This information could be obtained largely from the truck-based sample described above, but would need to be supplemented by specific surveys to obtain information for the non-road modes.

Major freight corridors. Planning and policy analysis may need to identify the major corridors for the movement of goods within the metropolitan area. Identification of the corridors would largely follow from the analysis of truck and commodity flows described above.

Where possible, the corridors should be described in terms of:

- commodity types moving along them;
- truck types using them; and
- freight type (intra-urban, intra-state, interstate, export-import, etc).

For each corridor, it would be helpful to list in as much detail as needed the specific problem locations along them. These might include:

- road network bottlenecks (e.g. points of congestion, delay, etc);

- road network deficiencies (e.g. route discontinuities, absence of through or direct links, etc);

- parking or access conditions (e.g. clearways, inadequate loading zones);

- specific site deficiencies (e.g. inadequate bridge clearances, sharp turns, poor sight distances);

- accident black spots; and

- residential areas under threat due to intrusion of extraneous truck traffic.

Methodology. In most urban areas, much of the information described above is not currently available. Thus, if it is desired to have this information to support planning or policy initiatives in relation to urban freight, new surveys are needed. As mentioned, much of the information could be obtained from a truck-based survey, and indeed the critical information on commodity flows can best be obtained in this way.

However, as noted previously, it is important that data are not collected for their own sake, but only if they are relevant to some explicit need. Any major data collection exercise must be carefully planned in a proper study design so that it:

- collects information which is relevant to explicit policy or planning needs;

- is efficient in the use of survey resources (i.e such aspects as sample size, and method of data analysis must be carefully considered);

- produces reliable and verifiable results (i.e. such aspects as sample frame, control of survey progress, and use of cross-checks on the output of the survey results must be built in to the survey design);

- is capable of expeditious analysis (e.g. questions must be carefully and unambiguously worded; pilot studies must be undertaken; the data should be capable of computer analysis; and reporting requirements specified); and

- facilitates subsequent monitoring of the freight system (i.e. on-going monitoring should produce relevant and timely information, and allow comparison with results obtained in the major survey).

Evaluation

There is no shortage of suggestions about ways to change aspects of the urban freight system, as the discussion in Part B of this book has indicated. The challenge is to select which suggestions are worthwhile.

One useful way of conceptualizing the evaluation issue is to consider that evaluation has three dimensions as shown in Figure 14.1. These dimensions define the complexity and completeness of the evaluation process (Richardson and Ogden, 1977, p 269):

- *Breadth* refers to the number of identifiable groups included in the evaluation. Freight evaluation may include three groups: trucks (and these may need to be further sub-divided, e.g. service trucks, large and small trucks, commercial and private trucks), other road users, and the freight system generally.

- *Width* refers to the geographical area over which the evaluation is to extend. It may be link or site specific, route or corridor specific, or area wide.

- *Depth* refers to the number of factors considered within the evaluation, namely specific impacts included in the six objectives discussed in Chapter 5.

The value of conceptualizing the task in this way is that it underscores the complexity of evaluation. Determining where to draw the line in any dimension is a major (possibly the key) decision in any given instance. For example, a decision concerning the provision of loading docks at a commercial site would likely focus on the first level of breadth (trucks serving the facility only), one level of width (the commercial site itself), and possibly two levels of depth (costs to vehicle operators and costs to building owners). Even quite substantial freight policy initiatives tend to be quite constrained within this framework. For example, the Los Angeles peak period truck restriction proposal discussed in Chapter 15 focused on a quite limited proportion of the truck fleet (breadth), was single minded in its concern for vehicle emissions (depth), and considered only a limited number of roads in the City of the Los Angeles (width).

It is not suggested of course that every evaluation should be wide, deep and broad (in these terms). Rather, we are arguing that each case must explicitly consider the extent to which different user and non-user groups are considered, the area concerned, and the objectives to be included in the evaluation.

The framework also emphasises the complexity of the real world, and the fact that freight impacts can be quite pervasive. Just because an evaluation process chooses to ignore a particular aspect of one of the three dimensions does not mean that impacts will not be felt there. Hence, ideally, this consideration should be the determinant of whether or not a given factor is included in the analysis. If it can be assumed that the consequences of a proposed action on a given factor is minimal, that factor can safely be left out of the analysis. On the other hand, if such an assumption cannot be made, then that factor ought, ideally, to be included.

Methodology. One of the main difficulties of any formal evaluation process is that different impacts are measured in different ways. This is revealed in the framework also. For example, a five minute delay to a car driver may be valued quite differently to a five minute delay to a truck driver, while a truck driver struggling to meet a 'just in time' delivery schedule is likely to value a five minute delay quite differently from another truck driver returning empty to home base at the end of the day. In the depth dimension, we have the classic 'apples and oranges' problem of trying to compare and trade off impacts on one objective (e.g. efficiency) against another (e.g. environment).

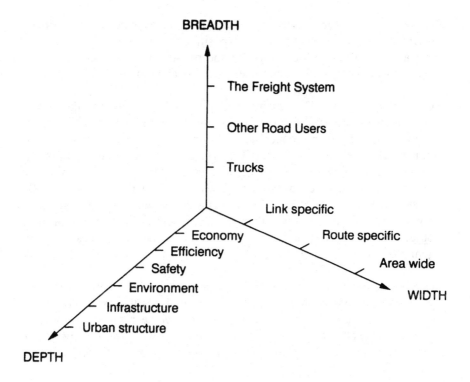

Figure 14.1 Dimensions of evaluation

There are only two ways out of this methodological problem - to attempt to reduce everything to a common measure (usually dollars), or to accept that the tradeoff between fundamentally different impacts is essentially subjective, and thus a political decision. While there have been attempts to do the former, most transport evaluation processes implicitly or explicitly do the latter.[3]

In general, these forms of evaluation are based upon a simple matrix presentation, showing the anticipated consequences of a range of alternative courses of action (Figure 14.2). It is considered that the analysts have completed their task when they have produced this matrix; selection of the best course of action is a political decision.

Evaluation of this sort is of two distinct types, *goals assessment*, which shows the extent to which alternative proposals achieve a range of pre-set goals; the goals usually include both quantifiable (e.g. economic) and non-quantifiable (e.g. social and environmental) consequences; and *impact assessment*, which shows the impacts (positive and negative) of alternative proposals, including both quantifiable and non-quantifiable impacts.

There are three specific techniques of goals assessment:

Cost-effectiveness: The main distinguishing feature of the cost-effectiveness approach is that it involves the prior identification of *objectives*, and it is thus concerned with how each alternative contributes to the attainment of those objectives. The basis of this assessment is the development of *measures of effectiveness* (i.e. the extent to which an alternative achieves each objective) (Meyer and Miller, 1984, p 318). Cost-effectiveness evaluation is only applicable where there is a single objective, and the aim is either to maximize the attainment of that objective for a given budget, or to determine the lowest cost way of achieving a given outcome.

Goals achievement matrix: This approach is similar to the cost-effectiveness approach, in that it too analyses the extent to which each alternative will meet objectives which have been set in advance. In general these objectives are the benefits to be derived, and it is the likely success or failure in doing so (as opposed to the costs involved) on which the plans are compared (Hill, 1968).

Multi-criteria decision analysis: The distinguishing feature of this method is that it attempts to involve the decision maker in the process, so that it is the decision maker's weightings that are used. As Crowley (1987) says: 'Its emphasis is on clarification, and on helping the decision maker to better understand the options; the final choice is based upon the decision maker's own priorities, which reflects the way that most decisions are made in practice'.

Techniques of impact assessment include:

Planning balance sheet: This term has become almost a generic for any presentation of the sort shown in Figure 14.2. However, the term was coined, and may still properly be used, to describe a specific technique. Its unique feature is that the utilities (i.e. entries in the matrix) are calculated for each affected group in the community (Lichfield, 1970).

Objectives or Impacts*	Alternative Number		
	A	B	C.....
Economic objectives			
Efficiency objectives			
Road safety objectives			
Environmental objectives			
Infrastructure objectives			
Urban structure objectives			

* Specified in quantifiable terms, if possible.

Figure 14.2 Evaluation matrix

Impact overlays: In this technique, the impacts of a particular alternative are specified on a spatial basis, and a contour map is drawn depicting the effects of these impacts on facility location (McHarg, 1971). It is also useful as a screening device in the context of infrastructure planning, identifying options which may then be subject to more rigorous analysis.

Environmental Effects Statement: Finally, brief mention should be made of a related evaluation process, namely the preparation of an Environmental Effects Statement (EES). These have become a formal legal or administrative requirement in most western industrialized countries (although they may be known by different names), and must be prepared for many transport proposals, especially large and/or controversial ones. These typically include, inter alia, a description of the likely environmental effects of the proposal, and a listing of safeguards to be taken.

An evaluation method of this general sort (Figure 14.2) has been developed for use in connection with truck management proposals in Britain. This is shown in Figure 14.3. It is interesting, in view of the above discussion, to note that its proponents developed this simple approach on the grounds that 'there is little justification for complex procedures because it is considered that the associated data requirements are too onerous to be cost effective in terms of the decisions that have to be made.'

Guidelines. An even simpler approach to evaluation is to not bother with any formal framework at all, but simply to rely on guidelines which purport to reflect good practice. If this approach to evaluation was considered appropriate, a useful set of guidelines might be the following (based on Kearney, 1975; Anon, 1978d; Hedges, 1985; Christiansen, 1979; Hall, 1982):

- Strategies should be planned and designed with both long range and short range objectives in mind. Specific circumstances may dictate that an immediate problem be addressed in the short term, but implementation should take cognisance of long term implications, which may be much broader in their impact.

- Similarly, the effects of proposed strategies on the wider geographical area should be evaluated. Effects of changes are not confined to the area which is the focus of the proposed strategy (e.g. central city streets), and this should be acknowledged and taken into account in evaluation.

- Both adverse effects and beneficial effects should be taken into account. Even minor changes to any system as complex as the urban freight system can have unexpected effects, and attempts should be made to anticipate these. For example, attempts to alleviate a problem in one area may simply transfer it to another area.

- Almost any measure that improves traffic flow will also improve truck flow. Exceptions to this are measures which aim to spread the commuter peak, which may lead to overlap between peak automobile and truck flows.

| Steps: | Core Calculations[1] | | Additional Check[2] |
	Traffic	Environmental	
1. Establish scale of problem	Heavy commercial vehicles (hcv): (i) % through (ii) % of total flow	Residences: (i) number affected	Schools, hospitals, other sensitive land uses; Pedestrians; Timing of hcv flows (night)? hcv weight characteristics; Safety hazards
2. Consider scheme(s) assess: (a) restricted route(s) (b) alternative routes(s) for diverted traffic (c) any other affected route(s)	(i) % change in flow of hcv (ii) % change in numbers of hcv (iii) change in total traffic flow	Residences: (i) number with increased flow (ii) number with decreased flow of hcv	As above plus likely violation rates
3. Check balance of gainers and losers		If a net benefit if apparent, proceed to step 4	Identify location/scale of effects
4. Examine cost and additional factors[3]	(i) operating cost changes[4] (ii) implementation costs		Road wear and maintenance implications; Accident effects; Congestion effects; Are individual hauliers/concerns severely affected?

Notes:
1 Core calculations are seen as the minimum necessary for sound decision-making except where the effects are fairly obvious.
2 The additional checks should be considered carefully and where they appear relevant, at least a qualitative assessment should be made on the basis of local knowledge and professional judgement. If the additional checks are both relevant and susceptible to quantification, then further detail may be sought.
3 Problems identified should not be used in the evaluation alone, but also cause the scheme design to be reconsidered to see if improvements can be made.
4 It is preferable to use resource costs (net of transfer payments), officially up-dated.

Source: Institution of Highway Engineers, 1981, p. 3.

Figure 14.3 Evaluation framework for truck management schemes

- Care must be taken when analysing situations where truck flow and automobile, pedestrian, or public transport flows are in conflict. Attempts should be made to include all likely effects, so that decisions about tradeoffs can be made on a well-advised basis. If possible, planning and design should attempt to find ways of satisfactorily accommodating all requirements.

- Where there is an expected net total benefit, questions of equity should be considered to be certain that the benefits do not accrue mainly to some groups with the disbenefits impacting mainly on other groups.

- Improvements to urban goods and services transport should be designed to reinforce the region's land use, economic, and environmental goals.

- Improvements should be acceptable, to the extent possible, to all affected parties. While it may not be possible to ensure that all parties favour the proposal, it is usually difficult to enact improvements that a strongly involved and politically connected group finds unacceptable or unreasonable.

- As noted previously, in all planning and policy initiatives, there should be effective dialogue between public and private sectors. Channels of communication (both formal and informal) should be established, and maintained on an on-going basis.

- Freight and truck considerations are more likely to be effectively dealt with if they are incorporated within the urban area's usual transport planning processes. Rather than dealing with issues on an ad hoc, crisis management basis, it is best to establish and maintain a degree of interest and expertise within the transport planning agency, so that freight needs are dealt with in a broader framework, e.g. regional economic planning, traffic management planning, urban development planning, economic strategies, etc.

- Where enforcement is necessary to achieve the objectives of a particular strategy, it should be vigorous and consistent. Enforcement feasibility and costs should be included in the evaluation of alternative strategies.

- Almost any logistics management practice which improves the efficiency of goods distribution (e.g. route scheduling, consolidation, off-hours operation) will reduce conflicts between freight and passenger vehicles and thus tend to improve traffic flow.

- While strategies aimed at truck movement and pick up and delivery operations are understandably at the forefront of concern, other truck related issues such as overnight parking, safety, facilities for out-of-town trucks, and delivery of services should not be overlooked.

- Finally, it is important to remember that each urban area is unique, so that a strategy which has worked in one area should not be adopted in another without careful evaluation to compensate for the differences in the two areas.

Research

The final, and potentially one of the most important, instruments for implementation of public policy in the urban freight field is research. It is important that freight research continues in order to provide the necessary theoretical and empirical underpinning of freight policy. Hicks (1977, p 117) has expressed the research role quite well:

If the urban freight transport problem is to be moved closer to solution, government should play an active part in the move. Government already plays a significant role in influencing the nature of the urban freight process and it is difficult to see how it could withdraw this influence if this were thought desirable. It follows then that government activities which have influence on urban freight need greater researched planning than has hitherto been the case.

There are many valid targets for increased research activity. Technological development, safety, economic viability, financial performance, freight terminal operations, freight location, transport planning and modelling, building codes and planning schemes, and traffic engineering, are some of the obvious areas where freight-related research has the potential to produce valuable results.

321

While research may be classified in many ways (basic vs applied, open ended vs constrained, etc), one useful way of thinking about research roles in urban freight is to distinguish between what might be called curiosity-based research ('intellectual prospecting') and mission-oriented research (research aimed at answering a specific need). Of course the distinction is not a precise one, since much 'prospecting' demonstrates the validity of the research topic, thus opening it to detailed investigation of a more directed sort, while much mission-oriented research arises because someone has shown that it is a potentially worthwhile project.

Curiosity-based research

Any suggestions for fruitful areas for intellectual prospecting inevitably reflect the background and experience of the person doing the suggesting. However, this writer's hunch as to where the biggest 'nuggets' may be found from intellectual prospecting are in four main areas (where a nugget may be defined in terms of discovery of new insights into ways of achieving the objectives for urban freight outlined in Chapter 5).

The first area is that of a better understanding of the freight system, its role and function, and the relationships between demand (shippers' and receivers' needs to move goods) and supply (trucks, terminals, etc). This research would be directed at attempting to better understand the increasingly complex nature of freight demand and supply side responses to it. The research need is to determine ways of estimating credible measures of freight system performance and response to exogenous changes in the economic system which creates the demand for freight transport. It may lead to (or require) new data and information, since lack of data has in the past limited the analysis or identification of freight problems and issues. It may lead to the identification of a need for a modelling capability - not models for their own sake, but models as a means of synthesizing and analysing the freight system and its interactions with other systems.

Second, there is potential value in developing means of assessing options for freight system improvement. The corollary to this is to develop means of assessing the impact on the freight system of policy changes elsewhere (including, but not only, policies aimed at restricting the movement of trucks in urban areas, improvement of safety, reducing the environmental impact of trucks, and fostering economic development through freight system changes). This may involve investigation through case studies, demonstration projects, or monitoring the effects of policy changes.

322

Third, there may be value in researching ways in which the urban transport (or land use, or economic planning) decision making process can better incorporate freight considerations. Freight tends to be neglected in these decision-making processes, and to the extent that it is taken into account at all, it is usually negative (i.e. a control or restriction of some sort). On the other hand, there are examples of urban areas that have deliberately included freight in their urban and transport planning processes, and developed pro-active plans to achieve explicit freight-related goals. Also relevant is research on ways of coordinating the responsibilities of various agencies (e.g. transport, land use planning, economic development planning, transport management, etc) in order to acknowledge and integrate freight objectives. One way may be to document 'success stories', and to develop guidelines for the inclusion of freight-related activities in the various planning and policy agencies. In particular, research to indicate the regional economic effects of more efficient freight transport systems could be especially cogent since cities are increasingly having to compete on an international basis to maintain their economic base.

Finally, since much of the difficulty in freight is that many of the external costs are not borne by the urban freight sector or its customers, research on the means of internalizing these costs could be fruitful. This may be directed not only at operating costs, but at noise, emissions, safety, and effects on urban form.

Mission-oriented research

The above discussion has necessarily been extremely cursory, because discussion of research needs and directions is difficult without an explicit frame of reference. However, discussion of the second type of research, namely mission-oriented or sponsored research, is even more difficult to do in the abstract. About all that one could do in a context-free discussion is to prepare an unstructured, unprioritized list of potential research projects, the value of which would be doubtful.

Nevertheless, it is relevant to discuss how such a research program may be developed and prioritized. Ogden and Bowyer (1985) have described one possible means of determining urban freight research needs and priorities. Their context was the development of an urban freight research program for the Australian Road Research Board (ARRB), involving firstly an assessment of the need for further research, secondly the preparation of research project statements, and thirdly the development of priorities and recommendations for ARRB involvement.

The method used to determine these research needs and priorities involved four stages:

- a statement of issues in relation to six freight-related objectives (service quality, economic efficiency, environment and safety, distributional (equity) effects, road infrastructure cost recovery, and energy);

- a series of interviews with people having relevant experience and/or representing key ARRB interest groups, to refine the statements of issues and identify research needs within them;

- on the basis of the above, the preparation of draft research proposals which appeared to have the potential to produce payoff from a greater research effort; and

- a workshop, to consider and refine (or reject) the draft research proposals, and to develop recommendations to ARRB for research needs and priorities in the urban freight field.

Ogden and Bowyer (op cit) reported that this procedure was useful and effective in not only developing research priorities, but also in stimulating interest among relevant user groups. More specifically, they noted that the procedure:

- facilitated the identification of a range of specific issues;

- provided a mechanism for generating research topics;

- provided a means of refining these topics into detailed research proposals;

- was an effective information exchange; and

- heightened awareness of the importance of freight issues within transport and other agencies.

Notes

1. Discussions related to the inclusion of freight in US metropolitan urban-wide transport planning agencies may be found in such sources as Institute of Transportation Engineers (1972), Anon (1978d), Anon (1982d), Southworth, et al (1983) and Robicheaux and Chatterjee (1978), while Hall (1982) has described various approaches adopted in Britain.

2. It is salutary to remember Forrester's (1969, p 110) observation that 'with a high degree of confidence we can say that intuitive solutions to the problems of complex systems will be wrong most of the time', or more succinctly (op cit, p 9) 'the intuitive process will select the wrong solution much more often than not'!

3. This is not the place for a detailed discussion of transport evaluation. There is a considerable literature on the subject (Stopher and Meyburg, 1976; Lockwood and Wagner, 1977; Wohl and Hendrickson, 1984; Meyer and Miller, 1984; Leitch, 1979). Only the bare essence of the methodologies used will be presented here.

15 Case studies

In the earlier chapters of this book, numerous references have been made to studies of urban goods movement conducted in cities around the world. In this final chapter, we focus more specifically on this aspect, presenting details of some case studies describing how various cities have made specific provision for urban freight in planning or policy areas. These case studies are as follows:

- New York City (freight activity in the Garment Centre);
- Dallas, Texas (provision of central city loading spaces);
- Los Angeles, California (peak hour truck restrictions);
- Los Angeles, California (transport corridor to the port area);
- Dallas, Texas (hazardous materials truck routes);
- New Orleans, Louisiana (central city freight access);
- Melbourne, Australia (freight needs in road investment);
- Perth, Australia (routes for large combination vehicles);
- London, England (environmental controls on trucks); and
- Tokyo, Japan (facilitating urban freight distribution).

New York City: Freight activity in the Garment Centre

The New York City Garment Centre is a forty block area in lower Manhattan, where, in the early 1970s, some 8,000 firms employed 116,000 workers to produce, sell and transport clothing. The high concentration of firms in multi-storey loft buildings, as well as the industry's operating characteristics, contributed to substantial truck activity and congestion. For example, in 1979, the average daily speed was about 10 km/h (6 mph), and only 5 km/h (3 mph) at midday; an average delivery was about 500 m

(1640 ft) and took around 30 minutes; trucks were parked three deep on some streets, completely stopping traffic; and truck waiting times of several hours were common. Small shipments predominated, with half of deliveries being less than 180 kg (400 lb). In addition to problems of congestion, noise, and air pollution, product prices were high, and transport costs of Manhattan apparel firms were three to four times higher than those of firms elsewhere in the United States (New York City, 1979; Hedges, 1985).

In 1972, the Manhattan Garment Centre Project was launched by the City of New York, with financial and technical support from the US Department of Transportation. Its aim was to develop and implement both short range and long range strategies to reduce the costs and environmental impacts of congestion in the Garment Centre.

The first phase of the study, completed in 1976, concentrated on low-cost, short-range improvements. A set of explicit criteria was developed, against which candidate proposals could be assessed. These criteria were (Hedges, 1985):

- primary objective;
- political feasibility;
- administrative feasibility;
- implementation cost to the private sector;
- implementation cost to the public sector;
- implementation time;
- whether an operational innovation was required;
- applicability to other areas;
- benefits and costs to the public sector; and
- benefits and costs to the private sector.

These criteria were used to assess twelve specific proposals. This resulted in the selection of five which were actually implemented. These five were:

Passenger vehicle ban. A ban on all automobiles without commercial licence plates was introduced between 10 am and 3 pm on weekdays for two city blocks on two streets. This was based on the observation that some 66 percent of vehicles entering the Garment Centre were autos, and 58 percent of these did not stop in the area (New York City, 1976).

328

Installation of turning lanes. A left turning lane was installed at one intersection by imposing a curbside parking ban for a distance of 17 m (50 ft) from the intersection.

Truck parking durations. The maximum permitted parking duration in the area was reduced from 4 h to 3 h, in order to encourage better utilization of curb space, and increase parking turnover. Surveys showed that 90 percent of the trucks stopping in the area were able to complete their transaction in this time (New York City, 1976).

Corner curb cuts and *midblock curb cuts.* Curb cuts were constructed at 21 sites at both intersection and midblock locations, to ease the movement of handcarts and clothing racks on and off sidewalks, and to reduce interference with vehicular and pedestrian traffic.

Other proposals which were either rejected or set aside for additional study during this phase included pedestrian crossing restrictions, off-hours pick up and delivery, street widening, special handcart lanes, overnight off-street parking, no-standing restrictions, and a parking reservation system (Hedges, 1985).

The results of implementing the above Phase 1 proposals were encouraging at first, leading to an overall increase in vehicle movements, a reduction of queues at turns, and better movement of handcarts. However, a reduction in enforcement effort over time led to an erosion of these gains, except for the smoother movement of handcarts due to the curb cuts.

The second phase of the study involved an examination of both long term and additional short term alternatives, including containerization, consolidated receiving rooms, parking reservation systems, elevated or underground conveyor systems, renovation of elevators, trucks designed for hanging garments, road pricing, and parking surcharges. The majority of the recommendations of this phase were concerned with improving truck movements through improved traffic signal control, removal or relocation of roadside obstacles, reduced on-street parking, and better management of curb loading zones (Hedges, 1985).

Most of these strategies have been implemented. Hedges (1985) has noted that while no formal 'before and after' measurements have been made, City officials report that traffic conditions are better so long as enforcement levels are adequate.

Dallas, Texas: Provision of central city loading spaces

The downtown area of Dallas, Texas, has experienced substantial growth over the last 20 years, and the City has taken a number of steps to accommodate the truck traffic associated with the need to service these developments. The measures adopted were of essentially three types: a revision of the off-street loading zone ordinance, the provision of underground truck terminals, and a regulatory revision of the use of on-street loading zones including an experiment with metered loading zones. Most of these measures stemmed from a major study conducted in the early 1970s, which involved all interested parties from both public and private sectors (Walters, 1982, p 242).

Off-street loading zone ordinance. Prior to the review of the off-street loading zone ordinance, Dallas had one of the lowest requirements for loading spaces of any US city, although the problems were not as great as they might have been since most developers (although not those in the downtown area) actually exceeded the ordinance requirements in providing off-street facilities (Habib, 1983, p 62).

The new ordinance, adopted in 1980, was based on the notion that a building developer would be required to provide loading spaces to fully accommodate peak hour demand at the site. This had the effect of changing Dallas' off-street requirements from one the lowest in America to one of the highest. (For example, the requirement for a downtown office building increased from one space per 46,500 m^2 (500, 000 ft^2) to one space per 9,300 m^2 (100,000 ft^2) (Walters, 1989a, p 55).

The ordinance featured three sizes of vehicle (tractor semi-trailer, single unit truck, and passenger vehicle or van, with the mix between them varying with land use). It also allowed up to 40 percent of the required spaces to be catered for at the curb where no negative traffic impacts would result. However this relaxation only applied to the spaces for autos or vans, not trucks (Walters, 1989a, p 56; Habib, 1985). Developments adjacent to a public truck terminal (see below) were exempt from the on-site requirements, but were required to connect to the public terminal.

The ordinance developed in Dallas was based on accommodating the peak hour pick up and delivery operations at the specific site. For most sites, this accommodation is off-street. The use of the on-street complement (if available) for the largest generators is unique amongst US cities (Habib, 1983). The combined off-street and on-street loading requirements address the differences between buildings in the city core (where there is little or

330

no spare curb space available) and those at the city fringe where curb space is more likely to be available. Walters (1989a, p 58) has noted that only one building in the core area has been able to utilize the option of on-street spaces as substitutes for off-street provision.

Another interesting feature of the Dallas ordinance is that it explicitly downgraded the importance of the tractor semi-trailer. This had the effect of allowing developers to provide a larger number of loading spaces with little or no increase in the total area devoted to truck loading and unloading. However, Habib (1985) has noted that while this change may be appropriate for central city developments, it is probably not applicable to fringe or suburban developments.

Some details of the Dallas ordinance are provided in Table 6.5. An important aspect of the development of the ordinance was the involvement of all interested parties, especially building developers.

Underground truck terminal. A 1969 master plan for the development of downtown Dallas envisaged a future city centre on several levels: street level for vehicular traffic, subways for pedestrians, and a lower level for interconnected trucking activities (Walters, 1982, p 242).

Although this was a very ambitious plan, two public underground truck terminals have been opened, one in 1977 and the other in 1984; together they serve over 600,000 m^2 (6.5 million ft^2) of downtown office space (Walters, 1989a, p 57-60).

The first terminal, the Bullington Truck Terminal at Thanksgiving Square, was provided by the City at a cost of $3.6 million (Walters, 1989b, p 69). The land for the facility was donated by a private foundation, and the surface level has a park, a chapel, and pedestrian facilities (Habib, 1985). It is accessed via a two block long portal under a former city street which was abandoned. Cartways connect the terminal to buildings in four adjacent blocks. The average haul length is 42 m (140 ft), but the most remote building served by the facility involves a haul length of over 110 m (350 ft) (Walters, 1989a, p 60).

It was designed with 43 docks suitable for single unit trucks, which was though to be adequate to cater for around 500,000 m^2 (5.4 million ft^2) of office space; this was expected to generate around 800 deliveries per day. However, by the mid 1980s, it was handling only 300 deliveries per day, although it was serving its expected floor space of around 500,000 m^2. Two dock spaces were permanently occupied by trash dumpsters and three were reserved for security personnel, leaving 38 operating spaces. During the peak hour (10 am to 11 am) the terminal is usually full, but there is seldom a queue. The pattern which has emerged is that the larger trucks use the underground facility, but smaller vehicles (pickups, vans and passenger vehicles) continue to deliver to the curbside, often illegally, because it is quicker and more convenient (Walters, 1989a, p 60).

The terminal is operated by the City, with the operating costs being recovered from the managers of the buildings served, on a pro-rata basis. In operation, each arriving vehicle is assigned a position number by the terminal manager as it enters, with an attempt being made to assign trucks to positions close to their respective destination building.

Commenting on this terminal, Habib (1985) noted that:

> The principal lesson of the facility is that a shared off-street facility for large office buildings is feasible. The facility has physical connections to each existing and future building site, and all connections run under tha adjacent street system. The facility could just as well have been in the basement of a new building (instead of the 'basement' of a park) and would have operated in a similar manner (except for the structural configuration and size of the internal columns). The point here is that new large buildings, many of them public, are routinely constructed in the central area and the opportunity to provide much-needed off-street truck spaces is not seized. New shared facilities do not have to be of the scale of Thanksgiving Square. However, many buildings adjacent to a redevelopment site that do not have adequate off-street parking facilities and adjacent buildings on principal arterials are the essential signals that should trigger consideration of opportunities for shared off-street loading facilities.

The second truck terminal, the Browder Truck Terminal, at present serves only a single building, and is operated by the building manager, not the City. Like Thanksgiving Square, it uses a former street as a portal. In the future, it may extend into an adjacent block to serve new a new development (Walters, 1989a, p 61). There has also been a feasibility study of a third truck terminal, which found that positive results could be obtained if there was a way of assigning rent from commercial development to repay capital costs (Walters, 1989b, p 70).

Walters (1989b, p 70) has summarized the City's involvement by noting that:

The City has incurred a major cost to pay for (one) truck terminal and after building one more (paying for the portal only, for the single user building to date) has so far not participated in another. The reasons are two-fold: first, the new off-street loading ordinance has shifted the responsibility for loading space provision to building owners, and they have opted to build their own facilities so far; second, the City has now identified as its primary benefit from public truck terminals the removal of *existing* curb loading spaces off-street.

Metered loading zones. As there are no alleys in downtown Dallas, a system had evolved whereby building occupiers could lease curb space outside their premises for a nominal fee; this practice was discontinued in 1979 because it was found that the spaces were often used for car parking, and because the arrangement of spaces was hardly optimal for loading purposes (Walters, 1989b, p 67).

This system was replaced by one which involved the provision of curbside loading zones, following a supply-demand analysis by the City. What was almost unique about the system however was that it featured metered loading zones, i.e. the spaces were reserved for trucks, but truck drivers were required to set the meter when they arrived. Two streets were treated in this fashion, one having a free meter, the other having a 5 cent fee. Habib (1985) described this as probably the first metered truck loading zone in America. Its objectives were to increase the curb space capacity for trucks by encouraging a higher rate of turnover.

However, the experiment has apparently not been successful, and the meters have been removed. The reasons for this were (Walters, 1989a, p 62):

- even with the free meters, truck drivers declined to flip the meters and start the clock running;

- the general public misunderstood, and parked in the metered spaces; and

- because of the variety of sizes of delivery vehicles, the curb space was not being used efficiently when the parking was restricted to one vehicle per space.

Los Angeles, California: Peak hour truck restrictions

The Los Angeles region experiences extensive and costly periods of traffic congestion, and has a major air quality problem, due in part to motor vehicle emissions. The population of the region has increased by some 40 percent over the last 15 years, while the region's major transport system, the famed freeway network, has seen little change in recent years. (During the 1960s, over 600 km (375 miles) of freeway were added, but the 1970s saw only some 160 km (100 miles) of new freeway, and the 1980s only about 16 km (10 miles).

These twin problems of congestion and emissions are being tackled in a wide variety of ways, including new freeway construction (e.g. the construction of the Imperial Freeway, and the development of several privately funded toll facilities), ride sharing programs, high occupancy vehicle lanes, tougher emission standards, construction of new public transport facilities, etc. (Southern California Association of Governments, 1989b). Included in the overall package of strategies are some aimed explicitly at trucks, of which the proposal for a ban on peak hour truck movements on most streets in the City of Los Angeles is one.

This proposal has been evolving for several years, and at the time of writing had not been actually enacted as law. The reasons for this are twofold. Firstly, a great deal of effort has been devoted to attempting to ensure that any City ordinance aimed at restricting truck activity will hold up in court. (Interestingly, virtually the only professional evaluation of the proposal has been concerned with the legality of the proposal; there has been almost no attention to other dimensions of evaluation, such as its effect on the economy, jobs, or even emissions.) Secondly, the City has been engaging in considerable negotiation with particular interest groups in an attempt to get either voluntary compliance in advance of the ordinance, or to get industry to agree to change its practices in exchange for an exemption from the ban when it is enacted. (For example, the construction industry agreed to commence work one hour earlier in the day and introduce ride sharing programs for its employees in exchange for an exemption from the peak hour ban.)

As mentioned, the proposal is still evolving (Nelson, et al, 1991), but the essence of the strategic approach intended by the City of Los Angeles is to require all trucks which operate in the City to be registered, an identification scheme to be developed to denote those trucks authorized to operate during peak hours (operators would be have only, say, one third of their fleet so authorized), and shippers and receivers of goods in the City to be required to operate during off-peak hours.

As an example, one proposal incorporated the following elements:

- to apply to all trucks having three or more axles, and shippers or receivers which generate trips by such vehicles;

- no such truck to be allowed to run on the streets of Los Angeles unless enrolled with the City;

- placards to be issued by the City and displayed on the vehicle to indicate that the vehicle is authorized to operate on streets within the City during the peak period (6 am - 9 am and 4 pm - 7 pm, Monday to Friday);

- operators would have various options as to the use of their fleet during peak periods, e.g. 60 percent of the fleet in one peak period and none in the other; 30 percent of the fleet in both peak periods, etc);

- exemptions to be available to particular operators, such as emergency vehicles; and trucks carrying specific commodities such as household goods, alcohol, hazardous materials, etc;

- also, operators to be exempt if their fleet is in use for 24 hours per day, and there is no flexibility possible in the operation without incurring additional costs, and/or if the operator would violate existing laws (e.g. noise) if they operated off-peak;

- the restrictions to apply to all streets under the jurisdiction of the City unless specifically exempted; the exemptions would include, inter alia, streets in the Port area and near major industrial and freight terminal areas (it should be noted that the region's major freeways are not under the jurisdiction of the City and therefore would not be subject to the peak hour restrictions, although most streets within the City connecting to the freeways would be);

- shippers/receivers to be limited to a maximum of five heavy truck movements per week during peak periods;

335

- shippers/receivers which generated eight or more heavy truck movements per week during peak periods to be required to schedule a minimum of one-third of all such shipments to a time between 8 pm and 5 am; and

- exemptions from the previous points to be given to certain shippers/receivers, including government facilities, those which can show that they would be in breach of a contract, or those which can show that they would suffer an adverse operational or economic impact to the extent that they would lose competitiveness or profitability if they were required to comply.

This is of course merely a sketch outline of the nature and extent of one peak period restriction proposal, but serves to indicate what the City has in mind.

As mentioned previously, no formal analysis of the impact of the proposal has been undertaken. However, a study of the impact of restrictions on truck use of Los Angeles freeways during peak periods concluded that the effect on congestion would be small, and likely to be lost within 6 weeks to 6 months as a result of other traffic shifting from the shoulder periods to the peak (Cambridge Systematics, 1988a,b; Grenzeback, et al, 1990). Perhaps the same conclusion would apply to a truck restriction aimed at City streets. Moreover, opponents of the proposal have argued that it may actually be counter-productive so far as emissions are concerned. For example, operators would adjust their activities to keep their trucks employed throughout the working day, and this may involve extra travel as their trucks move to operate in other parts of the Los Angeles region (i.e. not the City of Los Angeles) during the peak hours. Similarly, to the extent that trucks would operate earlier in the day, before the morning peak, the emissions are in the atmosphere for a longer time, and thus have longer to break down and form smog. Others point out that a truck can only do so much work in a day and if it operates for fewer hours, there would need to be more trucks on the road (Duncan, 1988, p 78).

City officials and supporters of the proposal counter by claiming that the proposal has been effective already, and will continue to be so even if it is never enacted into law, by acting as a catalyst for change. They cite cases where, for example, shippers/receivers have voluntarily moved to evening deliveries, and have found that it has produced cost savings, or at least minimal cost increases.

Los Angeles, California: Transport corridor to the port area

The Los Angeles area has two ports in the San Pedro Bay area, the Port of Long Beach and the Port of Los Angeles. Together they constitute one of the largest ports in the US, and form a link in the trade between Asian ports and US shippers and receivers. This has allowed a through transit time of 12 days from Japan to Chicago or Dallas (US Department of Transportation, 1990, p 5.32). Currently about 35 percent of containers passing through the ports are 'bridge' traffic (i.e. traffic not generated by Southern California), and this is expected to increase to 50 percent by 2020 (Southern California Association of Governments, 1989b, p 115).

In 1986, the Southern Pacific Railroad (SPR) opened an Intermodal Container Transfer Facility (ICTF) about 7 km (4 miles) from the port area; containers are trucked to and from the various shipping terminals, and unit trains of double-stacked containers move the traffic to and from locations in the US south, mid-west and east. Before the ICTF began operation, containers were trucked to and from the SPR intermodal yard near downtown Los Angeles, a distance of about 35 km (21 miles). This arrangement still applies for containers to be moved by other railroads, notably Union Pacific and Santa Fe.

Currently, one shipping terminal at the Port of Long Beach has an on-dock rail loading yard, and others are in prospect; these facilities do not require any trucking of containers, as the trains come directly to the shipping terminal for loading and unloading (see Chapter 11).

Notwithstanding these initiatives, access to the San Pedro Bay ports is regarded as unsatisfactory. Truck access is via freeways, which are heavily congested for many hours of the day, while the three rail lines are of a low geometric standard, are indirect, and feature numerous at-grade crossings. As a result, a major new Consolidated Transportation Corridor (CTC) is to be constructed between the port area and downtown Los Angeles. It will feature a rail corridor (probably triple-track) and an upgraded road corridor. Much of the facility is to be grade-separated, to minimize delay, noise, and interference with cross-traffic (Figure 15.1).

A Joint Powers Authority, with representation from local, county and state governments and the two port authorities, has been established to undertake the project. It has described the project as follows (Joint Powers Authority, 1990, p 2):

The project is designed to facilitate port access while mitigating potentially adverse impacts of port growth, including highway traffic congestion, air pollution, vehicle delay at grade crossings, and impacts of train noise in residential areas... The project will create a highway and rail system of national significance, connecting the economic center of the San Pedro Bay ports - the largest port complex in the United States - to the Interstate Highway system and the national railroad system, thereby facilitating the movement of international cargo.

More specifically, the CTC is expected to provide the following benefits (Joint Powers Authority, 1990, p 6):

Congestion and safety benefits: By facilitating the development of on-dock rail yards, there is an expected mode shift from road to rail for long distance container movements, leading to reduced truck travel and fewer truck crashes on Los Angeles' streets and freeways.

Reduced noise and traffic delays: The project is expected to result in a 50 percent reduction in train-related noise and vibration impacts in residential areas. The grade separations are expected to eliminate 90 percent of existing vehicle hours of delay at grade crossings.

Improved railroad operations: The project will reduce train operating hours by 30 percent, with a 75 percent reduction in the number of times trains have to stop for other trains to pass.

Improved air quality: Smoother flowing freeways and a reduction in truck traffic will reduce emissions, ceteris paribus. The reduction in train operating hours and train stoppages will further reduce emissions. There is a greater potential for electrification of rail services in the corridor, and this would further reduce emissions.

Increased economic activity: The CTC will allow the Ports of Long Beach and Los Angeles to implement their '2020 Plan', a $4 billion program to expand the land and terminal areas of the two ports (Vickerman, Zachary, Miller, Inc, 1988). It will yield a projected increase of $46 billion in economic output (gross sales) in Southern California over a 20 year period, and create an additional 37,000 trade-related jobs. Access improvements along the corridor will create redevelopment and employment opportunities. There will also be an anticipated 5,000 jobs created during the construction phase. Project cost is expected to be around $500 million in 1990 values.

338

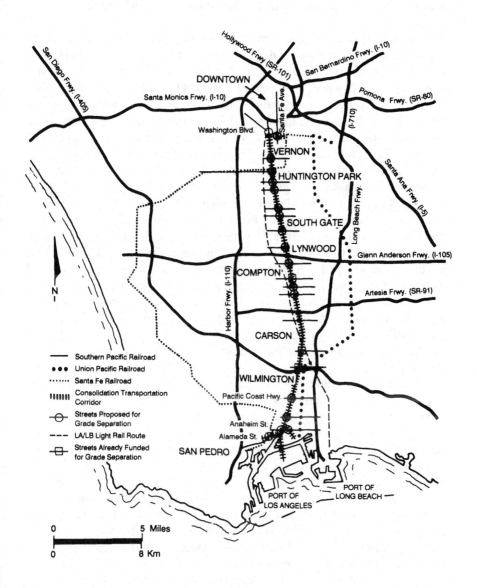

Figure 15.1 Consolidated Transportation Corridor, Los Angeles

Dallas-Fort Worth, Texas: Hazardous materials truck routes

Many urban areas worldwide have in recent years considered the question of how best to accommodate the movement of hazardous materials. One such case will be considered here, that of Dallas-Fort Worth, Texas. It has been selected firstly because its experience has been documented (Kessler, 1986), secondly because it used a systematic, analytical approach which could serve as an example to other cities, and thirdly because it was based upon the application of a widely known analysis procedure, that developed by the US Federal Highway Administration (Barber and Hildebrand, 1980).

In 1978, the City of Dallas introduced an ordinance to regulate the movement of hazardous goods, by restricting such movements to designated routes. The initial routes adopted included an outer freeway loop for through movements, and prohibited movement on elevated or depressed freeway segments in the central city area, including the underground truck terminals referred to above. In the following year, the adjacent City of Fort Worth also developed a hazardous materials route network, again based upon use of the loop freeway system for through shipments.

Increasing community concern about all facets of hazardous materials, including its transport and storage, led to the establishment of a Task Force, under the aegis of the North Central Texas Council of Governments, for the purpose of developing and implementing a work program for hazardous materials management.

In the area of hazardous materials management, a two-phase approach was used, firstly to establish a region-wide system, especially to cater for through shipments, and secondly, a local system, both to allow access to the regional system, and to allow intra-regional movements of hazardous materials. The aim was to develop an agreed region-wide system coordinated across all local government jurisdictions, which would then allow each jurisdiction to determine local needs on a case by case basis.

The essential task was therefore to develop an analysis method for evaluating candidate hazardous materials truck routes, and, as mentioned, the method selected was based upon that developed by the US Federal Highway Administration (Barber and Hildebrand, 1980). Importantly, this method addresses not only methodology, but also explicitly focuses upon institutional factors such as identification of participants and the responsibility of relevant jurisdictions.

The risk assessment methodology involved an estimation of the probability of an accident on any road segment, and the consequences of that accident should it occur. These two are then combined to form a total

340

risk measure for each segment, which can then be summed to form a total risk assessment for alternative routes. These calculations were performed for a regionwide network of some 800 km (500 miles), divided into 2800 segments. Accident input was based upon truck crash data for the three years 1980-82, while estimation of the consequences of a hazardous materials accident was based on a worst-case scenario involving the evacuation of all persons within 3.2 km (2 miles) of the crash site.

An important departure from the FHWA guidelines was that the measure of accident consequence involved multiplying the population or employment affected by a crash, by the length of the segment within which the crash occurred; the resultant measures were expressed as 'population exposure miles' or 'employment exposure miles'. In this way, a 'total risk' measure could be calculated for each candidate route.

In order to identify the best routes for hazardous materials shipments through the Dallas-Fort Worth area, a 'minimum risk' path algorithm was developed, by analogy with a minimum time algorithm as used in transport network analysis procedures. For comparison purposes, the minimum distance routes were also determined as a base case.

Comparing the base case risk with the level of risk associated with the 'minimum risk' network showed that the 'total risk' index for the latter was 62 percent lower. Risk comparisons on other criteria were that the 'minimum risk' network reduced the exposure (i.e. within a 3.2 km radius) from 72 percent of the region's population to 38 percent, while the employment exposure went from 86 percent of the region's workforce to 17 percent. However, the 'circuity' of travel (defined as the ratio of the minimum risk path length to the minimum distance path length) increased by 116.1 percent, i.e. on average, shipments would be required to travel over twice as far.

Thus, overall, a 'benefit' (in terms of the ratio of the total risk of minimum distance routes to total risk of minimum risk routes) of 2.625 had to considered in the light of a 'cost' (i.e. increased circuity) of 2.161. Since benefit exceeded cost, it was considered that the hazardous route network had a positive benefit. Although this is an unquantified measure, to convert these indices to dollar values would have required specific data on the frequency of hazardous materials shipments for each segment, and this data was not available.

Finally, a subjective assessment was made of a range of other non-quantifiable factors, using overlay maps. These factors included emergency vehicle access, proximity to population with special evacuation needs, proximity to municipal water supplies, traffic congestion, proximity to environmentally-sensitive areas, and exposure to special activity centres.

An important outcome of the study process was that there was general community support for the proposed routes; 'many of the suburban representatives commented that although they were concerned from an emergency response standpoint about the presence of the route through or adjacent to their community, they recognised that such a route must be provided.' (Kessler, op cit, p 87).

New Orleans, Louisiana: Central city freight access

In 1977, the Regional Planning Commission of New Orleans, Louisiana, began a study of goods movement in that metropolitan region (Regional Planning Commission, 1980; JHK and Associates, 1983; National Association of Regional Councils, 1984). This study was motivated by a previous study which found that traders and the public were concerned about congestion and insufficient parking in the downtown area.

The study had two phases, firstly to establish a data base concerning truck and commodity generators and movements, and secondly to identify the goods movement needs of the area, especially the downtown area. This second phase included extensive interview surveys of downtown businesses and the trucking industry. An important finding of this process was that while there was a consensus that freight delivery problems existed, and that individual firms had a view about problems that affected them directly, there was only a limited view of goods problems overall, or of how individual actions compound the problem (e.g. restrictions on delivery hours, non-supply of off-street facilities, or double parking of delivery vehicles).

Arising from these sources, the Commission identified a range of potential actions that could be taken at the governmental level to alleviate the problems. These included:

- minor changes to the downtown delivery system;
- more flexible delivery periods (including night time delivery);
- provision of additional delivery space;
- pickup and/or delivery terminal consolidation
- regulations and/or fee assessments for goods activities;
- design standards for new construction (e.g. loading space provision);
- modal alternatives;

- new technology, especially to alleviate truck queuing; and
- education and information programs aimed at people involved in downtown goods movement.

Following a qualitative evaluation of these options, four specific strategies were identified as being potentially feasible and practical.

The first strategy involved the adoption of a new zoning ordinance for off-street loading spaces. Hitherto, new downtown developments were only required to provide for 25 percent of their loading space needs, the balance being provided on-street. This not only perpetuated a congested atmosphere in the central city, but also placed the City of New Orleans at a continuing financial disadvantage by requiring more on-street spaces. Thus, the Commission recommended that the City adopt a new zoning ordinance that would increase the amount of loading spaces that a new development was required to provide (based upon the type of development), require major building additions to provide for increased loading needs, and make designs for access and egress subject to review and approval by the City. This recommendation was subsequently adopted.

The second strategy was aimed at curb space management, since some 80 percent of the downtown area's loading space was provided on-street. This involved discontinuance of the policy of leasing curb space to a business, and to more strictly enforce 'no parking' and 'loading zone' regulations. The Commission's surveys had indicated that some 10-25 percent of the vehicles using the curbside loading spaces were not involved in goods delivery. In order to ensure that only delivery vehicles used such spaces, the Commission recommended that commercial signs be mandatory on all vehicles using the loading spaces. Further, at critical locations, the City would provide additional loading spaces by converting car parking spaces to loading zones. This recommendation was also accepted.

The third strategy involved enforced night time deliveries, in order to relieve daytime traffic congestion. However, several practical and legal problems were identified, including security concerns, the extra costs which would be imposed throughout the transport and delivery chain due to additional employment needs, the need in many cases for direct personal contact between the carrier and the shipper/receiver, and the assumption of significant legal authority by the City in enforcing night time deliveries. For these reasons, the Commission recommended that such a policy be adopted only as a last resort.

The final strategy involved consolidation for downtown deliveries and/or receivals. The concept of *consolidated delivery* involved the establishment of a warehouse to which individual deliveries would be delivered initially, and then taken to the ultimate consignee on a downtown delivery round (see Chapter 12). However, this strategy was rejected because of cost, reduction of service levels, legal difficulties, and doubt about whether it would really have any effect on the number of freight vehicles required to serve the downtown area.

The concept of *consolidated receiving* was viewed as more practical and beneficial than the consolidation of delivery operations. This would involve goods destined to a downtown building to be delivered to a central location in or near the building, where a receiving clerk would be on duty to accept deliveries (see Chapter 12). Goods would again be on-delivered on a single delivery round. This would have the effect, in theory, of increasing the number of trucks using a single loading space and reducing the time required for a carrier to complete a delivery. The Commission recommended that the City and the Chamber of Commerce work with interested building owners and managers to explore further possibilities of consolidated receival.

Melbourne, Australia: Freight needs in road investment

In 1974, the Australian Federal Government designated a National Road System of major interstate highways. Since that date, a major program of road construction, fully Federally-funded, has been undertaken. However, in some parts of Australia, and particularly in the State of Victoria, by the mid-1990s the National Road System will have been improved to standards which are commensurate with the traffic flow experienced on the various parts of the network.

In Victoria, the National Road System consists of three routes terminating at the edge of the Melbourne Metropolitan Area. These routes, together with other State Highways, support the national economy by serving rural agricultural and mining sectors, and facilitating transport of goods and people between major cities.

By the mid-1980s it was clear that attention within the National Road strategy needed to be redirected to include metropolitan routes, especially those assisting the trade exposed sectors, i.e. road investment needed to be directed towards regions with the greatest intensity of relevant economic development and road transport demand and usage. This redirection was particularly cogent in the case of Melbourne, as nearly 30 percent of Australia's total manufacturing employment is located in that region.

In this context, the Victorian Government, through its State road authority (the Road Construction Authority) undertook a major examination of the significance of urban roads as they affected national economic performance. More specifically, this study, the so-called NATROV study, sought to examine the rationale for extending the National Roads System into the Melbourne metropolitan area, and, if such extension was found to be warranted, to define a development strategy for metropolitan National Roads (Road Construction Authority, 1987, p 2). This approach was based on the premise that if Australia is to respond to world economic trends and achieve sustained economic growth, effort is now required to increase the international competitiveness of its secondary (manufacturing) and service industries, particularly the trade-exposed portions of the manufacturing sector (i.e. exporting and import-competing industries.)

The study found that road transport costs were typically about 5 percent of product costs for the trade-exposed parts of the manufacturing sector. Strategic road investment could significantly increase the competitiveness of manufacturing firms by lowering transport costs, providing essential support for private investment, and acting as a catalyst for industrial relocation and structural economic change (op cit, p 24). In addition, the quality of the road network influences inventory costs incurred by firms, through its impact on reliability of delivery times. Thus, a major conclusion of the study was that 'benefits to the economy from urban road improvements directed at the trade-exposed manufacturing sector are substantially larger than might be expected, given that they directly impact a relatively small proportion of total costs' (op cit, p 5).

In particular, major urban road improvements, by reducing travel times and vehicle operating costs (and maybe fleet requirements), can directly improve the profitability and competitiveness of manufacturing firms. Firms may be able to use these cost savings to increase export sales or squeeze out imported competition, giving a direct benefit to the national balance of payments.

The report (op cit, p 5-6) went on to show how these benefits are multiplied through the national economy as follows:

Such balance of payments benefits could allow the pursuit of more expansionary economic policies, in principle to the point where the increased imports that result from the stimulation equal the initial balance of payments gain flowing from the road improvement. Research ... indicates that the ultimate increase in gross domestic product (GDP) flowing from this 'full expansion policy' is about *five to eight times* the value of the initial cost saving (i.e. initial balance of payments gain). By implication, infrastructure projects such as road improvements which can assist in improving Australia's net export position can reasonably be credited with some multiplier benefits for so doing. Indicative calculations suggest that, when demand elasticities are considered, the relative benefit multiplier on trade-exposed freight movements is about *three*, to reflect the potential gain to GDP from improved competitiveness. Allowing for the overall level of trade exposure in the Australian manufacturing sector, the benefit multiplier on all freight movements reduces to about 1.5. This means that estimates of ultimate benefits to the national economy from major urban road improvements should involve increasing the benefits conventionally calculated to the freight sector (for time and cost savings) by *about 50 percent.* (their emphases)

The report went on to develop criteria for evaluating the suitability of specific metropolitan corridors as National Roads (op cit, p 37). These criteria were:

-   link major freight generators;

-   connections to the port, airport, major industrial areas, and major ex-urban and interstate routes;

-   carry high freight flows;

-   address existing deficiencies (congestion, indirect routing, etc);

-   warranted on conventional cost:benefit economic grounds (allowing for the additional weightings to trade-exposed movements); and

-   supported as high priority by manufacturers and the freight sector.

On this basis, a number of key routes were identified. Several of these have been accepted as being eligible for Federal designation as National Routes, and Federal approval has been given in principle to several more, pending State decisions following planning review processes as to the future of the road reservations involved.

The net result of decisions made following the NATROV study is that a very high proportion of Melbourne's new road construction in the next decade or more will be predicated on benefits to the economy which accrue through the more efficient movement of freight, and directed towards roads which have a high freight and trucking importance, particularly those which assist trade-exposed manufacturing.

Perth, Australia: Routes for large combination vehicles

The largest vehicles to operate on public roads anywhere in the world are the so-called 'road trains' which serve the remote parts of Australia. These can be up to 50 m (164 ft) in length, and 136 t in mass. In the state of Western Australia, double bottom (i.e. twin trailer) road trains with an overall length of up to 33 m (108 ft) and GVM of up to 79 t are permitted to operate on the main northern highway out of the State capital, Perth, but are not permitted to operate in the Perth metropolitan area; they must assemble and disassemble at on off-road site located about 26 km (16 miles) north of downtown Perth. (Perth has a metropolitan population of 1.16 million, which is 71 percent of the total State population).

Following the improvement of sections of the urban road network within Perth, road train access to road transport depots (including terminal areas, markets, and livestock saleyards) was proposed by the road freight industry. In responding to this initiative, the Western Australian Main Roads Department commissioned a study into the practicality of allowing such operations (Pearson, et al, 1990).

The study involved extensive measurement of site and road conditions, as well as traffic and industry surveys, and addressed the following issues:

- the characteristics of road trains in an urban environment;

- the physical capabilities of road trains to negotiate the urban road network required to access terminal sites;

- vehicle performance issues;

- the interaction of road trains and traffic, now and in the future;

- future urban development patterns; and

- estimate of benefits and costs, to both the road freight sector and the community as a whole.

There was no prior Australian experience with double-trailered trucks in a large metropolitan area, so use was made of overseas experience, particularly the US experience with their so-called 'twins' (Transportation Research Board, 1989). Although most of these are shorter than the Western Australian 'doubles' (Geuy, 1989), the issues to be addressed were similar. These issues included: overtaking, braking, grades, horizontal curvature, lane width, shoulder width, roadside, railway level crossings, splash and spray, buffeting, driver vision, intersection geometry, intersection sight distance, and intersection capacity. In addition, computer simulation models of truck performance were used to assess acceleration and deceleration, and fuel consumption.

A model of vehicle swept paths was used to analyse low speed off-tracking to determine the adequacy of existing intersections and site entrances/exits. On this basis, an estimate was made of the extent (and cost) of site works and intersection re-construction which would be necessary to accommodate road trains. Lateral displacement at highway speeds was considered with the aid of the results of a study of road trains in the northern part of Western Australia (Sweatman, 1991).

Vehicle performance was assessed using models of vehicle dynamic behaviour, to determine steady state rollover threshold, rearward amplification, and performance under emergency braking.

All of these parameters were brought together to facilitate an analysis of the likely impacts of road trains on other traffic in an urban environment. The essential criterion here was that the introduction of road trains should not degrade the safety of the road network. Safety at intersections was assessed in terms of gap acceptance in right turn manoeuvres (Australian vehicles drive on the left) and left turn manoeuvres (merges). It was determined that because of the length and acceleration of the road trains, all right turn manoeuvres would need to be performed with exclusive right turn phases at signalized intersections. Similarly, all signal-controlled intersections would need advance warning of impending changes to a red signal to allow road trains to brake in safety. Safety between intersections was assessed on the basis of swept path and overtaking, together with the nature of abutting land use; in particular, it was considered that extensive land use controls to ensure control of access from abutting properties would be necessary in order to limit 'friction' from traffic (including pedestrian and bicycle traffic) generated by such development in the future.

An assessment of costs and benefits of the proposal was then made. Quantifiable benefits included savings in fuel use and savings in road wear (at present, after dissembling the road train, the second trailer is hauled to its destination by a 'block truck', i.e. a truck with a 10 t block of concrete mounted on it to provide traction.) It was found that savings in both of these were significant, with the major benefit coming from reduction in road wear due to the elimination of block trucks. Quantifiable costs were mainly those associated with once-off reconstruction of intersections and other sites, to cater for the larger swept path of the road trains. There was also a loss of revenue to the State government due to reduced fuel usage. Non-quantifiable impacts included reduction of theft and vandalism, reduction in employment opportunities, and compliance costs (e.g. increased surveillance and enforcement).

The result of the cost-benefit analysis showed a significant net present value over a 10 year period. However, this assessment of the feasibility of the proposal, with its associated cost and benefit calculations, needs to be set against community concerns about the presence of road trains in mixed urban traffic. At the time of writing, no decision had been made about allowing road trains to operate in metropolitan Perth.

London, England: Environmental controls on trucks

One of the major freight-related concerns in British cities is the environmental impact of heavy vehicles, and this concern goes back many years. For example, in 1973 the *Heavy Commercial Vehicles Control and Regulation Act* (usually referred to by the name of its proposer, the Dykes Act) was passed by Parliament. This gave local authorities the power to regulate heavy commercial vehicle movements and activities in order to promote environmental objectives (especially those related to noise).

In 1975, the Greater London Council (GLC) prepared a 'Lorry Routes and Bans' proposal, which paralleled the National Government's plans for nationwide truck routing (see Chapter 6), and the work done by other regional and local authorities under the Dykes Act outside London (Buchan, et al, 1985). This had four major elements (Hasell, Foulkes and Robertson, 1978c):

- overnight parking restrictions on-street;
- local street controls on moving traffic;
- local routing; and
- large area restrictions on moving traffic.

With all of these strategies (except perhaps for parking restrictions), the proposed controls would have caused a reallocation of traffic flow and nuisance from one street or area to another. Thus the GLC sought direct public reaction to ensure that before proposals were implemented, they had adequate public support, and that the technical and professional assessment of costs, benefits and impacts reflected community views. The views of the road freight industry and shippers/receivers of goods were also sought to ensure that the economic, employment and other impacts of the proposals were taken into account. The problem and the initial solutions in each of the above four areas are briefly described below (Hasell, Foulkes and Robertson, 1978c).

Trucks parked in residential streets create problems of noise, visual intrusion, safety and security. Prohibition of overnight parking in residential areas of London was commenced on a trial basis in 1971, and extended to cover most of London by 1980. This prohibition was made possible partly by the provision of public truck parks (see Chapter 11), and partly as a result of owners or operators making their own arrangements.

Local street controls were introduced to discourage trucks from using residential streets as alternative routes to the main arterials. As noted in Chapter 6, a common form of control was a width restriction, whereby bollards or other physical devices were installed to prevent the passage of vehicles in excess of (say) 2.1 m. However, such local restrictions were seen as having the potential to create region-wide problems unless carried out in the context of designated truck routes and area-wide traffic control.

The initial truck route network comprised some 690 km (425 miles) of main road in London; controls were to apply to all trucks in excess of 16 t gross vehicle mass (GVM). These routes were selected on the basis of physical standards, little residential or retail frontage, low pedestrian activity, and proximity to major truck trip generators. Quantitative assessment was made of four key environmental factors: noise levels, carbon monoxide levels, smoke levels, and pedestrian delay. These proposals were put out for public comment in 1975, and the reaction was overwhelmingly negative: those who stood to benefit from the proposal did not come forward and actively support it, while those who were disadvantaged were strident in their opposition. However, there was support for the principle of truck routing from both the public and the road freight sector, so long as it was 'not on my street'. As a result, the GLC determined not to proceed with the proposed network: 'the clear conclusion for London is that comprehensive lorry routing can only be a viable policy where there exists a main road network which is adequate in both environmental and geometric design terms.' (Hasell, Foulkes and Robertson, 1978c).

Two proposals for area wide restrictions on truck activity were considered in the 1970s. The first applied to a 15 km^2 (6 mile^2) area in Central London. Through movements of long vehicles (in excess of 12 m (40 feet)) were prohibited in 1973, and, in spite of a low level of enforcement, it was effective in reducing through truck flows in the area by about 85 percent. An assessment was made of a proposal to ban the movement of all such vehicles in that area, but it was found that most of those trucks entering the area with legitimate business could not be replaced by smaller vehicles (e.g. trucks carrying newsprint). This proposal was implemented, but with a permit system for those firms which could demonstrate need. A proposal for a larger scale area-wide truck restriction covering Inner London (325 km^2 (125 mile^2)) was also examined at this time, including the notion of a permit available for a fee to operators of vehicles who wished to bring them into the area. However, this was not proceeded with, largely because it was considered that it would have deleterious effects on London's economic base.

The problems remained however, and in 1982, a Panel was established to consider social, economic and environmental effects of introducing extensive truck bans in the Greater London area (Wood, 1983). The key elements of this work, as accepted by the Greater London Council in 1983, were that it would apply to all but about 400 km (250 miles) of road in Greater London, would cover all trucks in excess of 16.5 t GVM, and impose restrictions on truck movement (e.g. midnight to 7 am weekdays, midnight to 7 am and 1 pm to midnight Saturdays, and all day Sundays). There would however be exemptions available for specific operators, in particular where their inclusion would have adverse effects on London's economic base (Buchan, et al, 1984). When the GLC was abolished in 1983, the various London boroughs failed to reach a consensus on the future of the truck restrictions. This led eventually, in 1987, to the London Boroughs Transport Committee (a consortium of 23 of the 33 London boroughs) taking over responsibility, with a commitment to continuing the restrictions. Enforcement therefore now only occurs in boroughs which are members of the Committee. In these boroughs, the permit system has been maintained. However, new conditions are continually being added.

Tokyo, Japan: Facilitating urban freight distribution

There have been two major surveys of freight distribution in Tokyo, Japan, one in 1972 and one in 1982 (Miyamoto, 1989). These revealed some valuable information about the structure of freight services in Tokyo and trends over the ten-year period. Important changes in urban goods services over that decade were the increased value of goods which had reduced the size and mass of individual shipments while increasing the frequency of services; the rising needs of home-based delivery services such as express home deliveries; and the need for more advanced services, such as faster, round-the-clock delivery in response to manufacturing industry's 'just in time' production strategies.

Solutions to the distribution bottlenecks in Tokyo are being sought through two basic policies (Miyamoto, 1989): improving the flow of trucks and more efficient use of truck. Particular means of implementing these policies include the following:

First, building a network of major 'trunk roads dedicated to cargo distribution'. These are envisaged as part of a broader land use-transport policy which would involve three elements: building the trunk roads, building major distribution nodes along the roads, and introducing 'regulations and policies for inducing and controlling the construction of distribution bases and related facilities'.

Second, the use of existing road space by commercial vehicles needs to be rationalized, especially truck parking and loading/unloading. This is to be partly the responsibility of the private sector (regulations on the provision of truck loading and parking areas), and partly by Government provision of parking and 'cargo sorting' areas.

Third, the productivity of individual trucks needs to be improved. This is to be tackled by such means as more efficient distribution networks, greater use of commercial or hire and reward trucks rather than private trucks, and improved real time information systems.

References

Akcelik R (1981) Traffic signals: Capacity and timing analysis. *Research Report ARR 123.* 108 p. (Australian Road Research Board, Melbourne, Australia).

American Association of State Highway and Transportation Officials (1987) *Guide on Evaluation and Attenuation of Traffic Noise, 1985.* 28 p. (AASHTO, Washington, DC).

Ampt ES, Richardson AJ and Meyburg AH (1991) *Selected Readings in Transport Survey Methodology.* (Eucalyptus Press, Sydney, Australia).

Anderson DL (1983) Your company's logistics management: An asset or a liability in the 1980s. *Transportation Review (winter)*, pp 119-124.

Anon (1974a) The use of regulatory powers in improving urban goods transportation, in Fisher GP (ed) *Proceedings of the Engineering Foundation Conference on Goods Transportation in Urban Areas*, pp 57-80. (Engineering Foundation, New York).

Anon (1974b) Consolidated terminal for pickup and delivery in urban areas, in Fisher GP (ed) *Proceedings of the Engineering Foundation Conference on Goods Transportation in Urban Areas*, pp 123-148. (Engineering Foundation, New York).

Anon (1974c) The location of freight terminals in urban areas, in Fisher GP (ed) *Proceedings of the Engineering Foundation Conference on Goods Transportation in Urban Areas*, pp 81-120. (Engineering Foundation, New York).

Anon (1978a) Traffic engineering and design to facilitate urban goods movement, in Fisher GP (ed) *Proceedings of the 3rd Engineering Foundation Conference on Goods Transportation in Urban Areas*, pp 53-76. (Engineering Foundation, New York).

Anon (1978b) Locating and servicing major freight generators in urban areas, in Fisher GP (ed) *Proceedings of the 3rd Engineering Foundation Conference on Goods Transportation in Urban Areas*, pp 151-164. (Engineering Foundation, New York).

Anon (1978c) Impact of local government regulations on urban goods movement, in Fisher GP (ed) *Proceedings of the 3rd Engineering Foundation Conference on Goods Transportation in Urban Areas*, pp 77-100. (Engineering Foundation, New York).

Anon (1978d) Goods movement considerations in metropolitan planning, in Fisher GP (ed) *Proceedings of the 3rd Engineering Foundation Conference on Goods Transportation in Urban Areas*, pp 115-150. (Engineering Foundation, New York).

Anon (1982a) Freight movement in relation to urban land use, planning, terminal facilities and environment, in Fisher GP and Meyburg AH (eds) *Proceedings of the 4th Engineering Foundation Conference on Goods Transportation in Urban Areas*, pp 41-50. (Engineering Foundation, New York).

Anon (1982b) The role of regulation in urban goods movement, in Fisher GP and Meyburg AH (eds) *Proceedings of the 4th Engineering Foundation Conference on Goods Transportation in Urban Areas*, pp 69-84. (Engineering Foundation, New York).

Anon (1982c) Fuel conservation and contingency planning, in Fisher GP and Meyburg AH (eds) *Proceedings of the 4th Engineering Foundation Conference on Goods Transportation in Urban Areas*, pp 51-68. (Engineering Foundation, New York).

Anon (1982d) Integration of urban goods movement into the urban transportation planning process, in Fisher GP and Meyburg AH (eds) *Proceedings of the 4th Engineering Foundation Conference on Goods Transportation in Urban Areas*, pp 33-40. (Engineering Foundation, New York).

Anon (1989a) Issues and problems of moving goods in urban areas. *ASCE Journal of Transportation Engineering 115(1)*, pp 4-19.

Anon (1989b) Data requirements for policy, planning and design, in Chatterjee A, Fisher GP and Staley RA (eds) *Goods Transportation in Urban Areas*, pp 13-24. (American Society of Civil Engineers, New York).

Anon (1989c) Truck accommodation in urban areas, in Chatterjee A, Fisher GP and Staley RA (eds) *Goods Transportation in Urban Areas*, pp 1-7. (American Society of Civil Engineers, New York).

Arrow MM, Coyle JJ and Ketcham B (1974) Environmental impact of goods movement activity in New York City. *Transportation Research Record 496*, pp 80-92.

Australian Bureau of Statistics (1990) Survey of motor vehicle usage. *Catalogue 9208.0*. (ABS, Canberra, Australia).

Barber EJ and Hildebrand LK (1980) *Guidelines for Applying Criteria to Designate Routes for Transporting Hazardous Materials*. (Federal Highway Administration, Washington, DC).

Barnstead RC (1970) Truck activities in the city center. *The Urban Movement of Goods*, pp 83-94. (Organisation for Economic Cooperation and Development, Paris).

Bartlett RS and Newton WH (1982) Goods vehicle trip generation and attraction by industrial and commercial premises. *Laboratory Report 1059*. 65 p. (Transport and Road Research Laboratory, Crowthorne, UK).

Bixby RH and Reno AT (1982) Energy contingency planning for urban goods movement, in Fisher GP and Meyburg AH (eds) *Proceedings of the 4th Engineering Foundation Conference on Goods Transportation in Urban Areas*, pp 329-350. (Engineering Foundation, New York).

Black J (1978) Micro and macro planning techniques and the study of urban goods movement, in Fisher GP (ed) *Proceedings of the 3rd Engineering Foundation Conference on Goods Transportation in Urban Areas*, pp 413-438. (Engineering Foundation, New York).

Black WR (1972) Inter-regional commodity flows: Some experiments with the gravity model. *Journal of Regional Science 12(1)*, pp 107-118.

Blaze JR, Halagera RT and Miller MS (1973) *The Urban Transportation Planning Approach to Urban Goods Movement*. 7 p. (Chicago Area Transportation Study, Chicago, USA).

Blaze JR and Raasch N (1970) *Planning for Freight Facilities*. 24 p. (Chicago Area Transportation Study, Chicago, USA).

Bloch AJ (1978) Economic consequences of goods movement restrictions in the Manhattan CBD, in Fisher GP (ed) *Proceedings of the 3rd Engineering Foundation Conference on Goods Transportation in Urban Areas*, pp 337-348. (Engineering Foundation, New York).

Blower DF and Campbell KL (1988) Analysis of heavy duty truck use in urban areas. *Report Number UMTRI-88-31*. 76 p. (Motor Vehicle Manufacturers Association, Detroit, MI).

Bolger FT and Bruck HW (1973) *An Overview of Urban Goods Movement Projects and Data Sources*. (US Department of Transportation, Washington, DC).

Bowman BL and Lum HS (1990) Examination of truck accidents on urban freeways. *ITE Journal 60(10)*, pp 21-26.

Bowyer DP (1991) *Urban Freight Model Development*. 33 p. (Australian Road Research Board, Melbourne, Australia).

Bowyer DP, Akcelik RA and Biggs DC (1985) Guide to fuel consumption analysis. *Special Report 32*. 98 p. (Australian Road Research Board, Melbourne, Australia).

Bowyer DP and Ogden KW (1988) Impacts of urban road investment on road freight transport: Gateway Bridge case study. *Proceedings of the 14th Australian Road Research Board Conference 14(3)*, pp 224-235.

Brogan JD (1980) Improving truck trip generation techniques through trip end stratification. *Transportation Research Record 771*, pp 1-6.

Brown GE and Ogden KW (1988) The effects of vehicle category on traffic signal design: A re-examination of through car equivalents. *Proceedings of the 14th Australian Road Research Board Conference 14(2)*, pp 27-34.

Buchan K, Lattimore P, Lester N and Mackintosh M (1985) The environmental and economic impact of the GLC night and weekend lorry ban. *Proceedings of the 13th PTRC Summer Annual Meeting, Seminar K*, pp 13-42. (Planning and Transport Research and Computation, London).

Bureau of Transport and Communication Economics (1990) Transport and the greenhouse effect. *Transport and Communication Indicators, Bulletin 28*, pp 15-18. (Australian Government Publishing Service, Canberra, Australia).

Bureau of Transport and Communication Economics (1991) Greenhouse gas emissions in Australian transport. *Working Paper 1*. 83 p. (BTCE, Canberra, Australia).

Bureau of Transport Economics (1978) Outlook papers: Freight transport. *Proceedings of the 1978 Transport Outlook Conference*. (Australian Government Publishing Service, Canberra, Australia).

Button KJ (1978) A note on the road pricing of commercial traffic, *Transportation Planning and Technology 4(3)*, pp 175-178.

Button KJ and Pearman AD (1981) *The Economics of Urban Freight Transport*. 218 p. (MacMillan, London).

Cadotte ER, Chatterjee A, Judd M, Robicheaux RA and Wegman FJ (1977) *Planning for Urban Goods Movement*. 272 p. (University of Tennessee, Knoxville, USA).

California Department of Transportation (1987) *California Highway Cost Allocation and Tax Alternatives Study*. (California Department of Transportation, Sacramento, USA).

Cambridge Systematics Inc (1988a) *Urban Freeway Gridlock Study: Technical Report*. (California Department of Transportation, Sacramento, USA).

Cambridge Systematics Inc (1988b) *Urban Freeway Gridlock Study: Summary Report*. 38 p. (California Department of Transportation, Sacramento, USA).

Chambers Group Inc (1990) *Air Quality Benefits of Early Starting Time*. (Southern California Ready Mixed Concrete Association, Los Angeles).

Chappell CW and Smith MT (1971) Review of urban goods movement studies. *Highway Research Board Special Report 120*, pp 163-181. (HRB, Washington, DC).

Chatterjee A (1982) Facilitating urban goods movement through land use planning, in Fisher GP and Meyburg AH (eds). *Proceedings of the 4th Engineering Foundation Conference on Goods Transportation in Urban Areas*, pp 225-230. (Engineering Foundation, New York).

Chatterjee A, Wegmann FJ, Brogan JD and Phiu-Nual K (1979) Estimating truck traffic for analysing UGM problems and opportunities. *ITE Journal 49(5)*, pp 24-32.

Chatterjee A, Staley RA and Whaley JR (1986) Transportation parks: A promising approach to facilitate urban goods movement. *Transportation Quarterly 40(2)*, pp 211-220.

Chatterjee A, Robicheaux A, Cadotte ER and Wegman FJ (1979) Short range planning for urban goods movement. *Traffic Quarterly 33(3)*, pp 381-395.

Chatterjee A, Fisher GP and Staley RA (eds) (1989) *Goods Transportation in Urban Areas*. 163 p. (American Society of Civil Engineers, New York).

Chiang YS, Roberts PO and Ben-Akiva M (1980) Development of a policy-sensitive model for forecasting freight demand: Final Report. *Report Number DOT-P-30-81-04.* 231 p. (Department of Transportation, Washington, DC).

Chisholm M and O'Sullivan P (1973) *Freight Flows and Spatial Aspects of the British Economy.* 141 p. (Cambridge University Press, Cambridge).

Christiansen DL (1978) Off-street truck loading facilities in downtown areas: Requirements and design. *Transportation Research Record 668*, pp 10-14.

Christiansen DL (1979) *Urban Transportation Planning for Goods and Services.* (Department of Transportation, Washington, DC).

Christie AW (1977) Swindon freight study: Environmental and congestion models. *Supplementary Report 309: The Management of Urban Freight Movements*, pp 34-40. (Transport and Road Research Laboratory, Crowthorne, UK).

Churchill JDC (1970) Operation Moondrop: An experiment in out of hours goods delivery. *The Urban Movement of Goods*, pp 135-140. (Organisation for Economic Cooperation and Development, Paris).

Colston and Budd Pty Ltd and WD Scott and Company Ltd (1984) *Costs of Congestion on Truck Operations.* 76 p. (New South Wales Road Freight Transport Industry Council, Sydney, Australia).

Constantinou TP and Janus AM (1990) Alternative fuel options. *Operations Review 7(1)*, pp 7-10. (Chicago Area Transportation Study, Chicago).

Cooper JC (1983) Complying with area lorry bans: An evaluation of some operating alternatives. *Transportation Planning and Technology 8(2)*, pp 117-126.

Cooper JC (1990) Freight needs and transport policy. *Rees Jeffreys Road Fund, Discussion Paper 15.* 62 p. (Transport Studies Unit, Oxford University, Oxford, UK).

Corcoran PJ and Christie AW (1978) Review of the results of lorry planning studies. *Supplementary Report 381*. 16 p. (Transport and Road Research Laboratory, Crowthorne, UK).

Costa P (1988) Using input-output to forecast freight transport demand, in Bianco L and La Bella A (eds) *Freight Transport Planning and Logistics*, pp 79-120. (Springer-Verlag, Berlin).

Crowley JA (1987) The use of multi-criteria decision analysis in infrastructure investment appraisal. *Australian Road Research 17(3)*, pp 169-174.

Crowley KW, Sweeney DG, Ricondo R, Brugnoli IP and Helmsworth MC (1980) Urban goods movement: An overview and bibliography. *Report Number UMTA-PA-11-0020*. 108 p. (Urban Mass Transportation Administration, Washington, DC).

Cundill MA (1976) Swindon freight study: Assessment of 'no entry except for access' controls. *Supplementary Report 309*, pp 41-57. (Transport and Road Research Laboratory, Crowthorne, UK).

Currie A (1981) Utilisation of urban road freight vehicles. *Bureau of Transport Economics Occasional Paper 39*. 89 p. (Australian Government Publishing Service, Canberra, Australia).

DeCabooter PH and Solberg CE (1990) Operational considerations relating to long trucks in urban areas. *Transportation Research Record 1249*, pp 5-15.

de Neufville R, Wilson NHM and Fuertes L (1974) Consolidation of urban goods movements: A critical analysis. *Transportation Research Record 496*, pp 16-27.

Department of Transport (UK) (1979) *Lorries, People and the Environment: A Background Paper*. (DOT, London).

Department of Transport (UK) (1990) *Transport Statistics Great Britain 1979-1989*. 239 p. (HMSO, London).

Department of Transportation (US) (1972) *National Transportation Report.* (DOT, Washington, DC).

Department of Transportation (US) (1973) *Urban Goods Movement Task Force: Departmental Action Plan and Report to the Secretary.* (DOT, Washington, DC).

Department of Transportation (US) (1978) *Proceedings of the Workshop on Urban Freight Consolidation, Knoxville, Tennessee, July, 1976.* 178 p. (DOT, Washington, DC).

Department of Transportation (US) (1989) *Highway Statistics, 1988.* 185 p. (DOT, Washington, DC).

Department of Transportation (US) (1990) *National Transportation Strategic Planning Study.* (DOT, Washington, DC).

Dumble PL (1979) Aggregate models of goods vehicle trips. *Research Report ARR 96.* 64 p. (Australian Road Research Board, Melbourne, Australia).

Duncan DW (1988) Impact: higher costs, bigger headaches. *Fleet Owner* (September), pp 76-94.

Eckstein WE (1985) Goods distribution centres: A contribution to the systematizing of local goods traffic in towns. *Transport Policy and Decision Making 3(2)*, pp 135-148.

Erickson S (1989) Influence of advanced technology on future truck development, in Batten DF and Thord R (eds) *Transportation for the Future*, pp 195-210. (Springer-Verlag, Berlin).

Euler GW (1990) Intelligent vehicle/highway systems: Definitions and application. *ITE Journal 60(11)*, pp 17-22.

European Conference of Ministers of Transport (1984) *Goods Distribution Systems in Urban Areas: Report of the 61st Round Table on Transport Economics.* 80 p. (ECMT, Paris).

Federal Highway Administration (1980) *Urban Goods Movement.* 11 p. (FHWA, Washington, DC).

Federal Highway Administration (1982) *Final Report of the Federal Highway Cost Allocation Study.* (FHWA, Washington, DC).

Federal Highway Administration (1987) *Allocation of Life-Cycle Highway Pavement Costs.* (FHWA, Washington, DC).

Fisher GP (ed) (1974) *Proceedings of the Engineering Foundation Conference on Goods Transportation in Urban Areas.* 415 p. (Engineering Foundation, New York).

Fisher GP (ed) (1976) *Proceedings of the 2nd Engineering Foundation Conference on Goods Transportation in Urban Areas.* 449 p. (Engineering Foundation, New York).

Fisher GP (ed) (1978) *Proceedings of the 3rd Engineering Foundation Conference on Goods Transportation in Urban Areas.* 815 p. (Engineering Foundation, New York).

Fisher GP (1989) Preface, in Chatterjee A, Fisher GP and Staley RA (eds) *Goods Transportation in Urban Areas.* (American Society of Civil Engineers, New York).

Fisher GP and Meyburg AH (eds) (1982) *Proceedings of the 4th Engineering Foundation Conference on Goods Transportation in Urban Areas.* 431 p. (Engineering Foundation, New York).

Fisher GP and Meyburg AH (1983) Urban goods movement in the 1980s. *Transportation Research Record 920*, pp 49-53.

Fisk CS (1990) Effects of heavy traffic on network congestion. *Transportation Research 24B (5)*, pp 391-404.

Forrester JW (1969) *Urban Dynamics.* 285 p. (MIT Press, Cambridge, USA).

Foster Committee (1979) *Road Haulage Operators' Licensing*. (Report of the Independent Committee of Enquiry into Road Haulage Operators' Licensing). 162 p. (HMSO, London).

Franz LS and Woodmansee J (1990) Computer-aided truck dispatching under conditions of product price variance with limited supply. *Journal of Business Logistics 11(1)*, pp 127-139.

French RL (1990) Intelligent vehicle/highway systems in action. *ITE Journal 60(11)*, pp 23-31.

Friedlaender AF (1969) *The Dilemma of Freight Transport Regulation*. (Brookings Institution, Washington, DC).

Friesz TL and Tobin RL (eds) (1983) Intercity freight modelling. *Transportation Research 17A (6)*, pp 407-525.

Garber NJ and Gadiraju R (1990) Effects of truck strategies on traffic flow and safety on multi-lane highways. *Transportation Research Record 1256*, pp 49-54.

Garrison WL and Scapinakis D (1990) Adoption of advanced positioning and communications technology by the trucking industry. *Report Number UCB-ITS-RR-90-9*. 29 p. (Institute of Transportation Studies, University of California, Berkeley).

Geuy BL (1989) An industry perspective on longer combination vehicle operations in the western USA. *Transportation Planning and Technology 14(2)*, pp 101-115.

Gilmour P (1987) Logistics management: Introduction, in Gilmour P (ed) *Logistics Management in Australia*, pp 3-10. (Longman Cheshire, Melbourne, Australia).

Goddard C (1980) Urban goods movement: Management solutions to an energy problem. *Special Report 191: Consideration in Transportation Energy Contingency Planning*, pp 84-85. (Transportation Research Board, Washington, DC).

Goetschalckx M and Taylor W (1987) A decision support system for dynamic truck dispatching. *Computers and Industrial Engineering 13(1)*, pp 120-123.

Goettee D and Cadotte ER (1977) Freight movement: A crucial component of transportation system management. *Special Report 172: Transportation System Management*, pp 37-43. (Transportation Research Board, Washington, DC).

Goodwin AB (1986) Design considerations for intermodal container transfer facilities. *State of the Art Report 4: Facing the Challenge; The Intermodal Terminal of the Future*, pp 48-51. (Transportation Research Board, Washington, DC).

Gordon RA, Aitken RN and Clark RR (1982) Area truck control. *Proceedings of the 11th Australian Road Research Board Conference 11(4)*, pp 206-213.

Goss DN, Heilmann RL, Rinehart DJ, et al (1967) *Urban Goods Movement Demand*. (Department of Housing and Urban Development, Washington, DC).

Gray R (1982) Behaviourial approaches to freight transport modal choice. *Transport Reviews 2(2)*, pp 161-184.

Greater London Council (1976) *Freight in London: Background Paper 20a, Freight Land Use Review*. 29 p. (GLC, London).

Grenzeback LR, Reilly WR, Roberts PO and Stowers JR (1990) Urban freeway gridlock study: Peak-period urban freeway congestion. *Transportation Research Record 1256*, pp 16-26.

Grenzeback LR, Stowers JR and Boghani AB (1988) Feasibility of national heavy vehicle monitoring system. *National Highway Cooperative Highway Research Program Report 303*. 68 p. (Transportation Research Board, Washington, DC).

Habib PA (1975) *Accommodating Goods Movement Vehicles in the City Center*. PhD dissertation, Department of Civil Engineering, Polytechnic Institute of New York. 139 p. (unpublished).

Habib PA (1981) Curbside pickup and delivery operations and arterial traffic impacts. *Report Number FHWA/RD-80/020*. 114 p. (Federal Highway Administration, Washington, DC).

Habib PA (1982) Off-street loading facilities: Some new approaches, in Fisher GP and Meyburg AH (eds) *Proceedings of the 4th Engineering Foundation Conference on Goods Transportation in Urban Areas*, pp 257-270. (Engineering Foundation, New York).

Habib PA (1983) Practices in urban freight. *Report Number UMTA-NY-11-0023-F*. 91 p. (Urban Mass Transportation Administration, Washington, DC).

Habib PA (1985) Urban freight practice: An evaluation of selected examples. *Transportation Research Record 1038*, pp 40-51.

Habib PA and Crowley KW (1976a) Economic approach to allocating curb space for urban goods movement. *Transportation Research Record 591*, pp 18-24.

Habib PA and Crowley KW (1976b) Economic rationale for establishing off-street loading requirements in the city center. *Transportation Research Record 591*, pp 25-31.

Habib PA and Crowley KW (1978) Space allocation guidelines for off-street loading facilities. *Transportation Research Record 668*, pp 7-9.

Hall MS (1982) Local authorities and planning for freight. *Research Report 49*. 68 p. (Transport Operations Research Group, University of Newcastle upon Tyne, UK).

Hall MS and Worden P (1982) A review of parking and service facilities for goods vehicles and their drivers. *Research Report 47*. 53 p. (Transport Operations Research Group, University of Newcastle upon Tyne, UK).

Hall RW (1990) *LTL Trucking in Los Angeles: Congestion Relief Through Terminal Siting*. (University of California, Transportation Center, Berkeley).

Hansen JCS, Palmer SL and Khan AM (1988) Planning urban access for large combination trucks. *Transportation Research Record 1166*, pp 22-30.

Haritos Z (1973) *Rational Road Pricing Policies in Canada.* (Canadian Transportation Commission, Ottawa, Canada).

Harker PT (1985) The state of the art in the predictive analysis of freight transport systems. *Transport Reviews 5(2)*, pp 143-164.

Harker PT (1987) *Predicting Intercity Freight Flows.* 261 p. (VNU Science Press, Utrecht, The Netherlands).

Harper DV (1982) *Transportation in America: Users, Carriers, Government. (2nd edition).* 645 p. (Prentice-Hall, Englewood Cliffs, USA).

Harris NC, Roodbool GC and Ale BJM (1986) Risk assessment of alternative transport modes for hazardous materials. *State of the Art Report 3: Recent Advances in Hazardous Materials Transportation Research*, pp 47-52. (Transportation Research Board, Washington, DC).

Hasell BB, Foulkes M and Robertson JJS (1978a) Freight planning in London: The existing system and its problems. *Traffic Engineering and Control 19(1)*, pp 60-63.

Hasell BB, Foulkes M and Robertson JJS (1978b) Freight planning in London: Assisting efficient freight operation. *Traffic Engineering and Control 19(2)*, pp 126-129.

Hasell BB, Foulkes M and Robertson JJS (1978c) Freight planning in London: Reducing the environmental impact. *Traffic Engineering and Control 19(3)*, pp 182-185.

Hasell BB, Foulkes M and Robertson JJS (1978d) Freight planning in London: The total strategy. *Traffic Engineering and Control 19(4)*, pp 231-235.

Hasell BB and Christie AW (1978) The Greenwich-Lewisham freight study. *Supplementary Report 407.* 37 p. (Transport and Road Research Laboratory, Crowthorne, UK).

Hedges CA (1971) Demand forecasting and development of a framework for analysis of urban commodity flow: Statement of the problem. *Special Report 120: Urban Commodity Flow*, pp 145-148. (Highway Research Board, Washington, DC).

Hedges CA (1978) Transportation systems management: The urban freight component, in Fisher GP (ed) *Proceedings of the 3rd Engineering Foundation Conference on Goods Transportation in Urban Areas*, pp 227-250. (Engineering Foundation, New York).

Hedges CA (1985) Improving urban goods movement: The transportation system management approach. *Transport Policy and Decision Making 3(2)*, pp 113-133.

Hensher DA (1989) Behaviourial and resource values of travel time savings: A bicentennial update. *Australian Road Research 19(3)*, pp 223-229.

Hicks SK (1977) Urban freight, in Hensher DA (ed) *Urban Transport Economics*, pp 100-130. (Cambridge University Press, Cambridge, UK).

Highway Research Board (1971) *Special Report 120: Urban Commodity Flow*. 207 p. (Highway Research Board, Washington, DC).

Hill C and Davies P (1990) Help is on the way. *ASCE Civil Engineering Journal 60(2)*, pp 64-65.

Hill M (1968) A goals achievement matrix in evaluation of alternative plans. *Journal of the American Institute of Planners 34(1)*, pp 19-29.

Hills PJ (1990) Automated vehicle pricing for the use of roadspace: An idea whose time has arrived. *Rees Jeffreys Road Fund, Discussion Paper 7*, (Transport Studies Unit, Oxford University, Oxford, UK).

House RK and Associates Ltd, with Clayton, Sparks and Associates Ltd (1979) *The Economics of Urban Goods Movement*. (Transport Canada, Montreal, Canada).

Hummer JE, Zegeer CV and Hanscom FR (1989) Effects of turns by larger trucks at urban intersections. *Transportation Research Record 1195*, pp 64-74.

Hussain I (1990) Road investment benefits over and above transport cost savings and gains to newly generated traffic. *Proceedings of the 18th PTRC Summer Annual Meeting, Seminar J*, pp 101-104. (Planning and Transport Research Corporation, London).

Hutchinson BG (1974) Estimating urban goods movement demands. *Transportation Research Record 496*, pp 1-15.

Hutchinson BG (1981) Urban transport policy and policy analysis methods. *Transport Reviews 1(2)*, pp 169-188.

Hutchinson BG (1988) Geometric, capacity and safety impacts of large trucks in urban areas. *Proceedings of the Roads and Transportation Association of Canada Annual Meeting*, pp D3-D33.

Hutchinson BG and Parker DJ (1989) Large truck braking capabilities and the inadequacies of geometric design and traffic operations standards. *Proceedings of the Roads and Transportation Association of Canada Annual Meeting.*

Hutchinson NE (1987) *An Integrated Approach to Logistics Management.* 251 p. (Prentice-Hall, Englewood Cliffs, USA).

Institute of Transportation Engineers (1972) *Goods Transportation in Urban Areas.* 40 p. (ITE, Washington, DC).

Institute of Transportation Engineers (1981) *New Technology and Applications for Urban Goods Movement: An Informational Report.* 41 p. (ITE, Washington, DC).

Institute of Transportation Engineers (1987) *Trip Generation (4th edition).* 1372 p. (ITE, Washington, DC).

Institution of Highway Engineers (1981) *Guidelines for Lorry Management Schemes.* 59 p. (IHE, London).

InterState Commission (1990) *Road User Charges and Vehicle Registration: A National Scheme* (2 vols) (Australian Government Publishing Service, Canberra, Australia).

Jeffs VP and Hills PJ (1990) Determinants of modal choice in freight transport: A case study. *Transportation 17(1)*, pp 29-48.

JHK and Associates (1983) *Comprehensive TSM Grant Recipient Technical Exchange: Operational Study, Urban Goods Movement.* 20 p. (Federal Highway Administration, Washington, DC).

Johnson DM, Joyce FE and Williams HE (1977) Environmental policy and the heavy goods vehicle in conurbations. *Supplementary Report 309: The Management of Urban Freight Movements*, pp 111-134. (Transport and Road Research Laboratory, Crowthorne, UK).

Joint Powers Authority (1990) *Southern California Consolidated Transportation Corridor.* 19 p. (City of Los Angeles, Los Angeles).

Kearney AT, Inc (1975) Urban goods movement demonstration project design: Final report on phases I and II. *Report Number UMTA-IL-06-0030-75-1.* (Urban Mass Transportation Administration, Washington, DC).

Kearney AT, Inc (1976) *A Primer on Urban Goods Movement.* 29 p. (Urban Mass Transportation Administration, Washington, DC).

Keisling MK, Euritt MA and Walton CM (1991) *The Coordination of Container Weight Limits Between Ocean Carriers and Truckers.* 26 p. (Paper presented at 70th Annual Meeting of the Transportation Research Board, Washington, DC).

Kessler D (1986) Establishing hazardous materials truck routes for shipments through the Dallas-Fort Worth area. *State of the Art Report 3: Recent Advances in Hazardous Materials Transportation Research*, pp 79-90. (Transportation Research Board, Washington, DC).

Kimber RM, McDonald M and Hounsell NB (1986) The prediction of saturation flows for road junctions controlled by traffic signals. *Research Report 67.* 18 p. (Transport and Road Research Laboratory, Crowthorne, UK).

Kirby RF, Tagell MT and Ogden KW (1986) Traffic management in Metro Manila: Formulating traffic policies. *Traffic Engineering and Control 27(5)*, pp 262-269.

Lawlor L (1982) Road pricing and cost recovery: A review of approaches to allocating road system costs. *Bureau of Transport Economics Reference Paper 38*. 59 p. (BTE, Canberra, Australia).

Lay MG (1984) Costing truck infrastructure effects. *International Transport Congress: Transportation Towards the Year 2000*, Vol 4, pp 21-39. (Roads and Transportation Association of Canada, Ottawa, Canada).

Lay MG (1986) *Handbook of Road Technology* (2 vols). 712 p. (Gordon and Breach, London).

Lea ND and Associates (1971) *An Evaluation of Urban Transport Efficiency in Canada*. (Canadian Ministry of Transport, Ottawa, Canada).

Leitch G (1979) *Trunk Road proposals: A Comprehensive Framework for Appraisal*. (HMSO, London).

Levinson HS (1982) Urban goods movement information needs, in Fisher GP and Meyburg AH (eds) *Proceedings of the 4th Engineering Foundation Conference on Goods Transportation in Urban Areas*, pp 205-214. (Engineering Foundation, New York).

Lichfield N (1970) Evaluation methodology of urban and regional plans: A review. *Regional Studies 4(2)*, pp 151-165.

Lockheed Information Management Services Company (1990) *Truck Operations Pilot Survey*. 74 p. (South Coast Air Quality Management District, Los Angeles).

Lockwood SC and Wagner FA (1977) Methodological framework for the TSM planning process. *Special Report 172: Transportation System Management*, pp 100-118. (Transportation Research Board, Washington, DC).

Loder and Bayly (1981) *On-road Management of Trucks in Urban Areas.* 67 p. (Road Safety and Traffic Authority of Victoria, Melbourne, Australia).

Magee JF, Copacino WC and Rosenfeld DB (1985) *Modern Logistics Management.* 430 p. (Wiley, New York).

Mahoney JH (1985) *Intermodal Freight Transportation.* 214 p. (Eno Foundation, Westport, USA).

Maring G and Politano A (1982) The urban goods movement and energy interface, in Fisher GP and Meyburg AH (eds) *Proceedings of the 4th Engineering Foundation Conference on Goods Transportation in Urban Areas,* pp 319-328. (Engineering Foundation, New York).

Marino JH (1974) Freight terminal operations and location: Problems and prospects, in Fisher GP (ed) *Proceedings of the Engineering Foundation Conference on Goods Transportation in Urban Areas,* pp 199-216. (Engineering Foundation, New York).

May AD and Patterson NS (1984) Transport problems as perceived by inner city firms. *Transportation 12(3),* pp 225-241.

May TE, Mills G and Scully T (1984) *National Road Freight Industry Inquiry.* 519 p. (Australian Government Publishing Service, Canberra, Australia).

McHarg I (1971) *Design with Nature.* 197 p. (Doubleday, New York).

Mele J (1988) Congestion takes its toll. *Fleet Owner* (September), pp 59-72.

Meyburg AH (1976) Modelling in the context of urban goods movement problems, in Fisher GP (ed) *Proceedings of the 2nd Conference on Goods Transportation in Urban Areas,* pp 127-168. (Engineering Foundation, New York).

Meyburg AH (1979) The applicability of behaviourial modelling to the analysis of goods movement, in Hensher DA and Stopher PR (eds) *Behaviourial Travel Modelling,* pp 624-635. (Croom Helm, London).

Meyburg AH and Stopher PR (1974) A framework for the analysis of demand for urban goods movement. *Transportation Research Record 496*, pp 68-79.

Meyer MD and Miller EJ (1984) *Urban Transportation Planning: A Decision-Oriented Approach.* 524 p. (McGraw Hill, New York).

Miernyk WH (1967) *The Elements of Input-Output Analysis.* 156 p. (Random House, New York).

Millendorf SF (1989) Facilitation of goods movement in the New York City area, in Chatterjee A, Fisher GP and Staley RA (eds) *Goods Transportation in Urban Areas*, pp 25-30. (American Society of Civil Engineers, New York).

Miyamoto S (1989) Urban distribution within the context of traffic problems. *The Wheel Extended 19(1)*, pp 2-9.

Mohr E (1974) Some fallacies in urban goods movement. *Transportation Research Record 496*, pp 105-109.

Molina CJ (1987) Development of passenger car equivalents for large trucks at signalized intersections. *ITE Journal 57(11)*, pp 33-37.

Muller GT (1989) *Intermodal Freight Transportation.* 243 p. (Eno Foundation, Westport, USA).

National Association of Regional Councils (1984) *Linking Goods Movement and Economic Development: A Case Study Analysis.* 108 p. (Department of Transportation, Washington, DC).

National Highway Traffic Safety Administration (1989) *Fatal Accident Reporting System, 1986: A Review of Information on Fatal Traffic Accidents in the US in 1988.* (NHTSA, Washington, DC).

Nelson C, Siwek S, Guensler R and Michelson K (1991) *Managing Trucks for Air Quality.* (Paper presented at 70th Annual Meeting of Transportation Research Board, Washington, DC).

Nelson PM and Underwood MCP (1982) Operational performance of the TRRL quiet heavy vehicle. *Supplementary Report 746.* 31 p. (Transport and Road Research Laboratory, Crowthorne, UK).

New York City (1976) Manhattan garment center urban goods movement study: Phase I final report. *Report Number UMTA-UPM-02-80-1.* (Urban Mass Transportation Administration, Washington, DC).

New York City (1979) Manhattan garment center urban goods movement study: Phase II final report. *Report Number DOT-05-30053.* (Department of Transportation, Washington, DC).

Nicolin C (1989) Future goods transport in Europe, in Batten DF and Thord R (eds) *Transportation for the Future*, pp 13-16. (Springer-Verlag, Berlin).

Nix FP (1990) Potential impact on Canada of new container standards. *Journal of the Transportation Research Forum 31(1)*, pp 109-118.

Noortman HJ (1984) Goods distribution in urban areas. *Goods Distribution Systems in Urban Areas: Report of the 61st Round Table on Transport Economics*, pp 5-64. (European Conference of Ministers of Transport, Paris).

O'Day J and Kostyniuk LP (1985) Large trucks in urban areas: A safety problem? *ASCE Journal of Transportation Engineering 111(3)*, pp 303-317.

Ogden KW (1976) *An Overview of Freight Systems in the Context of Urban Transportation Planning.* 179 p. (Ontario Ministry of Transportation and Communications, Toronto, Canada).

Ogden KW (1977a) Modelling urban freight generation. *Traffic Engineering and Control 18(3)*, pp 106-109.

Ogden KW (1977b) *Urban Goods Movement.* 365 p. (Monash University, Melbourne, Australia).

Ogden (1977c) An analysis of urban commodity flow. *Transportation Planning and Technology 4(1)*, pp 1-9.

Ogden (1977d) *Basic Requirements for the Analysis of Urban Freight.* 109 p. (Ontario Ministry of Transportation and Communications, Toronto, Canada).

Ogden KW (1978) The distribution of truck trips and commodity flow in urban areas: A gravity model analysis. *Transportation Research 12(2)*, pp 131-137.

Ogden KW (1980) Licensing and environmental controls on freight transport. *Research Report 32.* 35 p. (Transport Operations Research Group, University of Newcastle upon Tyne, Newcastle, UK).

Ogden KW (1984) A framework for urban freight policy analysis. *Transportation Planning & Technology 8(4)*, pp 253-266.

Ogden KW (1985) Shore-based shipping costs: The urban freight component. *Transport Policy and Decision Making 3(2)*, pp 181-198.

Ogden KW (1988a) Urban freight perspectives - past, present and future. *Proceedings of the 14th Australian Road Research Board Conference 14(1)*, pp 157-174.

Ogden KW (1988b) Road cost recovery in Australia. *Transport Reviews 8(2)*, pp 101-123.

Ogden KW (1990) *Strategic Issues in Urban Freight Transport with Particular Reference to Perth.* 119 p. (Western Australia Department of Transport, Perth, Australia).

Ogden KW (1991) Truck movement and access in urban areas. *ASCE Journal of Transportation Engineering 117(1)*, pp 72-91.

Ogden KW and Bowyer (1985) Directions for urban freight research in Australia. *Transportation Research Record 1038*, pp 51-58.

Ogden KW and Richardson AJ (1978) Reducing the cost of urban freight through transport system management, in Fisher GP (ed) *Proceedings of the 3rd Engineering Foundation Conference on Goods Transportation in Urban Areas*, pp 251-274. (Engineering Foundation, New York).

Ogden KW and Tan HW (1989) Truck involvement in fatal urban road accidents in Australia, in Chatterjee A, Fisher GP and Staley RA (eds.) *Goods Transportation in Urban Areas*, pp 133-158. (American Society of Civil Engineers, New York).

Organisation for Economic Cooperation and Development (1970) *The Urban Movement of Goods: Proceedings of the Third Technology Assessment Review*. 236 p. (OECD, Paris).

Organisation for Economic Cooperation and Development (1977) *Integrated Urban Traffic Management*. 70 p. (OECD, Paris).

Organisation for Economic Cooperation and Development (1985) *Technico-Economic Analysis of the Role of Road Freight Transport*. 131 p. (OECD, Paris).

Organisation for Economic Cooperation and Development (1988) *Transporting Hazardous Goods by Road*. 144 p. (OECD, Paris).

Organization for Economic Growth, Inc (1979) Requirements and specifications for off-hours delivery. *Report Number FHWA-RD-79-60*. 123 p. (Federal Highway Administration, Washington, DC).

Parsons, Ralph M Company (1974) *A Study of the Transportation Center Facilitation Concept*. (Department of Transportation, Washington, DC).

Pearson, RA and Associates (1988) *Application of New Technology in Road Freight Operations*. 39 p. (Road Traffic Authority of Victoria, Melbourne, Australia).

Pearson RA, Ogden KW, Sweatman PF and Jarvis JR (1990) A study of the practicality of allowing double bottom road trains into metropolitan Perth. *Proc. Workshop on Integration of Large Vehicles into Urban Networks, 15th Australian Road Research Board Conference*, 13 p.

Pijawka KD, Foote S and Soesilo A (1985) Risk assessment of transporting hazardous material: Route analysis and hazard management. *Transportation Research Record 1020*, pp 1-6.

375

Pitfield DE (1978) Freight distribution model predictions compared: A test of hypotheses. *Environment and Planning A 10(7)*, pp 813-836.

Plant Location International Pty Ltd (1983) *Freight Transfer Facilities Study, Sydney.* (New South Wales Road Freight Transport Industry Council, Sydney, Australia).

Plowden SPC (1983) Transport efficiency and the urban environment: Is there a conflict? *Transport Reviews 4(3)*, pp 363-398.

Port Authority of New York and New Jersey (1988) *Truck Commodity Survey: Overall Analysis and Summary.* 39 p. (PANYNJ, New York).

Prentice AS and Ogden KW (1988) Truck accidents in the City of Melbourne. *Australian Road Research 18(1)*, pp 1-10.

Quarmby DA (1989) Developments in the retail market and their effect on freight distribution. *Journal of Transport Economics and Policy 23(1)*, pp 75-87.

Radzikowski P (1983) Rail and water terminal interface. *Transportation Research Record 907*, pp 4-7.

Rawling FG (1989) Information needs for policy, planning and design, in Chatterjee A, Fisher GP and Staley RA (eds.) *Goods Transportation in Urban Areas*, pp 95-118. (American Society of Civil Engineers, New York).

Rawling FG and Reilly JP (1987) CATS commercial vehicle survey of 1986: A discussion of project management issues. *CATS Research News 26(1)*, pp 5-28. (Chicago Area Transportation Study, Chicago).

Recker WW, Golob TF, Hsueh CW and Nohalty P (1988) An analysis of the characteristics and congestion impacts of truck-involved freeway accidents. *Report Number RTA 13945-55D281.* (California Department of Transportation, Sacramento, USA).

Regional Planning Commission (1980) *Regional Planning Commission's Goods Movement Analysis for the New Orleans Metropolitan Area.* (RPC, New Orleans, USA).

Reilly JP and Hochmuth JJ (1990) Effects of truck restrictions on regional transportation demand estimates. *Transportation Research Record 1256*, pp 38-48.

Reilly JP, Rosenbluh A and Rawling FG (1987) Factoring and analysis of the commercial vehicle survey. *CATS Research News 26(1)*, pp 29-46. (Chicago Area Transportation Study, Chicago, USA).

Rimmer PJ (1978) Urban goods movement in Sydney. *Bureau of Transport Economics Occasional Paper 17*. 76 p. (Australian Government Publishing Service, Canberra, Australia).

Rimmer PJ and Hicks SK (1979) Urban goods movement: Process, planning approach and policy, in Hensher DA and Stopher PR (eds) *Behaviourial Travel Modelling*, pp 525-552. (Croom Helm, London).

Rimmer PJ and Tsipouras A (1977) Ports and urban systems: Framework and research needs in resolution of port generated conflicts. *Proceedings of the 3rd Australian Transport Research Forum*. (Victorian Ministry of Transport, Melbourne, Australia).

Road Construction Authority (1987) *Metropolitan National Roads Study*. 55 p. (Road Construction Authority of Victoria, Melbourne, Australia).

Road Traffic Authority (1988) *Central Area Transport Strategy. Issue Paper 6A, Freight and Commercial Vehicle Movement*. 38 p. (Road Traffic Authority of Victoria, Melbourne, Australia).

Roberts N and Felts W (1983) Intermodal freight transfer facilities in California. *Transportation Research Record 920*, pp 68-72.

Roberts PO and Kullman BC (1979) Urban goods movement: Behaviourial demand forecasting procedures, in Hensher DA and Stopher PR (eds) *Behaviourial Travel Modelling*, pp 533-576. (Croom Helm, London).

Robeson JF (1978) Urban freight consolidation: Legal, attitudinal, and operational considerations associated with implementation. *Report Number UMTA-OH-0001-78-2*. (Urban Mass Transportation Administration, Washington, DC).

Robicheaux RA and Chatterjee A (1978) Injecting UGM considerations into the transportation planning process, in Fisher GP (ed) *Proceedings of the 3rd Engineering Foundation Conference on Goods Transportation in Urban Areas*, pp 401-412. (Engineering Foundation, New York).

Ross P (1978) Improving urban traffic through truck-oriented measures. *Public Roads 42(3)*, pp 91-98.

Rothbart LS (1988) (ed) Sources of information in transportation: Part 5, trucking (4th edition). (Vance Publications, New York).

Rowe WD (1983) Risk assessment processes for hazardous materials transportation. *National Cooperative Highway Research Program Synthesis of Highway Practice 103.* 27 p. (Transportation Research Board, Washington, DC).

Ryder A (1990) The cost of clean burn. *Heavy Duty Trucking 69(6)*, pp 64-71.

Saccomanno FF and Chan CC (1985) Economic evaluation of routing strategies for hazardous road shipments. *Transportation Research Record 1020*, pp 12-18.

Sach ND (1984) Road traffic regulations, in Ogden KW and Bennett DW (eds) *Traffic Engineering Practice (3rd edition)*, pp 76-79. (Monash University, Melbourne, Australia).

Scanlon RD and Cantilli EJ (1985) Assessing the risk and safety in the transportation of hazardous materials. *Transportation Research Record 1020*, pp 6-11.

Schuster AD (1978) The economic feasibility of the urban freight consolidation terminal concept, in Fisher GP (ed) *Proceedings of the 3rd Engineering Foundation Conference on Goods Transportation in Urban Areas*, pp 559-583. (Engineering Foundation, New York).

Schuster AD (1982) Fuel conservation in urban goods distribution, in Fisher GP and Meyburg AH (eds) *Proceedings of the 4th Engineering Foundation Conference on Goods Transportation in Urban Areas*, pp 351-370. (Engineering Foundation, New York).

Schwerdtfeger W (1978) Goods movements of retail and service businesses in Germany, in Fisher GP (ed) *Proceedings of the 3rd Engineering Foundation Conference on Goods Transportation in Urban Areas*, pp 439-468. (Engineering Foundation, New York).

Schwerdtfeger W (1982) Urban goods movement in the context of urban transportation planning in Germany, in Fisher GP and Meyburg AH (eds) *Proceedings of the 4th Engineering Foundation Conference on Goods Transportation in Urban Areas*, pp 161-174. (Engineering Foundation, New York).

Scodari PF and Fisher A (1988) How Uncle Sam values mortality risk reductions, in Stammer RE (ed) *Highway Safety: At the Crossroads*, pp 182-198. (American Society of Civil Engineers, Washington, DC).

Simons N, Hamilton CW, Leis RD and Cheaney ES (1972) *Urban Goods Movement Program Design*. (Urban Mass Transportation Administration, Washington, DC).

Slavin HL (1976) Demand for urban goods vehicle trips. *Transportation Research Record 591*, pp 32-37.

Small KA, Winston C and Evans CA (1989) *Road Work: A New Highway Pricing and Investment Policy*. (Brookings Institution, Washington, DC).

Smist TE and Ranney TA (1983) Heavy truck accident causation: Analysis of the CPIR-B File. *Report Number DOT-HS-806-425*. 42 p. (Department of Transportation, Washington, DC).

Smith BL and Mason JM (1988) *Accommodation of Trucks on the Highway: Safety in Design*. 179 p. (American Society of Civil Engineers, New York).

Smith KJG (1976) Constraints affecting the use of a public transhipment depot. *Research Report 19*. (Transport Operations Research Group, University of Newcastle upon Tyne, UK).

Smith MG and Douglass M (1982) Goods movement in urban areas. *RRU Bulletin 58*. 57 p. (Road Research Unit, Wellington, New Zealand).

Smith RA (1990) *Action Plan to Reduce Cargo Delays Associated with Trucks*. 19 p. (Port of Melbourne Authority, Melbourne, Australia).

Smith, Wilbur and Associates (1969) *Motor Trucks in the Metropolis*. 208 p. (Automobile Manufacturers Association, New York).

Sonntag H (1985) A computer model of urban commercial traffic - analysis, basic concept and application. *Transport Policy and Decision Making 3(2)*, pp 171-180.

Southern California Association of Governments (1983) *The Importance of Goods Movement and Regional Transportation to the Southern California Economy and International Trade*. 31 p. (SCAG, Los Angeles).

Southern California Association of Governments (1988) *Congestion in the Los Angeles Region: Costs Under Future Mobility Strategies*. 14 p. (SCAG, Los Angeles).

Southern California Association of Governments (1989a) *International Trade and Goods Movement: The Southern California Experience and its Future*. (SCAG, Los Angeles).

Southern California Association of Governments (1989b) *Air Quality Management Plan: South Coast Air Basin. Final Report, Appendix IV-G*. 326 p. (SCAG, Los Angeles).

Southworth F (1982a) Logistic demand models for urban goods movement, in Fisher GP and Meyburg AH (eds) *Proceedings of the 4th Engineering Foundation Conference on Goods Transportation in Urban Areas*, pp 189-204. (Engineering Foundation, New York).

Southworth F (1982b) *The Spatial Accessibility of Truck Terminals in the Presence of Multi-destination Truck Circuits*. 15 p. (Civil Engineering Department, University of Illinois at Urbana-Champaign, USA).

Southworth F (1983) *Improved Urban Goods Movement Planning: The Energy Implications*. 26 p. (Department of Civil Engineering, University of Illinois, Urbana-Champaign, USA).

Southworth F, Janson B, Papathanassopoulos E and Zavattero D (1981) Direct and indirect energy consumption by Chicago's urban trucking industry. *Transportation Research Record 834*, pp 20-27.

Southworth F, Janson B, Papathanassopoulos E and Zavattero D (1982) Accounting for energy consumption in Chicago's urban trucking industry, in Fisher GP and Meyburg AH (eds) *Proceedings of the 4th Engineering Foundation Conference on Goods Transportation in Urban Areas*, pp 371-386. (Engineering Foundation, New York).

Southworth F, Lee YJ, Griffin CS and Zavattero D (1983) Strategic motor freight planning for Chicago in the year 2000. *Transportation Research Record 920*, pp 45-48.

Spielberg F (1982) The planner's role in urban goods movement, in Fisher GP and Meyburg AH (eds) *Proceedings of the 4th Engineering Foundation Conference on Goods Transportation in Urban Areas*, pp 215-224. (Engineering Foundation, New York).

Spielberg F and Smith SA (1981) Service and supply trips at federal institutions in Washington, DC area. *Transportation Research Record 834*, pp 15-20.

Stadden K (1989) Truck technology. *Heavy Duty Trucking 68(10)*, pp 70-75.

Staley RA (1978) Motor carrier terminals: Criteria for site selection, in Fisher GP (ed) *Proceedings of the 3rd Engineering Foundation Conference on Goods Transportation in Urban Areas*, pp 543-558. (Engineering Foundation, New York).

Staley RA (1982) A profile of service-type trucks, 1977, in Fisher GP and Meyburg AH (eds) *Proceedings of the 4th Engineering Foundation Conference on Goods Transportation in Urban Areas*, pp 271-276. (Engineering Foundation, New York).

Staley RA (1983) Land use constraints in locating intermodal terminals. *Transportation Research Record 907*, pp 1-4.

Staley RA (1989a) Urban intermodal freight management, in Chatterjee A, Fisher GP and Staley RA (eds) *Goods Transportation in Urban Areas*, pp 8-12. (American Society of Civil Engineers, New York).

Staley RA (1989b) Moving intermodal containers over urban/suburban highways, in Chatterjee A, Fisher GP and Staley RA (eds) *Goods Transportation in Urban Areas*, pp 78-82. (American Society of Civil Engineers, New York).

Staley RA (1989c) Assessing the role of regulation in urban goods movement, in Chatterjee A, Fisher GP and Staley RA (eds) *Goods Transportation in Urban Areas*, pp 49-52. (American Society of Civil Engineers, New York).

Starkie DNM (1967) Intensity of commercial traffic generation by industry. *Traffic Engineering and Control 7(10)*, pp 558-560.

Stopher PR and Meyburg AH (1975) *Urban Transportation Modelling and Planning*. 345 p. (DC Heath, Lexington, USA).

Stopher PR and Meyburg AH (1976) *Transportation Systems Evaluation*. 179 p. (DC Heath, Lexington, USA).

Stover VG (1988) *Transportation and Land Development*. 239 p. (Institute of Transportation Engineers, Washington, DC).

Strauss-Wieder A, Kang K and Yokel M (1989) The truck commodity survey in New York-New Jersey metropolitan area, in Chatterjee A, Fisher GP and Staley RA (eds) *Goods Transportation in Urban Areas*, pp 83-94. (American Society of Civil Engineers, New York).

Sudgen R and Williams A (1978) *The Principles of Practical Cost-Benefit Analysis*. 275 p. (Oxford University Press, Oxford).

Swan Wooster Engineering Co Ltd (1979) *Evaluation of Urban Trucking Rationalization in Vancouver - Phases 1 and 2*. (Transport Canada, Montreal, Canada).

Sweatman PF (1991) Dynamic performance and traffic impacts of road trains. *Research Report ARR 176*. 73 p. (Australian Road Research Board, Melbourne, Australia).

Teal RF (1988) *Estimating the Full Economic Costs of Truck Incidents on Urban Freeways*. 47 p. (AAA Foundation for Traffic Safety, Washington, DC).

Technical Advisory Group (established pursuant to the California Clean Air Act) (1990) *Guidelines for Local Air Districts Considering Transportation Control Measures Directed at Heavy-duty Truck Operations*. 35 p. (California Air Resources Board, Sacramento).

Tee Consulting Services Inc (1979a) *A Framework for Urban Goods Movement Information in Canada*. 291 p. (Transport Canada, Montreal, Canada).

Tee Consulting Services Inc (1979b) *Consolidated Building Receiver Demonstration*. 194 p. (Transport Canada, Montreal, Canada).

Thompson T (1990) Road user charging: The current state of technology. *Traffic Engineering and Control 31(10)*, pp 526-533.

Traffic Authority (1982) *Policy and Guidelines for Traffic Generating Developments*. (Traffic Authority of New South Wales, Sydney, Australia).

Transportation Development Agency (1974) *Profile of Urban Goods Flow in Calgary, Alberta*. (TDA, Montreal, Canada).

Transportation Research Board (1986a) *State of the Art Report 4: Facing the Challenge: The Intermodal Terminal of the Future*. 142 p. (TRB, Washington, DC).

Transportation Research Board (1986b) *Special Report 211: Twin Trailer Trucks*. 388 p. (TRB, Washington, DC).

Transportation Research Board (1989) *Special Report 223: Providing Access for Larger Trucks*. 316 p. (TRB, Washington, DC).

Travers Morgan Pty Ltd (1987) *Commodity Movement Framework* (2 Vols). (Road Traffic Authority of Victoria, Melbourne, Australia).

Treichler B (1990) Competitors share deliveries: Portland area florists decide they'd switch than fight, *P and D Magazine 3(6)*, pp 20-21.

Tri-State Transportation Commission (1968) *Truck Transportation: Regional Profile 1(8)*. (TSTC, New York).

Trucking Research Institute (1990) *Incident Management: Executive Summary*. 25 p. (TRI, Alexandria, USA).

TTM Consulting Pty Ltd (1987) *Traffic Management Strategies for Freight*. (Road Traffic Authority of Victoria, Melbourne, Australia).

TTM Consulting Pty Ltd (1989) *Guidelines for the Planning and Design of Road Freight Access for Commercial and Industrial Developments*. 33 p. (Road Traffic Authority of Victoria, Melbourne, Australia).

Urban Consortium for Technology Initiatives (1980) *Urban Goods Movement*. 28 p. (Department of Transportation, Washington, DC).

Van Vliet D (1982) Saturn: A modern assignment model. *Traffic Engineering and Control 23(12)*, pp 578-581.

Vickerman Zachary Miller Inc (1988) *2020 Cargo Handling Operations, Facilities and Infrastructure Requirements Study Summary*. 15 p. (San Pedro Bay Ports of Los Angeles and Long Beach).

Walters CA (1982) CBD Dallas: A case study in development of urban goods movement regulations, in Fisher GP and Meyburg AH (eds) *Proceedings of the 4th Engineering Foundation Conference on Goods Transportation in Urban Areas*, pp 241-256. (Engineering Foundation, New York).

Walters CH (1989a) Dallas urban goods movement changes: The decade after, in Chatterjee A, Fisher GP and Staley RA (eds) *Goods Transportation in Urban Areas*, pp 53-63. (American Society of Civil Engineers, New York).

Walters CH (1989b) Economic impact of alternative downtown UGM strategies, in Chatterjee A, Fisher GP and Staley RA (eds) *Goods Transportation in Urban Areas*, pp 64-73. (American Society of Civil Engineers, New York).

Watson PL (1975) *Urban Goods Movement*. 110 p. (DC Heath, Lexington, USA).

Winston C (1981) A disaggregate model of the demand for intercity freight transportation. *Econometrica 49(4)*, pp 981-1006.

Wohl M and Hendrickson C (1984) *Transportation Investment and Pricing Principles: An Introduction for Engineers, Planners and Economists*. 380 p. (Wiley, New York).

Wood D (1983) *Inquiry Into the Effects of Bans on Heavy Lorries Within London*. (Greater London Council, London).

Wood RT and Leighton RA (1969) Truck freight in the tri-state region. *Traffic Quarterly 23(3)*, pp 323-340.

Wood WG (1979) *Urban Goods Movement Research: A Framework and Results*. 276 p. (Transport Canada, Montreal, Canada).

Wood WG, Suen L and Ebrahim A (1982) Urban goods movement research: Canadian experience in the seventies. *Transportation Planning and Technology 7(2)*, pp 121-133.

Wooltorton A and White M (1978) Freight transport in St Helens: The value of traffic improvements. *Traffic Engineering and Control 19(4)*, pp 343-345.

Wyckoff DD (1979) *Truck Drivers in America*. 138 p. (DC Heath, Lexington, USA).

Young W, Richardson AJ, Ogden KW and Rattray AL (1982) Road-rail freight mode choice: The application of an elimination-by-aspects model. *Transportation Research Record 838*, pp 38-44.

Young W, Ritchie SG and Ogden KW (1980) Factors that influence freight-facility location preference. *Transportation Research Record 747*, pp 71-77.

Zavattero DA (1976) Suggested approach to urban goods movement and transportation planning. *Transportation Research Record 591*, pp 41-43.

Zavattero DA and Weseman SE (1981) Commercial vehicle trip generation in the Chicago region. *Transportation Research Record 834*, pp 12-15.

Index

Printed in the United States
by Baker & Taylor Publisher Services